WITHDRAWN

Illinois Central College
Learning Resource Center

New Plays for Red Letter Days

by ELIZABETH HOUGH SECHRIST

New Plays for

Illustrated

PHILADELPHIA: 1953

and JANETTE WOOLSEY

Red Letter Days

by Guy Fry

MACRAE SMITH COMPANY

COPYRIGHT, 1953

Elizabeth Hough Sechrist and Janette Woolsey

The plays in this volume are royalty
free, but permission must be granted
by the authors for any commercial use.

Library of Congress Catalog Card Number 53–7890

5310

Eighth Printing

Manufactured in the United States of America

TO

Nellie Dodge Woolsey

AND

Lydia Druck Sechrist

Preface

New Plays for Red Letter Days, the third volume in the "Red Letter Days" series, like its predecessors, is an outgrowth of a round-the-calendar demand for holiday material. Librarians are constantly asked for plays for holidays and special days and weeks. Elementary and junior high school teachers need plays for classroom and assembly programs. Parent Teacher Associations, Scout leaders, Cub mothers, playground and club workers—all these and many others working with children are searching for "just the right play" for some special occasion. It is for all these anxious seekers we have written the twenty-five plays presented in this book.

ELIZABETH HOUGH SECHRIST
JANETTE WOOLSEY

York, Pennsylvania

Contents

New Plays for Red Letter Days

Days and Days

CHARACTERS

LARRY, *nine years old*
HIS MOTHER
MR. MOON
FORGOTTEN DAYS
    (*three or more*)

NEGLECTED DAYS (*three or more*)
REMEMBERED DAYS (*three or more*)
RED LETTER DAYS (*three or more*)
JUNE 16
DECEMBER 25

COSTUMES

LARRY *in pajamas.* MOTHER *in ordinary dress.* MR. MOON *in yellow suit, a crescent-shaped hat fitting around his face.* FORGOTTEN DAYS *in dark suits, calendars fastened below waists like aprons, cardboards with days and dates hanging from shoulders i.e. Monday, 16, Tuesday, 22, etc; they may wear masks with faces painted on them, mouths are turned down at corners so they look unhappy.* RED LETTER DAYS *are dressed in gay colors, calendars at waist but their days are across their chests instead of on shoulders, days are numbered in red; two are marked December 25 and June 16.*

PROPERTIES

Any simple bedroom furniture may be used. There should be a bed, night table and chair at least and a book for LARRY *to read.* LARRY'S *clothes are hanging on the back of the chair. In Act Two the bed should be pushed to rear of stage to make more room on stage for the characters.*

ACT ONE

TIME: *January second, at bedtime.*

PLACE: LARRY'S *bedroom.* LARRY *is in bed and* HIS MOTHER *has just come in to say good night to him. As the scene opens* LARRY *is sitting up in bed with a book open on his knees. He is turning the pages.* HIS MOTHER *is hanging his clean clothes for the next day over the back of a chair. She seats herself on the chair, looks at* LARRY, *and speaks.*

MOTHER

Larry, it's eight-thirty. You must put your book away and go to sleep.

LARRY

O.K., but I'm not very sleepy.

(*He slides down between the bedclothes and the book falls to the floor.* HIS MOTHER *picks it up and puts it on the table.*)

MOTHER

Were you studying your geography lesson for tomorrow?

LARRY

Oh, I was just reading about the moon. Miss Brown says the moon controls the tides and the tides control the calendar—or something like that!

MOTHER

She probably told you that long ago people used the tides as a measure of time. They counted sixty tides to a month.

LARRY

Something like that. Say, Mother, where do the days go when they are—well, gone?

MOTHER

(*Laughing.*) Where do the days go? I guess that's something nobody knows. But I'm sure we all wonder where the days *get* to, and why they fly by so quickly.

LARRY

Yes, but I'd just like to know where they go!

MOTHER

That's a funny thing for a boy to be wondering about, I must say!

LARRY

(*Persistently.*) Where did yesterday go?

MOTHER

The same place that today is going, darling, and it's almost over and you aren't asleep yet. Good night, Larry. (*She leans over and kisses him.*)

LARRY

I'm not very sleepy.

MOTHER

Shall I bring you a glass of milk?

LARRY

Mmmm. I guess so. Mother, when you were young did you ever think much about where the days went to?

MOTHER

Of course. When I was a school librarian I often thought about that.

LARRY

Why?

MOTHER

Well, you see, when I was a librarian I had to change the date every school day. In the dater, that is.

LARRY

The dater? What's that?

MOTHER

That was what I used to stamp the books so that the boys and girls would know when to return them. And I guess changing the stamp every morning made me conscious of the date. Anyway, I know that often on Monday morning when I pushed the numbers around three times, omitting the Saturday and Sunday dates, it made me think.

LARRY

Think what?

MOTHER

Oh, it made me wonder, just as you've been saying, what had happened to those other dates—those two other days.

LARRY

They'd just gone by, hadn't they?

MOTHER

Yes, dear; gone forever.

LARRY

(*Sleepily.*) That's exactly . . . 'zactly . . . what I mean. Where . . . had they gone . . . I wonder.

(LARRY *closes his eyes.* HIS MOTHER *puts out the light and quietly leaves the room.*)

curtain

ACT TWO

PLACE: *Same as Act One. The bed has been pushed to rear of stage. When the scene opens* LARRY *is standing before* MR. MOON, *a fat, round-faced roly-poly of a man dressed all in yellow.* LARRY *is still in his pajamas and is rubbing his eyes sleepily.*

MR. MOON

How did you get here, little boy, and what is your name?

LARRY

I don't know how I got here. In my dream, I suppose. My name is Larry, but I know who *you* are without asking!

MR. MOON

You do?

LARRY

You're Mr. Moon, and you control the tides and the months and things like that.

MR. MOON

I still don't see how you got here! But if you came in a dream, I suppose you'll have to stay. I can't do a thing about it. Dreams are harder to control than the ocean tides. Just ask the days, if you don't believe me.

LARRY

Oh, is *this* where the days go? I might have known they would return to the moon! Just wait until I tell my mother. She's been trying for years to find out where they went.

MR. MOON

You earth people certainly do worry over the most trivial nonsense! If you were more careful how you *spend* your days, you wouldn't need to give them a second thought after they've passed. Furthermore, if anyone had told you where the days went, you wouldn't have believed him. Now, would you?

LARRY

Probably not. Say, if the days live here with you, where are they now?

MR. MOON

(*Pointing with a fat finger to door at left.*) Here come some of them now.

(FORGOTTEN DAYS *and* NEGLECTED DAYS *come on stage from left. They all have sad expressions on their faces, with the corners of their mouths turned down. They walk slowly up to* LARRY.)

FORGOTTEN DAYS

(*In unison.*) Who are you?

LARRY

I'm Larry. Who are you?

FORGOTTEN DAYS

We—boo-hoo—are the Forgotten Days, the Neglected Days, the days which have passed unnoticed by you human beings!

LARRY

I'm sorry.

NEGLECTED DAYS

Sorry! You should be sorry! (*They all point accusing fingers at him.*) It's all your fault.

LARRY

Why? I don't see how it's *my* fault!

FORGOTTEN DAYS

It is! It's your fault. How would *you* like people to forget your name?

LARRY

I told you I'm sorry. I didn't mean—I didn't *want* to hurt your feelings. I don't even know what days you are. If you would only tell me, perhaps I could remember *something* about you.

ONE OF THE FORGOTTEN DAYS

How do we know? That's the worst of it. Even we can't remember now who we were. Don't you think we'd have our dates showing on our calendars if we knew them?

(*They all turn around and start to walk sadly from the stage, heads bent. As they start to walk off, the dates on their backs can be seen.* LARRY *runs after them, calling to them.*)

LARRY

Wait! Now I know you. (*He reads off the dates as he sees them on their backs.*) You are Tuesday the twenty-second. And *you* are Thursday . . .

(*The* FORGOTTEN DAYS *turn on him angrily.*)

ONE OF THE FORGOTTEN DAYS

Don't do that! Don't try to recall our dates, you foolish boy! You should be wise enough to know that no day can be recalled, ever, ever!

(*They turn and run off stage at right.*)

LARRY

(*Turning to* MR. MOON.) Oh, I'm sorry. Honestly I am, Mr. Moon. But (*brightly*) there are lots of days I *do* remember!

MR. MOON

I'm glad to hear it, my boy. You are referring, no doubt, to these days?

(*He points toward a group of* DAYS *who at that moment come skipping merrily on stage from left. Each of these not only has the calendar pinned on at the waist, but also wears across the chest a prominent date, like those on the backs of the* FORGOTTEN DAYS. *They are dressed in colorful clothes, mostly in red. When* LARRY *sees them he cries out in recognition.*)

LARRY

(*Pointing.*) Oh, I know you! And you! And I remember you, too!
(*He goes forward to meet them. He clasps their hands one by one.*)

MR. MOON

Of course you remember them. These are the Remembered Days and the Red Letter Days of your life. I dare say there are some, however, that in the years to come you will gradually forget.

LARRY

Well, I know I'll never forget *these* two! (*He walks over to two of the Days and stands between them. They are marked December 25 and June 16.*) I'll always remember them, because they are Christmas and my birthday!

DECEMBER 25

Do you notice that our calendars are marked with red letters?

LARRY

Sure, 'cause you two are Red Letter Days. I have lots of fun on Christmas Day, and so I like you *almost* the best. But I guess I like my birthday best of all. You see, that's the day that belongs 'specially to me.

JUNE 16

Oh, thank you. I always try to be a happy day for you, Larry.

ALL THE DAYS

We are *all* Happy Days!
(*They form a ring around* LARRY *and begin to dance and chant.*)
Oh, we are the Happy Days,
The good Remembered Days,
Your own Red Letter Days,
    And we hope that you'll recall us
    Forever and forever
    And for always!
Yes, forever and for always!

LARRY

(*From the center of the ring.*) Oh, I will! I promise!
(*Suddenly the first group, the* FORGOTTEN *and* NEGLECTED DAYS, *rush on stage with roars of anger, swinging their arms about wildly.*

They rush upon the other group, who turn in fright and run off stage.)

LARRY

Oh, you mean old things! Why did you drive them away? Couldn't you see that we were having a wonderful time?

MR. MOON

They're jealous. They're always jealous! They have very mean dispositions.

THE FORGOTTEN DAYS

You treated us badly. We want to treat *you* badly!

NEGLECTED DAYS

We're going to teach you a lesson.

LARRY

No, no! I told you I didn't mean to forget you.

FORGOTTEN DAYS

We'll see to it that you *never* forget us! Come on, boys, let's help him to remember us.

LARRY

What are you going to do?

NEGLECTED DAYS

We're going to make you remember us, now and always! Who am I? Who am I? Who am I?

(*They all rush upon him, pointing their fingers in his face and shouting "Who am I?" until* LARRY *begins to cry.*)

LARRY

I can't remember.

NEGLECTED DAYS

How shall we make him remember?

FORGOTTEN DAYS

I know. We'll stamp him!

NEGLECTED DAYS

Yes, that's what we'll do. We'll stamp him with our dates and then he'll have to remember us!

LARRY

Oh no, please don't do that!

MR. MOON

Perhaps you'd better not. His mother won't like it. The ink is very hard to get off.

LARRY

Tell them not to, Mr. Moon.

MR. MOON

Don't you think you'd better reconsider? After all, what is passed is done, and I'm sure Larry will do much better in the future.

ALL THE DAYS

No! We must teach him a lesson!

(*They all reach into their pockets and bring out dating stamps and ink pads. Simultaneously they press the stamps onto the ink pads, then all rush upon* LARRY.)

ALL THE DAYS

At him, let us at him!

(LARRY *tries to run but they surround him, and all press the date stamps upon him, his clothing, his hands and face. He holds his hands up to his face and cries out.*)

LARRY

No, no, no!

curtain

ACT THREE

PLACE: *Same as Act One.* LARRY *is in bed. He flays his arms about wildly and shouts.*

LARRY

No, no, no! Mr. Moon, make them stop!

(LARRY'S MOTHER *enters carrying a glass of milk. She sets the milk down upon the bedside table and bends over* LARRY, *shaking him until he wakens.*)

MOTHER

Larry, Larry, wake up! You're dreaming.

(LARRY *sits up and looks at her dazedly.*)

LARRY

Oh, it was only a dream.

MOTHER

It must have been a nightmare, the way you were yelling. For goodness sake, Larry! You had me frightened.

LARRY

You were frightened! You weren't even there. That was awful! I don't see why Mr. Moon couldn't have made them stop.

MOTHER

Don't talk nonsense. It was only a dream.

LARRY

(*Putting one hand up to his face.*) Mother, are there dates on my face?

MOTHER

Dates? How could there be? There isn't a date in the house.

LARRY

I mean *dates!* The Forgotten Days were stamping me with their daters, and it hurt. And Mr. Moon said the ink is very hard to get off.

MOTHER

There isn't any ink on you. (*She laughs.*) You were getting your dreams confused with what I told you about stamping the books when I was a librarian. (*She reaches for glass of milk and hands it to* LARRY.) Here, Son; drink your milk. Then you will sleep properly and forget all about "Forgotten Days."

LARRY

Oh, my goodness, Mother! That's just what I *mustn't* do, forget about them! That's what made them so angry. Mr. Moon said they were jealous because I forgot them but remembered the other days, like my birthday and Christmas.

MOTHER

It's only natural to forget some days and remember others, dear. We particularly remember the happy days of our lives.

LARRY

(*Thoughtfully, as he sips his milk.*) Yes, but there should be some way, Mother, that we could remember *all* the days.

MOTHER

Oh, but there is!

LARRY

There is?

MOTHER

Of course. You can keep a diary. I'll buy you one tomorrow when I go downtown.

LARRY

Gee, that's a swell idea! The days I forget about I can just look up in my diary. I'll write in it every night. Every day will seem important then!

MOTHER

Today is only the second of January. You can fill in for these first two days so that you will have a complete record of the year.

LARRY

Yes, the whole 365 days! And you know what, Mother?

MOTHER

What?

LARRY

If I keep a record of all the days, there won't really be any Forgotten Days!

MOTHER

That's right, Son. Then let's hope that in this year ahead there will be many Red Letter Days.

(*She sees that* LARRY *has fallen asleep. She bends over, kisses him on the cheek, and quietly leaves the room.*)

curtain

E.H.S.

Lincoln's Secret Journey

CHARACTERS

ABRAHAM LINCOLN	SECOND GENTLEMAN
JOHN NICOLAY	ALLAN PINKERTON
MRS. LINCOLN	GOVERNOR CURTIN
ROBERT LINCOLN	JUDGE DAVIS
WILLIE LINCOLN	COLONEL SUMNER
TAD LINCOLN	WARD LAMON
FIRST LADY	NORMAN JUDD
SECOND LADY	THOMAS SCOTT
FIRST GENTLEMAN	A. K. McCLURE

COSTUMES

The costumes of the men, with the exception of COLONEL SUMNER, *are much the same: long trousers, vests, long frock coats, and bow ties with long flowing ends. In Act One,* LINCOLN *carries a tall hat. In Act Two, he carries a soft hat and has a shawl over his arm.* COLONEL SUMNER *wears a Union Army uniform. The three boys wear long, tight-fitting trousers, white shirts and eton jackets. The women wear long full dresses over hoop skirts. Their hats are little bonnets which tie under the chin.*

PROPERTIES

Act One requires living room furniture while the setting for Act Two is a dining room. The telegram used in Act Two is the only other property needed.

ACT ONE

TIME: *February 21, 1861.*

PLACE: *The living room of a Philadelphia hotel suite. As curtain opens we find two ladies and gentlemen engaged in conversation.*

FIRST LADY

Was the train on time?

FIRST GENTLEMAN

We'll know in a few minutes.

SECOND LADY

I'm really *very* excited. It is thrilling indeed to shake hands with the President of the United States.

FIRST LADY

He isn't President yet.

SECOND LADY

But he will be in a few days.

FIRST LADY

Do you suppose Mr. Lincoln is actually as ugly as his pictures portray him?

SECOND GENTLEMAN

My dear madam, if we had been looking for handsome features I am sure a good tailor's model could have been elected. But Abraham Lincoln possesses far more important qualities. He has wisdom and a keen understanding of this country's problems.

FIRST GENTLEMAN

Philadelphia has been looking forward to this day for a long time. We feel that it will be most fitting to have Mr. Lincoln raise the flag of the United States over Independence Hall.

SECOND LADY

Oh dear, I do hope nothing goes wrong at the inauguration.

FIRST LADY

Are you planning to attend?

SECOND LADY

Why, of course! I wouldn't miss it for the world.

(JOHN NICOLAY *enters.*)

JOHN NICOLAY

(*He bows to ladies and shakes hands with the gentlemen.*) Good evening ladies—gentlemen.

FIRST GENTLEMAN

Mr. Nicolay, we are happy to see you. You are not alone, I trust. Is Mr. Lincoln in the hotel too?

JOHN NICOLAY

Yes, we arrived just a moment ago. Mr. Lincoln is still greeting some well-wishers who were waiting for him downstairs in the lobby. He will be here presently. I suppose the plans for tomorrow are all completed?

SECOND GENTLEMAN

Yes, they are just as I wrote you. In the morning Mr. Lincoln will raise the flag over Independence Hall. Then he will entrain for Harrisburg. He will be met at the station by Governor Curtin and proceed to the capitol to speak to the legislature. I hope these plans were agreeable to Mr. Lincoln.

JOHN NICOLAY

Certainly. He is prepared for both of these addresses.

(MR. LINCOLN *enters. He is followed by* MRS. LINCOLN, ROBERT, WILLIE *and* TAD LINCOLN.)

JOHN NICOLAY

Ladies and gentlemen. May I present our next President of the United States, Abraham Lincoln. (*The ladies all curtsy and the gentlemen bow low.*) And may I also present Mrs. Lincoln, and their three sons, Robert, Willie and Tad.

(*The ladies and gentlemen shake hands with* MR. *and* MRS. LINCOLN. *As each one shakes hands he must say something such as,* "It is a pleasure to know you, Mr. Lincoln," *or* "I trust you had an enjoyable trip, madam." *There must not be a dead silence while the greetings are taking place.*)

JOHN NICOLAY

And now if you don't mind, I know both Mr. and Mrs. Lincoln are very tired. Perhaps a rest would be most welcome to them.

FIRST GENTLEMAN

Of course, Mr. Nicolay, we all understand and sympathize. No doubt a trip like this proves quite a strain.

MR. LINCOLN

On the contrary. I've enjoyed every bit of it since I left Illinois. I'm sure my wife and children have too.

MRS. LINCOLN

Oh, yes indeed! I really had no idea people would be so friendly and kind.

SECOND GENTLEMAN

Well, we shall leave you to yourselves now. Mr. Nicolay, there are still a few arrangements to be made. May I confer with you for a short time?

JOHN NICOLAY

Certainly.

(*After bowing again to the* LINCOLNS *everyone leaves the room except the Lincoln family.*)

MR. LINCOLN

(*Turning to* MRS. LINCOLN.) Well my dear, are you happy?

MRS. LINCOLN

Oh, yes! And I am looking forward to seeing Washington. (*Musingly.*) I wonder what condition the White House is in.

ROBERT

Father, I think you should speak to Willie and Tad. They have been behaving quite disgracefully. Do you know that at several stations where we stopped I heard them saying to people in the crowd, "Do you want to see Old Abe?" and then they would point to someone else!

(MR. LINCOLN *starts to laugh and then quickly covers it with a cough.*)

MRS. LINCOLN

(*Speaking sharply.*) Willie! Tad! I am surprised at you. Do you want people to think you have not been trained properly?

ROBERT

And that's not all, sir. I overheard two of the servants saying at the Buffalo Hotel that the boys had been playing leapfrog in the upstairs hall.

(*At this* WILLIE *and* TAD *both begin to giggle. They try to stifle it by holding their hands over their mouths. At the same time they are casting sly looks at their father.*)

MR. LINCOLN

(*Somewhat sheepishly.*) I'm afraid I can't scold them for that, Robert. You see, I played with them.

MRS. LINCOLN

(*Shocked.*) Mr. Lincoln! You didn't!

TAD

Yes, he did. And he was good too.

WILLIE

Well, his legs were longer. That's why he was so good.
(*At this moment there is a knock at the door.*)

MR. LINCOLN

Open the door, Tad.
(TAD *opens the door and* JOHN NICOLAY *enters.*)

JOHN NICOLAY

I'm sorry to disturb you, Mr. Lincoln, but there's a gentleman to
see you and it is very urgent.

MR. LINCOLN

Of course, John, I shall see him. Mrs. Lincoln, will you excuse me?

MRS. LINCOLN

Certainly. Come, boys.
(MRS. LINCOLN *and boys leave.*)

MR. LINCOLN

(*Calling after them.*) Remember, boys, no more leapfrog! (*Turning to* JOHN NICOLAY.) Who is this, John, with such an important
message for me?

JOHN NICOLAY

Mr. Allan Pinkerton of Chicago, sir. He's a detective in the employ
of the Wilmington and Baltimore Railroad. He says he must talk
to you at once.

MR. LINCOLN

All right, John, but you stay here too.
(JOHN *leaves and returns in a second with* ALLAN PINKERTON.)

JOHN NICOLAY

Mr. Lincoln, may I present Mr. Allan Pinkerton of Chicago?

MR. LINCOLN

(*Shaking hands with* MR. PINKERTON.) It's nice to meet you, Mr.
Pinkerton. John tells me that you wish to speak with me on urgent
matters.

MR. PINKERTON

I do indeed, Mr. Lincoln. I only wish it were not necessary for me
to do so. I hear that there is a plot afoot to assassinate you as your

train passes through Baltimore on your way to Washington from Harrisburg. I have investigated very carefully and I am convinced the report is accurate.

MR. LINCOLN

Nonsense! Why should anyone wish to assassinate me?

MR. PINKERTON

I'm afraid you do not understand, Mr. Lincoln, that some persons have come to consider you the symbol of the forces working against slavery. I beg of you to cancel your published plans and to depart for Washington at once.

MR. LINCOLN

Mr. Pinkerton, I believe you are sincere. However, I am going to carry out the plans which have been made. Tomorrow morning I shall speak at Independence Hall and in the afternoon at Harrisburg.

MR. PINKERTON

But after that is over, sir, will you accept the arrangements we shall make to get you to Washington safely?

MR. LINCOLN

What do you think, John?

JOHN NICOLAY

I'm afraid Mr. Pinkerton is right. Surely you do not want to endanger your life. Think of the chaos the country would be in if anything should happen to you.

MR. LINCOLN

Very well. Plan it as you will. But I wish it were not to be. After all, I am not a coward.

MR. PINKERTON

No one will believe that of you, sir.

MR. LINCOLN

I sincerely hope not.

MR. PINKERTON

Mr. Nicolay will be informed of the plans. I shall not have to bother you again.

(MR. PINKERTON *and* MR. LINCOLN *shake hands and then* JOHN

NICOLAY *and* MR. PINKERTON *leave.* MR. LINCOLN *stands a moment lost in thought. He looks unhappy.*)

curtain

ACT TWO

TIME: *February 22, 1861.*

PLACE: *The dining room of a Harrisburg hotel. As curtain opens we find* ABRAHAM LINCOLN, GOVERNOR CURTIN, JUDGE DAVIS, COLONEL SUMNER, A. K. McCLURE, WARD LAMON, THOMAS SCOTT *and* NORMAN JUDD *sitting around the table.*

GOVERNOR CURTIN

That was an excellent speech, Mr. Lincoln. I feel certain that the Pennsylvania legislature will back you one hundred percent.

MR. LINCOLN

Thank you, Governor Curtin.

(JOHN NICOLAY *enters.*)

JOHN NICOLAY

I beg your pardon, gentlemen. I just wanted to set your mind at rest, Mr. Lincoln. Robert has found your valise.

MR. LINCOLN

Good! (*Turning to men at table.*) I gave my valise containing my inaugural address to my son Robert. Usually he's very reliable but in the excitement of the occasion he mislaid it. I confess I have been somewhat worried.

JUDGE DAVIS

I don't blame you, Mr. Lincoln. It would have been a serious matter if it had not been found in time.

MR. LINCOLN

Thank you, John, for coming in to tell me. We were about to ring for some more coffee. Will you join us? (*Turning to other men.*) Gentlemen, this is my valuable secretary and friend, John Nicolay. John, this is Governor Curtin of Pennsylvania, Colonel Sumner of the United States Army, Mr. A. K. McClure of the Pennsylvania legislature, Mr. Thomas Scott of the Pennsylvania Railroad and of course you know my good friends Norman Judd and Ward Lamon.

(NICOLAY *bows to each one as he is introduced.*)

JOHN NICOLAY

I believe I shall not take any coffee now, Mr. Lincoln. I still have a great deal to do. And, sir, Mrs. Lincoln begs me to ask you if you will please see her again before you leave.

(MR. LINCOLN *rises. Immediately the others do too.*)

MR. LINCOLN

I shall go to her immediately. Will you excuse me, gentlemen? I had intended to tell you of the change in my plans but I shall let Mr. Lamon do that now.

(MR. LINCOLN *and* JOHN NICOLAY *leave the room.*)

COLONEL SUMNER

(*Excitedly.*) Did I understand Mr. Lincoln to say there had been a change in his plans?

MR. LAMON

I'm sorry to say that we have been forced to make some. Mr. Judd, you talked with Mr. Pinkerton in Philadelphia. Can you explain to our friends what has happened?

MR. JUDD

Mr. Allan Pinkerton, a detective in the employ of the Wilmington and Baltimore Railroad, discovered a plot to assassinate Mr. Lincoln when his train passes through Baltimore tomorrow.

COLONEL SUMNER

Outrageous! Why, we will take a squad of cavalry and cut our way through it if necessary!

MR. JUDD

I quite understand your feeling, Colonel Sumner, but Mr. Lincoln insists that there be no violence.

JUDGE DAVIS

I hope you've made plans, Mr. Judd, that will completely insure Mr. Lincoln's safety.

GOVERNOR CURTIN

A plot like this must be the work of insane men!

MR. LAMON

Insane or not, it is without doubt a real plot. Continue please, Mr. Judd.

MR. JUDD

Our plan is this. Through the aid of Mr. Scott we have arranged for a special train to take Mr. Lincoln and Mr. Lamon back to Philadelphia tonight. There they will board the regular New York to Washington sleeper. They will occupy berths in the sleeping car and will be in Washington tomorrow before anyone knows that they have left Harrisburg. The inaugural train will leave tomorrow as scheduled.

MR. McCLURE

Is there not danger that someone will recognize Mr. Lincoln at the station tonight and send word out that he is leaving?

MR. SCOTT

I've taken care of that. All telegraph wires leading into Harrisburg have been cut and service will not be restored until tomorrow morning.

JUDGE DAVIS

You gentlemen seem to have provided for any emergency.

(MR. LINCOLN *and* JOHN NICOLAY *enter.* MR. LINCOLN *is carrying a soft hat instead of his customary tall one. There is a shawl hanging over one arm. Everyone stands as he comes in.*)

MR. LINCOLN

I presume you gentlemen are now informed of my plans. Please believe me when I say I would much prefer not to be doing this.

GOVERNOR CURTIN

Mr. Lincoln, I think you have made a wise decision.

MR. LINCOLN

I sincerely hope you're right, Governor. (*Turning to* NICOLAY.) John, look after Mrs. Lincoln and the boys. Mrs. Lincoln is very much disturbed right now. I hadn't told her until just before dinner because I wanted to spare her the worry as long as possible.

JOHN NICOLAY

Yes, sir. Everything will be all right and your family will join you at the Willard Hotel in Washington tomorrow.

MR. LINCOLN

I believe I'm ready then. Ward, shall we go?

(MR. LINCOLN *shakes hands with all of them and then he and* MR. LAMON *leave. There is a silence for several seconds.*)

GOVERNOR CURTIN

There goes a courageous man. Let us pray that for our country's future as well as his own sake he arrives safely.

JUDGE DAVIS

What time do you expect wire service to be restored to Harrisburg, Mr. Scott?

MR. SCOTT

Around six o'clock. We should have a message through from Washington by then. Are you all going to wait?

ALL

Yes! We'll wait.

(*They all sit down.*)

GOVERNOR CURTIN

Shall we have more coffee, gentlemen? (*He rings a bell.*)

(*Curtain closes for a few seconds to show the lapse of several hours. When it opens again the same persons are sitting there. Most of them are resting their heads in their hands and they look utterly weary. Suddenly* JOHN NICOLAY *rushes in with a telegram in his hand. He hands it to* THOMAS SCOTT. *Everyone sits up and weariness seems to fade away.*)

MR. SCOTT

(*Opening wire and reading.*) "Plums delivered nuts safely." (*Turning to others.*) This is the code message Mr. Pinkerton agreed to send. Gentlemen, Abraham Lincoln is safe in Washington!

GOVERNOR CURTIN

And the United States has been spared the life of one who may be the means of preserving the Union!

curtain

J.W.

The Queen of Hearts' Party

CHARACTERS

KING OF HEARTS

QUEEN OF HEARTS

PAGE

CINDERELLA

CINDERELLA'S PRINCE

SLEEPING BEAUTY

SLEEPING BEAUTY'S PRINCE

RAPUNZEL

RAPUNZEL'S PRINCE

SNOW WHITE

SNOW WHITE'S PRINCE

PRINCESS MATHILDE

BOOTS

CHEF

KNAVE OF HEARTS

FIVE PERSONS WITH BOOTS

SOLDIERS

COSTUMES

Crowns for QUEEN *and* KING. *Their costumes and that of* KNAVE *should have red hearts sewn on them.* PRINCESSES *can be in evening dresses.* PRINCES *should wear short trousers, long stockings, gay, colored shirts or jackets, tightly belted, caps with feathers hanging down or placed at a jaunty angle.* CHEF *should wear a big apron and tall chef's hat. People with* BOOTS *should have on something to represent their trades: painter, overalls and cap; baker, white apron; housewife, apron and dust cap; carpenter, overalls; shoemaker, leather apron.*

PROPERTIES

Thrones for QUEEN *and* KING; *chairs if desired; handkerchiefs for* KING *and* MATHILDE; *apron for* QUEEN; *bag for* CINDERELLA'S *slippers; toy goose; apron and brush for painter; rolling pin for baker; broom for housewife; saw for carpenter; shoe and hammer for shoemaker.*

PLACE: *The throne room of the palace of the* KING *and* QUEEN OF HEARTS. *There is practically no furniture, just a few scattered chairs. In the center of the room, so that they attract attention, are two thrones mounted on a low platform. As the curtains part the* KING OF HEARTS *is seen pacing up and down, glancing occasionally at his watch.*

KING

Oh dear—oh dear! What can the matter be! Why doesn't she come! The guests will be arriving soon. I can't understand it. (*He walks over and pulls on the long bell rope hanging beside the door.* PAGE *enters.*) Run quickly and see if you can find the Queen. Tell her I desire her to come to the throne room.

(*The* PAGE *starts to leave hurriedly and is almost knocked over in the doorway by the* QUEEN, *who rushes in at the same instant. She has a large gingham apron over her fine dress and her crown is crooked. There are dabs of flour on her face.*)

KING

Where have you been? I've been worried about you. It's practically time for our party to begin.

QUEEN

Oh, I've been in the kitchen making the tarts. After all, I couldn't let anyone else bake them. But now everything is all ready.

(*The* QUEEN *goes over to her throne and sits down with a contented sigh.*)

KING

(*Clearing his throat.*) Ahem! My dear, haven't you forgotten something?

QUEEN

(*Worriedly.*) I don't believe so. (*She begins to check off on her fingers.*) Let me see. The silver is clean, the napkins are on—

KING

(*Interrupting.*) No, no, I don't mean that. I'm sure you have everything perfectly arranged. I mean—(*he pauses, then points to her apron*) *that!*

QUEEN

(*Looking down at herself.*) My goodness! I *am* getting forgetful.

(*She removes crown and hands it to* KING. *Then she takes off the apron. She beckons to* PAGE, *who has been standing in the doorway, and hands it to him.* PAGE *takes the apron out and then returns to take his post in the doorway. In the meantime the* QUEEN *takes her crown again and puts it on.*)

QUEEN

How do I look now?

(*The* KING *looks at her critically. Then he goes over to her and straightens her crown. He takes a handkerchief from a pocket and dusts the flour off her face. He steps back, looks her over again and then nods his head.*)

KING

Beautiful, my dear, and charming as usual.

QUEEN

Thank you. Oh, I do hope that all our guests arrive safely.

KING

I feel sure they will. After all, every one of their stories end, "And they all lived happily ever after." It would never do for anything unpleasant to happen.

QUEEN

I know, I know. I try to keep remembering that. But you know how traffic is on the highway these days. And all of them just live in their castles, paying no attention to what is happening in the

world. I even expect that they will all come by coach and horses.
I can't help feeling uneasy until they are all safely here.

KING

Now don't worry or you won't be able to enjoy yourself. You had
such a wonderful idea. Nothing could be more suitable than for
the Queen and King of Hearts to give a Valentine's Day party. And
the guests you invited—princesses, princes and peasant boys. Each
one has had a most unusual romance.

QUEEN

Well, I certainly hope everything goes off smoothly. Sometimes
princesses can get pretty temperamental—especially when there
are several present.

(*Bell rings.* KING *hastily takes his place on throne.* PAGE *disappears a second and then returns. He stands very straight just inside doorway.*)

PAGE

Her Royal Highness, Cinderella!

(CINDERELLA *enters, carrying a small bag. She goes to throne and curtsies before* QUEEN *and* KING.)

QUEEN

Good evening, my dear.

CINDERELLA

Don't tell me that I'm the first one here!

KING

We're happy that you are, Princess Cinderella.

CINDERELLA

You know, I was so in the habit of leaving parties early that I just
can't seem to realize that now I can stay as long as anyone else. I
always want to arrive early so I will have a longer time to stay.

QUEEN

Would you like to have the Page take your bag?

CINDERELLA

No thank you. I'll just keep it right with me. (*Speaks confidentially to* QUEEN.) You see, it's an extra pair of slippers in case I should
lose one of mine. I seem to have the worst luck nowadays. When-

ever one slips off someone puts it in his pocket for a souvenir. The last dance I attended I had to go home in my stocking feet.

KING

Didn't your husband, the Prince, come with you?

CINDERELLA

Yes, but he went along to the stables to see that the horses are all right. We almost had an accident.

QUEEN

(*To* KING.) See? I told you so. (*To* CINDERELLA.) What happened, my dear?

CINDERELLA

Oh, a huge monster came roaring down the road toward us. At first I thought it was a dragon and that it would surely devour us. However, it rushed right on past. But our horses were so frightened that they simply raced down the road. I declare, I'm still all a-tremble.

QUEEN

What a dreadful, dreadful experience. I'm sure I don't know what this world's coming to!

(*Bell rings.* PAGE *disappears, then returns.*)

PAGE

Cinderella's Prince!

(*Enter* PRINCE. *He comes over and bows low over* QUEEN'S *hand.*)

CINDERELLA'S PRINCE

I hope your Highnesses will forgive me for being late.

QUEEN

You are not late. The other guests have not yet arrived. Oh dear, oh dear! I *do* hope that nothing has happened to them.

KING

(*To* PRINCE.) The Queen is *such* a worrier! I trust that Cinderella is more calm.

CINDERELLA'S PRINCE

She's always nervous around midnight. She just can't seem to remember that our coach won't turn into a pumpkin if we stay out after that hour.

(*Bell rings.* PAGE *leaves, then returns.*)

PAGE

The Sleeping Beauty and her Prince!

(*Enter* SLEEPING BEAUTY *and her* PRINCE. *They go over and greet the* KING *and* QUEEN. SLEEPING BEAUTY *curtsies and* PRINCE *bows.*)

QUEEN

I hope *you* didn't have any difficulty on the way.

SLEEPING BEAUTY

Oh no! Nothing happened to us. That's just the trouble. Nothing ever *does* happen.

SLEEPING BEAUTY'S PRINCE

The Princess is always expecting something exciting to happen. Each morning she asks how many years she has slept.

SLEEPING BEAUTY

(*To* CINDERELLA.) My dear, you really ought to try it some time. It's so restful. But it's frightfully expensive. After I woke up I had to buy an entire new wardrobe. It's amazing what a hundred years can do to styles! Nothing I had was fit to wear!

(*Bell rings.* PAGE *leaves, then returns.*)

PAGE

The Princess Rapunzel and her Prince!

(RAPUNZEL *and her* PRINCE *go over before* QUEEN *and* KING. RAPUNZEL *curtsies and* PRINCE *bows.*)

QUEEN

My dear Rapunzel! I hardly recognized you. What has happened to your beautiful hair?

RAPUNZEL

(*Laughing.*) Don't you like my new hair-do? (*She turns around so that the* QUEEN *can see it from all sides.*) I just *love* short hair! How I ever stood hair that dragged on the ground is more than I can see.

RAPUNZEL'S PRINCE

Somehow I just can't get used to it. Rapunzel's hair attracted me to her first of all.

RAPUNZEL

(*Sharply.*) *You* didn't have to spend hours and hours combing it every day. When I think of those snarls!

CINDERELLA

(*Aside to* SLEEPING BEAUTY.) I don't think she's nearly so attractive, do you?

SLEEPING BEAUTY

(*To* CINDERELLA.) I for one am glad it's off. Now she looks like the rest of us. I used to get a little tired of all the "Ohs" and "Ahs" that went around every time she came in a room trailing all that hair behind her.

(CINDERELLA'S PRINCE *has been standing close by listening to this conversation. The others are grouped around the throne talking quietly to each other and not hearing* CINDERELLA *and* SLEEPING BEAUTY *talk.*)

CINDERELLA'S PRINCE

Now, now girls. You don't have to worry, either one of you. (*To* CINDERELLA.) Didn't I choose you from all the girls in my kingdom? Personally I prefer small feet instead of lots of hair.

(CINDERELLA *looks down at her feet then smiles at her* PRINCE.)

CINDERELLA

I know—and I'm sorry. It's foolish to be jealous, isn't it?

(*Bell rings.* PAGE *leaves, then returns.*)

PAGE

Snow White and her Prince!

(SNOW WHITE *and* PRINCE *enter and go over to* QUEEN *and* KING. SNOW WHITE *curtsies and* PRINCE *bows.*)

QUEEN

(*To* SNOW WHITE.) You're looking very lovely, my child. Your cheeks are as rosy as apples.

SNOW WHITE

(*Quickly.*) No, no, don't say that!

(*She looks as though she were about to faint and her* PRINCE *supports her.*)

SNOW WHITE'S PRINCE

The truth is, your Majesty, that my Princess Snow·White can't bear to hear the word "apples." You may recall that it was an apple that very nearly caused her death.

QUEEN

To be sure, to be sure. It was stupid of me to forget. What I meant, dear Snow White, was that your cheeks are as red as roses.

SNOW WHITE

(*Completely recovered.*) Forgive me, your Majesty, for seeming to speak to you so rudely. You are indeed gracious to be so understanding.

KING

(*To* QUEEN.) Are the guests all here, my dear?

QUEEN

All but Princess Mathilde and her husband Boots.

RAPUNZEL

Are *they* coming?

QUEEN

Of course. Why not?

RAPUNZEL

(*Haughtily.*) I am not so sure that I, a princess of royal blood, care to associate with a peasant boy. (*Glances at* CINDERELLA.) And especially one who used to poke in the ashes.

SLEEPING BEAUTY

I agree with you, Princess Rapunzel.

CINDERELLA

Well, I don't. Probably you don't want to associate with me either. That remark about the ashes was meant for me, I know. You never fail to remind everyone that I used to be a poor girl.

QUEEN

(*To* KING.) Now what shall I do? I told you something unpleasant would happen.

(*Bell rings.* PAGE *leaves, then returns.*)

PAGE

The Princess Mathilde!

(PRINCESS MATHILDE *enters. She is weeping and has her handkerchief to her eyes.*)

QUEEN

Oh, no! Now I *know* something has happened. (*She gets off the throne and rushes toward* MATHILDE.) What has happened? An accident? Where is your husband? Did something happen to him?

PRINCESS MATHILDE

(*Wiping her eyes.*) No, it's just that I feel so depressed. (*She begins to cry again and then speaks between sobs.*) Boots will be here directly. He had to walk.

KING

Walk? What do you mean? Couldn't he ride with you?

PRINCESS MATHILDE

Boots is bringing the Golden Goose with him. That's the only thing that cheers me up when I'm in one of these moods.

(*The* QUEEN *goes back over to her throne and sits down. She puts her hand up to see if her crown is still straight, then she smooths her dress.*)

QUEEN

(*Tactfully.*) How nice. I've heard about that famous goose for years and now I'll actually see it.

(*Bell rings.* PAGE *leaves. A scuffle is heard outside and then the* PAGE *enters looking slightly disheveled.*)

PAGE

Your Majesties! There is a whole crowd of people out here. I don't think they all want to come in but the one leading them insists he was invited. Shall I call the soldiers and have them removed from the palace?

KING

No, let them enter.

QUEEN

(*To* KING.) I certainly hope the tarts hold out. I didn't expect this many.

(*Enter* BOOTS *carrying Goose. He is followed by a baker in white apron with rolling pin, a carpenter with his saw, a woman in apron carrying a broom, shoemaker in leather apron carrying shoe and hammer, working man carrying shovel, and a painter with his brush and pail. Each one is hanging on to the person in front of him and at the same time appears to be struggling to get free. They are all loudly protesting their predicament.* PRINCESS MATHILDE, *as soon as they come in, begins to laugh and laugh. Soon she is joined by all the others.* CINDERELLA *and* RAPUNZEL *cling to each other and the* QUEEN *and* KING *almost fall off their thrones as* BOOTS *and his party parade around the room. Suddenly in the midst of all this the* CHEF *dashes in.*)

CHEF

(*Speaking loudly to make himself heard.*) Your Majesty, your Majesty! A terrible calamity has befallen us!
(*Everyone becomes quiet.*)

CHEF

The Knave of Hearts, he stole your tarts and then he ran away!
(*The* QUEEN *shrieks.*)

QUEEN

I *knew* something terrible would happen. (*She faints. All the* PRINCESSES *crowd around her and begin fanning.*)

SLEEPING BEAUTY'S PRINCE

Command us, your Majesty. What will you have us do? Shall we pursue the Knave?

KING

No. No. Just keep calm and everything will turn out all right.
(*Enter soldiers dragging the* KNAVE *with them.*)

SOLDIER

Here he is, your Majesty! We caught him before he ever got out of the courtyard. And the tarts are safe. He didn't have a chance to eat even one.
(*The* QUEEN *suddenly sits up straight and adjusts her crown. Apparently she hadn't been in a real faint after all.*)

QUEEN

And my party is saved?

KING

Of course it is, my dear. I *told* you nothing would happen to spoil it.

CINDERELLA

Why were you so sure, your Majesty?

KING

Because this is Saint Valentine's day, the day when love and romance are honored and nothing can happen to persons like you when all of your stories end "And they all lived happily ever after." I kept telling the Queen that, but she never really believed me.

(*Just then music is heard. The* KING *gets up and offers the* QUEEN *his arm.*)

KING

Come, my dear, let us lead the way to the banquet hall. We shall all honor Saint Valentine, patron of romance. We shall be merry! We shall be gay!

QUEEN

Just one minute. Because this is Saint Valentine's Day I declare that the Knave of Hearts is forgiven.

(*The* KNAVE *rushes over to the* QUEEN, *throws himself on the floor, and kisses the hem of her skirt. He gets up and rushes out, followed by the soldiers.*)

QUEEN

(*To* KING.) After all, I don't suppose he could resist the temptation to sample one of my tarts!

(*The* KING *and* QUEEN *start slowly toward the door, arm in arm. The other couples fall in line behind them,* PRINCESS MATHILDE *and* BOOTS *being last.* BOOTS *is still carrying the Goose and the people are still attached to each other. They are still struggling and protesting but no one seems to be paying any attention to them. Everyone is happy.*

curtain

J.W.

My Honest Friend

CHARACTERS

CHRISTOPHER LUDWIG, *formerly Baker General of the Continental Army*
JAMIE, *a neighbor's child*

BETSY, *his sister*
MR. LEWIS, *a friend of Christopher Ludwig*

COSTUMES

BETSY *in a dress to her ankles; she wears a little apron and a kerchief is around her neck and brought together in a point halfway to her waist.* JAMIE *is in blouse and knee britches which hang loose just below knees.* CHRISTOPHER LUDWIG *has on blouse and knee britches which are fastened tightly just below knees. He wears long stockings.* MR. LEWIS *is dressed like* CHRISTOPHER *except that he wears a long frock coat and a three-cornered hat.*

PROPERTIES

In addition to the furniture, there will have to be a pan of bread dough, a similar pan of bread to be taken from the oven, and a pan of gingerbread.

TIME: *February 1799.*

PLACE: CHRISTOPHER LUDWIG'S *kitchen. A large crude table stands near the front of the stage. Several chairs or benches are scattered throughout the room. At the back of the stage is a fireplace. This can be made of cardboard and painted to look like stone. It should have an oven door so that the bread can be put in. If possible, have some antique kitchen utensils around to lend authenticity to the scene. These may be an iron pot, frying pan, platter, old dishes, spoons, etc. As the scene opens Jamie and Betsy are watching old* CHRISTOPHER LUDWIG *bake bread.*

BETSY

Master Ludwig, my mother says you are too old to live alone.

LUDWIG

And perhaps your mother is right. So will you come, then, and be my housekeeper, and bake my bread?

BETSY

(*Laughing.*) Oh, no! I'm too young.

JAMIE

Besides, she can't bake bread!

LUDWIG

Then, indeed, she will not do! I must have my bread. (*He gives a last pat to a loaf and places it in the pan.*)

BETSY

How old are you, Master Ludwig?

LUDWIG

Seventy and eight, and I still stand straight!

BETSY

That's a rhyme! Seventy and eight and you still stand straight. Isn't that funny, Jamie? Master Ludwig made a rhyme.

JAMIE

Our mother says you are still the best baker in Philadelphia.

LUDWIG

Your mother is kind, but she is wrong! *I* am the best baker in all of the United States.

BETSY

(*Laughing.*) Oh, you are so funny! Always making jokes. I guess that's why we like to come here so well.

JAMIE

Yes. And also in hopes that Master Ludwig will give us a slice of warm bread when it comes from the oven.

BETSY

Shame on you!

LUDWIG

That's all right, Jamie boy. Old Uncle Christopher will be glad to give his little friends warm bread from the oven. Besides, if you will but allow me to get on with my work with less of your chatter, there may be some gingerbread too.

JAMIE

Gingerbread! Now, *that's* the thing you can do the best of anyone in the whole world, Master Ludwig—bake gingerbread.

LUDWIG

Ach, and why not? Did I not return to England in my youth for the express purpose of learning to bake the best gingerbread in the world?

BETSY

Tell us how you baked bread for the Continental Army!

LUDWIG

You have heard it often, Miss Betsy.

JAMIE

Tell us how you baked bread for General Washington too.

LUDWIG

That you have heard also, but I am not too modest to repeat it. Baker General of the Army! That was the title conferred upon me by General George Washington himself. I wonder to this day what our soldiers would have done without old Christopher's bread. It was good bread too. Christopher Ludwig gave them the best.

JAMIE

Tell us what you said to the Congress, Master Ludwig.

LUDWIG

It was like this. Back in '77 when the Continental Congress told me that I had been appointed Baker General of the Army, they said: "We expect, sir, one pound of bread for every pound of flour." Yes, and what did I say to them, my kinder?

BETSY and JAMIE

What?

LUDWIG

I said to them, "Gentlemen, you have made a mistake! I am an honest man and have not forgotten that yeast and water add weight to a loaf of bread. For every hundredweight of flour you give me," I said, "you shall receive one hundred and thirty-five loaves of bread!"

BETSY

I guess they were surprised.

LUDWIG

Ach, yes! They forgot that it was Christopher Ludwig with whom they were dealing. Why should I want to get rich by the war? No, I had money.

JAMIE

Father says that you gave a lot of it to the government to help win the war. The people of Philadelphia know that you're a great patriot, Master Ludwig.

BETSY

Now tell us about General Washington.

LUDWIG

That, too, you have heard many times. General Washington was my friend. Many times have I dined with him. He liked to hear my jokes and stories. He always called me his friend. "My honest friend," he always called me.

JAMIE

Not many people have a letter from General Washington like yours.

LUDWIG

Ah, my letter! (*He pats the pocket of his coat.*) Always I carry his letter with me. It shall go with me to my grave.

(*A knock is heard at the door.* BETSY *opens it.* MR. LEWIS *enters.*)

MR. LEWIS

Good day to you, Christopher. I see you're busy with your loaves.

LUDWIG

Good day to you, Master Lewis. Yes, an old man does not eat much bread, but what he eats must be good. Besides, I have many friends who like my bread.

MR. LEWIS

I stopped in to thank you for the loaf you sent Mistress Lewis and me last week. But I have come for another purpose too.

LUDWIG

When these loaves are done you shall take one to Mistress Lewis.

MR. LEWIS

I'm afraid I haven't time to wait, Christopher. But if I may, I shall stop by for it on my way out of the city.

LUDWIG

You are going away?

MR. LEWIS

Yes, I'm leaving for Virginia by this afternoon's stagecoach. I'm going to see an old friend of yours, Christopher.

LUDWIG

Not General Washington?

MR. LEWIS

Yes. President Adams is sending me to Mount Vernon with messages for the General's birthday. Washington's birthday is next week and if the weather holds I should be in Mount Vernon for the occasion. That's why I have come here, Master Ludwig. We— that is, the Congress, Mr. Adams and I—thought perhaps you might have a greeting to send to your good friend.

LUDWIG

Ach, what an addlehead I am! So old I am getting that I could forget it is soon to be my General's birthday. And here I have no gift for him!

(*He sits at the table and holds his head in his hands.*)

MR. LEWIS

Oh, don't let that worry you. Send him your good wishes. I shall be happy to take the message for you.

LUDWIG

(*Slowly.*) Not just a greeting. I must send him a gift! He calls me his honest friend, and wrote me such a letter.

BETSY

Master Lewis, General Washington is a very *special* friend of Master Ludwig's.

JAMIE

He wrote a letter about Master Ludwig which is very dear to him.

BETSY

He carries it about with him always.

MR. LEWIS

I've heard of that letter.

BETSY

Read it to him, Master Ludwig!

LUDWIG

(*Wistfully.*) I *could* read it to you, Master Lewis, if you have a minute.

MR. LEWIS

I should like to hear it, Christopher.

LUDWIG

It is my dearest treasure on earth. (*He takes the letter from his pocket, clears his throat, and reads, while all eyes are turned on him.*)

"I have known Christopher Ludwig from an early period in the war, and have every reason to believe, as well from observation as information, that he has been a true and faithful servant to the public; that he has detected and exposed many impositions, which were attempted to be exercised by others in his department; that he has been the cause of much saving in many respects; and that his deportment in public life has afforded unquestionable proofs of his integrity and worth.

"With respect to his losses, I have no personal knowledge, but have often heard that he has suffered from his zeal in the cause of his country." And it is signed, "George Washington."

MR. LEWIS

Ah, that is indeed something to be proud of, Christopher. I can see why you want to send General Washington a gift for his birthday.

LUDWIG

Yes, but what shall I give him? There is so little time!

BETSY

Perhaps you have something about the house that you could send.

MR. LEWIS

(*Rising.*) Well, I'll tell you what. I shall stop by in an hour or so to pick up the loaf for Mistress Lewis. Perhaps by that time you will have thought of something.

(MR. LEWIS *goes out.*)

LUDWIG

(*Still sitting at the table thinking.*) I have nothing to send. Nothing!

JAMIE

I think I smell your bread burning, Master Ludwig.

LUDWIG

(*Jumping up and going to the oven.*) My bread! (*He removes the loaf pans from the oven and puts them on the table.*) No, it is not yet burned, but it is good that you spoke up, Jamie.

BETSY

Mmmm! That smells good. I'll bet that General Washington would like to have a warm slice of that right now.

JAMIE

I know *I* would!

LUDWIG

(*Turning the loaves out on a cloth.*) The General always liked my bread. But his favorite was my gingerbread. He always said that I made the best gingerbread in the world. (*Chuckles.*) Which I do!

BETSY

Oh, now I know! I know what to send him. Master Ludwig, send him some of your gingerbread for his birthday!

LUDWIG

(*Looking at* BETSY *with surprise.*) My gingerbread? Gingerbread for a birthday gift?

BETSY

Why not?

LUDWIG

Ach, it is not good enough!

JAMIE

You said yourself it is the best in the world.

BETSY

And just think how good it will taste to him 'way down there in Virginia. Gingerbread baked by his own favorite baker. Oh, I think it's a wonderful idea, Master Ludwig.

LUDWIG

Well, I don't know. Of course, he *might* want it!

JAMIE and BETSY

Oh, he would!

LUDWIG

I'd *like* to make the General some of my gingerbread.

BETSY

Then do! We'll help you.

(*The curtain goes down to show the passing of an hour. When it rises again* BETSY *and* JAMIE *are still in the kitchen and* MASTER LUDWIG *is lifting a large loaf of gingerbread out of the oven. The two children are watching.*)

LUDWIG

It is done.

BETSY

It smells delicious!

JAMIE

It *looks* delicious!

LUDWIG

Well, now, so it does! Let me put it on the cloth to cool. Master Lewis will be coming any minute. Ach, he'll think me a crazy old man to send such a gift to our beloved General, our first President. He'll think it is not a dignified gift.

(*A rap is heard on the door and* MR. LEWIS *enters.*)

MR. LEWIS

Mmm! I smell gingerbread! I've never smelled anything so good in all my life.

BETSY

(*Clapping her hands.*) It's Mr. Washington's present from Master Ludwig!

MR. LEWIS

What a wonderful idea, Christopher.

LUDWIG

The children thought of it. But I don't know. It's not a conventional gift, Master Lewis.

MR. LEWIS

I can think of nothing that would please the General more. He will be happy to know that you thought of him, and also to know that you remembered how fond he is of gingerbread. Is it too hot, think you, for me to take along? I am in great haste to be off.

LUDWIG

It is hot, yes. But you must keep it wrapped in this cloth. Also I have put a loaf of bread in this little basket for Mistress Lewis, with my compliments.

MR. LEWIS

Thank you, Christopher. I know my wife will enjoy it.

BETSY

I wish I could see General Washington's face when he sees what Master Ludwig has sent him.

JAMIE

Or when he tastes it!

LUDWIG

Ach, such a little gift. Only a poor loaf of gingerbread.

MR. LEWIS

But the best in the land, from the best baker in the United States of America! And is there a message from you to go with it, Christopher?

LUDWIG

(*Slowly.*) Tell him—tell my General that I send my respects and fondest greetings for his birthday, Master Lewis. Tell him that I am proud to share in my humble way in celebrating his birthday. (*A pause while all eyes are turned on* LUDWIG.) The birthday of George Washington; a famous man, a famous birthday!

curtain

E.H.S.

George Washington Serves His Country

CHARACTERS

Act One

MISS CRAWFORD	CHARLES
TOMMY	LARRY
ELAINE	MICHAEL
DICKIE	SUSAN
BETTY	SAMMY
ROBERT	RUTH
SHIRLEY	OTHER BOYS AND GIRLS

Act Two has the same children in it as in Act One. They may take parts in each scene or other children may be used instead. This will depend on how many children are available to be used in the play. The listing of characters for Act Two has been planned to show how the play may be given with a cast of seventeen, but this can be changed to include more if desired.

Act Two

NARRATOR (DICKIE)	GENERAL LAFAYETTE (LARRY)
GEORGE WASHINGTON (TOMMY)	FIRST OFFICER (MICHAEL)
JOHN HANCOCK (ROBERT)	SECOND OFFICER (SAMMY)
JOHN ADAMS (CHARLES)	THIRD OFFICER
EDMUND PENDLETON (LARRY)	SOLDIER
FIRST MEMBER OF CONGRESS (SAMMY)	MARTHA WASHINGTON (ELAINE)
SECOND MEMBER OF CONGRESS (MICHAEL)	SERVANT (MICHAEL)
MESSENGER	CHARLES THOMSON (ROBERT)
THOMAS JOHNSON	NELLIE CUSTIS (BETTY)
GENERAL STEUBEN (ROBERT)	LAWRENCE LEWIS (SAMMY)
DOCTOR (CHARLES)	OTHER COUPLES (SHIRLEY, SUSAN, RUTH, CHARLES, LARRY, MICHAEL)

COSTUMES

If desired the whole play may be presented without costuming. If Act Two is presented as a rehearsal, MISS CRAWFORD'S *speech at beginning of the act should be used. If costuming is preferred this speech should be omitted and Colonial dress used for all characters in Act Two.*

PROPERTIES

Act One, a desk for MISS CRAWFORD. *Act Two: Scene I, chairs for* MEMBERS OF CONGRESS; *table for* JOHN HANCOCK; *Scene II, a few chairs and a table; Scene III, living room furniture; Scene IV, same as Scene III.*

ACT ONE

TIME: *The present. A few weeks before Washington's Birthday.*

PLACE: *A schoolroom. Children are around in groups talking to one another. Teacher goes to her desk and raps for order.*

MISS CRAWFORD

Boys and girls, will you all please be quiet for a moment and listen to what I have to tell you. As you all know, it will soon be our turn to have charge of an auditorium program for the rest of the school. That day happens to be Washington's Birthday, so I thought we might have a play based on his life.

TOMMY

(*Excitedly.*) That sounds swell, Miss Crawford. May I be George Washington?

MISS CRAWFORD

(*Laughing.*) Just a minute, Tommy. Don't go so fast. First of all we must decide *what* we are going to do and then we will decide on the parts.

ELAINE

Are we going to give a long play, Miss Crawford? And will the girls be in it too?

MISS CRAWFORD

Well, it can't be *too* long, but the plan I have in mind should make it possible for all of you to take part, Elaine.

DICKIE

Tell us, Miss Crawford.

MISS CRAWFORD

If you will all stop talking long enough for me to explain, we can discuss the details afterward.

SEVERAL CHILDREN

(*Together.*) We'll listen, Miss Crawford.

(*The children all sit down and look at* MISS CRAWFORD *attentively.*)

MISS CRAWFORD

I think perhaps the best thing to do is a series of scenes, each one portraying something important that happened in Washington's life. You can divide into groups and each group can work out its own little play. None of them should be very long. It shouldn't be too hard to do. We have just finished studying the Revolutionary War in history and tomorrow you will hear the last chapter of the biography of Washington I have been reading to you.

BETTY

I hate to have that book end. Are you going to start another one soon?

MISS CRAWFORD

Yes, but I'll tell you about that another time. *Now* we are going to talk about our auditorium play. Let's first decide on what incidents we want to use.

TOMMY

Let's do Valley Forge. (*He gets up, places one hand inside his coat, bows his head and begins to pace up and down.*) See, don't I look like Washington?

(*The children all laugh.*)

MISS CRAWFORD

To tell the truth, Tommy, you look more like Napoleon than Washington.

ROBERT

Who was Napoleon?

MISS CRAWFORD

(*Sighing.*) Robert! Not now, please. We're talking about *Washington*. All right now—are you all agreed we should have a scene about Valley Forge?

CHORUS OF VOICES

Yes. Of course. Sure. Let's.

SHIRLEY

Couldn't we do one with a dance in it? Like when Nellie Custis got married. Remember how the biography said that Washington danced the minuet with spirit?

CHARLES

Isn't that just like a girl! A wedding and dancing! I'd rather do a scene about when he fought the Indians with Burgoyne.

SHIRLEY

Oh, you boys and your Indians! Anyway, Washington didn't win that time.

CHARLES

So what? He was there, wasn't he? And I'll bet the other kids would rather see a good Indian fight than any old dancing!

MISS CRAWFORD

(*Interrupting.*) Now stop arguing. We are here to *discuss* plans, not to *quarrel* about them. Shirley, I think your idea is splendid. It will give you girls a chance to work out something quite different from the rest. And Charles, we'll find a scene for you that will be exciting enough.

LARRY

I'll tell you. Put in one about Washington crossing the Delaware and let Charles fall overboard. *That* ought to be exciting.

(*Children and* MISS CRAWFORD *laugh.*)

MISS CRAWFORD

Now, let's get serious again. We've decided on Valley Forge and Nellie's wedding. Anything else?

MICHAEL

Couldn't we tell about Benedict Arnold? It was awfully important when Washington found out that his favorite general had turned traitor.

MISS CRAWFORD

We'll put that suggestion down, Michael. Any others?

SUSAN

I think we should tell about when he was elected first President of the United States.

SAMMY

Aren't we going to do a scene about the cherry tree?

RUTH

Oh, Sammy! Don't you remember that Miss Crawford told us that wasn't really true at all?

MISS CRAWFORD

I said, Ruth, that that old story was told long ago in a book about Washington written by Parson Weems. And while there is no foundation for it, people like to tell it because it seems to be a symbol of Washington's honesty. But I don't think we want to include it in our play.

DICKIE

Will we have the scenes in the order they really happened?

MISS CRAWFORD

Yes, and I think we should have a narrator; that is, someone to introduce each scene and explain what has happened between each one.

SUSAN

Miss Crawford, Dickie is the president of our class. I think he should do that.

CHILDREN

Yes. Dickie should. I nominate Dickie. He's the one.

MISS CRAWFORD

Dickie, it seems as though the class has already decided on your part. Now let's divide up into groups and we'll get started. Susan, you suggested the wedding. Suppose you take care of that.

(*Children all begin talking at once.*)
curtain

ACT TWO

(MISS CRAWFORD's *speech may or may not be used to introduce this act. If the production is staged without background or costuming, it should be included. Otherwise the action of the Washington scenes may begin at once. The* NARRATOR's *speeches may be read instead of spoken. When curtain opens all the boys and girls taking part are on the stage.*)

MISS CRAWFORD

All right, boys and girls! We are ready now for a full rehearsal. Each group has been working for two weeks on its own play and now we are going to put them together for the first time. We will close the curtains and those in the first scene take their places. All others please leave the stage. Dickie, you stand outside the curtain over to the right and remain there throughout the play.

curtain

NARRATOR

Today, February 22nd, is the anniversary of the birth of a famous American—George Washington, first President of the United States. We are going to present a few scenes which will portray some memorable events in his life. Our first scene takes place during the meeting of the Second Continental Congress at Philadelphia in May, 1775. Although the events which you are about to see took place over several weeks we are presenting them as though they all happened at one time. George Washington is a member of this Congress as a delegate from his state of Virginia. Benjamin Franklin is here, too, and John Adams. John Hancock is presiding as President of the Congress. For some days the discussion has been centered on whether or not the different states would willingly free themselves from loyalty to England even if doing so meant war.

curtain rises

SCENE I: *The Continental Congress.*

(JOHN HANCOCK *is seated at table and rest of the members sit facing him.*)

JOHN HANCOCK

Gentlemen, word has reached us that Boston is still in a state of siege. We have not yet heard from the expeditions of Ethan Allen and Benedict Arnold, who are conducting campaigns in the north.

(*He is interrupted by a messenger who hurries up to him and hands him a dispatch.* HANCOCK *reads it and almost shouts to the assembly.*)

I spoke too hastily, gentlemen. Allen and Arnold have been successful, and Fort Ticonderoga and Crown Point are in their possession!

JOHN ADAMS

Mr. Hancock?

JOHN HANCOCK

Yes, Mr. Adams.

JOHN ADAMS

Is it not time for us to declare ourselves and organize an army which will show everyone that we mean what we say?

JOHN HANCOCK

But we cannot make war without a general commander. We must have someone who would unite all parts of the country under him.

EDMUND PENDLETON

Mr. President.

JOHN HANCOCK

Yes, Mr. Pendleton?

EDMUND PENDLETON

We already have a most able general in the field. Why not have General Artemus Ward, who is now commanding the army outside of Boston, assume the entire command?

JOHN ADAMS

But I do not believe that southern companies would join and serve under him. We must influence the South through one of its own sons.

JOHN HANCOCK

Have you a suggestion, Mr. Adams?

JOHN ADAMS

I have indeed! There is in this very Congress a gentleman from

Virginia who is both skilled and experienced as a commander of men.

(WASHINGTON *gets up quietly and leaves the room.*)

JOHN ADAMS

And that gentleman is as modest as he is brave. I observe that he has left the room so we can discuss him freely without embarrassment. I refer, gentlemen, to Colonel George Washington of the Virginia militia.

FIRST MEMBER OF CONGRESS

But sir, Colonel Washington has never had a single military victory to his credit.

SECOND MEMBER OF CONGRESS

He is a fox-hunting planter. New Englanders would never stand for a man of wealth like that.

JOHN ADAMS

To be sure he is a wealthy man, but he is an honest one and I know you would never regret such a choice. And as a New Englander, I can assure you that my section of the country would concur in such an appointment.

THOMAS JOHNSON

Mr. President, I, Thomas Johnson of Maryland, should like to make a motion that the name of Colonel George Washington of Virginia be placed in nomination for commander in chief of the Colonial forces.

EDMUND PENDLETON

I second the motion.

JOHN HANCOCK

You have heard the motion, gentlemen. All those in favor signify by saying "Aye."

ALL

Aye.

JOHN HANCOCK

Opposed? (*Pauses.*) The motion is carried. Mr. Pendleton, will you please ask Colonel Washington to return?

(PENDLETON *goes out and returns immediately with* WASHING-TON.)

JOHN HANCOCK

Colonel Washington, the Continental Congress has just voted you commander in chief of the Continental army.

GEORGE WASHINGTON

Mr. President and Members of the Congress, I deeply appreciate the honor which has been conferred upon me, but I beg it be remembered by every gentleman in the room that I this day declare with the utmost sincerity that I do not think myself equal to the command with which I am honored.

JOHN HANCOCK

General Washington, for I may call you that now, you are hereby vested with full power to act as you see fit for the good and welfare of the service. And we who are assembled here resolve that we will assist and maintain you with our lives and our fortunes in this great cause to which you are dedicated.

GEORGE WASHINGTON

With everyone's cooperation and prayers I feel confident we shall succeed in our struggle for independence and that victory will be ours. May the people of our country realize that what we have undertaken today marks the beginning of a new life and a new independence from tyranny.

curtain

NARRATOR

Two years have passed since that day. It is now the winter of 1778. The American Army has had many defeats and some of its leaders have become very discouraged. The British Army is in Philadelphia enjoying the pleasures and comforts of that city. But the American Army, encamped at Valley Forge, is suffering from cold and hunger. Our next scene takes place in Washington's headquarters at Valley Forge.

curtain rises

SCENE II: *Washington's Headquarters at Valley Forge.*

(WASHINGTON, STEUBEN, LAFAYETTE, DOCTOR *and three officers are seated around a table.*)

GEORGE WASHINGTON

General Steuben, you have been in camp some time now. Can you tell us what you think should be done to improve the conditions here?

GENERAL STEUBEN

General Washington, the discipline of your army is very poor. I have been working at drilling your soldiers, but sometimes I think it is very hopeless indeed. Why, the first day I came I saw many of your men using their bayonets as spits on which to cook their meat!

GEORGE WASHINGTON

I admit, General, that such things may strike you as strange. But do not forget that our army is made up of men who have been recruited from farms, offices and, in fact, all walks of life. They are not the professional soldiers to which you have been accustomed.

GENERAL STEUBEN

But General Washington, in Europe I drill a man three weeks to make him into a recruit. Here I am expected to turn him into an officer in the same length of time. But I must admit that *your* soldiers have a spirit I have never observed before.

GEORGE WASHINGTON

(*Turns to* DOCTOR.) Doctor, has the epidemic of fever grown any less?

DOCTOR

I'm afraid not, sir. Only yesterday at least one-third of the men in camp were sent to hospitals. We are using every farmhouse, church and meeting house around this section for emergency hospitals. The disease is hard to control because we do not have the proper medicines or the right food to give sick men strength to get well.

GEORGE WASHINGTON

Perhaps things will improve soon. I believe that more wagons are getting through the snow, now, bringing us provisions.

FIRST OFFICER

Some barrels of fish came in yesterday, sir, and the men were so starved they seized them and ate the fish raw before we had a chance to have them cooked.

SECOND OFFICER

A joke is going around that our beef is so lean that you can see the butcher's britches through it.

(*Everyone laughs a little at this story.*)

GEORGE WASHINGTON

If the men can keep a sense of humor through this we have something to be thankful for. (*Turns to* LAFAYETTE.) General Lafayette, I hear that you are responsible for some of the new shirts that were just sent into camp.

GENERAL LAFAYETTE

Yes, General Washington. Some of the ladies living near here invited me to a party. I told them I appreciated an invitation from such pretty ladies but asked them if they knew that our soldiers had no shirts. They turned the party into a sewing bee instead.

GEORGE WASHINGTON

There is another matter about which I must again warn the officers. I have had many protests from farmers around here that their supplies of food are disappearing. We must not cause our friends such hardships.

THIRD OFFICER

We shall issue warnings, sir. But the men are desperate for food.

GEORGE WASHINGTON

While the men were on parade for me yesterday, I observed that even though their clothes were in tatters, some of them had decorated their hats with greens. I honored them for their spirit.

FIRST OFFICER

I understand too, sir, that one young soldier wrote to his mother that he was living on the fat of the land.

(SOLDIER *enters.*)

SOLDIER

General Washington, the sentry reports that a little Negro girl is outside. She has a small bundle of potatoes, apples, and nuts hidden under her coat and she says they are for the soldiers. She insists upon seeing you sir. She says she has come to join the army.

(*All* OFFICERS *laugh.*)

GEORGE WASHINGTON

Of course her master will have to be informed, but take the little girl to Mrs. Washington. She will know what to do with her. Perhaps she can have her help to distribute baskets of food and medicines to the sick soldiers. (*He pauses a moment and then stands up very straight with head held high.*) Gentlemen. We have many problems but with the examples of one young soldier and one little girl before us we can face the future with the assurance that such spirit will overcome any obstacle and will triumph in the end.

curtain

NARRATOR

So the war years passed. The American army defeated the British and in May, 1787, another convention of the states was held in Philadelphia. This time the purpose was to write a constitution. Again Washington attended. Afterward he returned to his home at Mt. Vernon. In March of the next year George Washington had a visitor at Mt. Vernon.

curtain rises

SCENE III: *Mt. Vernon.*

(MARTHA *and* GEORGE WASHINGTON *are seated in their living room. A servant enters.*)

SERVANT

General Washington, Mr. Charles Thomson is here to see you.

GEORGE WASHINGTON

Bring him in immediately.

(CHARLES THOMSON *enters.* WASHINGTON *arises and goes over and takes his hand.*)

GEORGE WASHINGTON

Mr. Thomson, I am happy to welcome you to Mt. Vernon.

(*He leads him over to* MARTHA WASHINGTON.)

GEORGE WASHINGTON

My dear, may I present to you Mr. Charles Thomson, who was Secretary of the Continental Congress?

(MRS. WASHINGTON *extends her hand and* MR. THOMSON *bows low over it.*)

MR. THOMSON

General Washington, I am sent here to inform you that the Electoral College has completed its vote and you have been unanimously elected the first President of the United States.

(WASHINGTON *bows his head and stands silent for a moment.*)

GEORGE WASHINGTON

Sir, I can do no other than accept. I am much affected by this fresh proof of my country's esteem and confidence. I hope that there may never be reason for regretting the choice. All I can promise is to accomplish that which can be done by honest zeal.

MR. THOMSON

Our country is fortunate, sir, that it will have your wisdom to guide us through our first years as an independent nation. We are indeed to be congratulated.

curtain

SCENE IV: *Same as Scene III.*

NARRATOR

And so once again George Washington served his country. For eight years he was President and then he returned to his beloved Mt. Vernon. On his birthday following his retirement, Mt. Vernon was filled with happiness. His ward, Nellie Custis, was married to Lawrence Lewis.

curtain

(*Minuet music is playing and several couples are dancing.* GEORGE *and* MARTHA WASHINGTON *are seated at one side. When dance is over* NELLIE *and* LAWRENCE *go over to them.*)

GEORGE WASHINGTON

Nellie, my child, you look very beautiful and happy this night. It is my wish for you that you will always find the happiness that I have.

(*He places his hand over* MARTHA'S *as he speaks. The music begins again.*)

NELLIE

Will you not join us in a last dance?

(WASHINGTON *arises and offers his arm to* MARTHA. *They join the dancers on the floor and begin the steps of the minuet.*)

curtain

J.W.

The Donkey's Mission

CHARACTERS

KENNY   FREDDY

BILL   AUNT BESSIE

JIMMY   UNCLE HARRY

COSTUMES

In Act One AUNT BESSIE wears a hat and coat, in Act Two she wears a house dress and apron. The boys are dressed in ordinary clothes. Some of them may wear jeans.

PROPERTIES

Scene I: a keg, watering can, cigar box, lantern, bin of oats, bucket, and tools of all kinds. Scene II: living room furniture, school books, and newspaper.

ACT ONE

SCENE I

TIME: *The present, two weeks before Easter.*

PLACE: *Barn with rough walls, tools leaning against the walls, and a keg and watering can on the floor. At rear is a stall where the donkey is supposedly tied. The walls of the stall should be high enough so that donkey (which is not there) won't be seen. An opening provides entrance to the stall. When the scene opens* KENNY *is standing at this opening or doorway talking to the donkey.*

KENNY

Boy, oh boy! You're the prettiest donkey I ever saw. And to think that you belong to me. You're all mine, Mr. Donkey. At least, you will be just as soon as I have you all paid for. I'll have to give you a name. Now let me see. (*Stands thinking for a moment.*) I know. I'll name you Jocko! That's a good name for a donkey. How about it, Jocko?

(BILL, JIMMY, *and* FREDDY *rush into the barn all excited, calling* KENNY'S *name. When they stop before the opening into the stall they stand and stare.*)

BILL

Gosh! It's really true. When did you get him?

JIMMY

Boy! A real live donkey! I thought you were kidding.

FREDDY

We thought you were kidding, Kenny. But there he is big as life! What's his name?

KENNY

Jocko. I just named him. Here, Jocko, eat some oats. (*He thrusts a pan into the opening and holds it there.*) Look at him eat. Yeah, look at him *eat!* I guess that's the trouble with donkeys. They're always hungry.

BILL

Where'd you get the oats?

KENNY

Mr. Burrows gave me some. But I'm going to the feed store and get more on my way home from work. I'm going to get a dollar's worth.

JIMMY

I bet he eats a lot.

KENNY

Yeah, *look* at him eat!

FREDDY

Does he really *belong* to you?

KENNY

Sure he does. I saved for him for a long time. Mr. Brown pays me two dollars and fifty cents a week for delivering groceries. So when I had enough saved up I just went over to the horse farm and bought him!

BILL

Is he all paid for?

KENNY

Well, not all. I'm going to give Mr. Burrows all my pay until he's mine. How about it, Jocko?

BILL

How you going to feed him if you pay *all* your money to Mr. Burrows?

JIMMY

Oh, Kenny's uncle will buy oats for him, I bet.

KENNY

(*Slowly.*) Well, you see—no, Uncle Harry can't. He can't afford to. I've gotta buy the feed myself, fellas.

(*The boys all look very serious.*)

BILL

With what?

KENNY

I dunno.

(*They stand silent.*)

KENNY

Well, fellas, I've got to get over to the store. You can come and see Jocko tomorrow after school.

BILL

Say, I'll tell you what. Why don't you rent out rides on Jocko? All the kids will want to ride him. I'll pay you to let me ride on him.

FREDDY

So will I!

KENNY

That's a swell idea, Bill.

JIMMY

How much?

KENNY

Let's say five cents a ride. (*He picks up a cigar box from a shelf.*) We can keep the money in this cigar box, and when we've got enough we'll buy oats with it!

ALL THE BOYS

That's great! We'll be over this time tomorrow to ride him. So long, Jocko!

curtain

SCENE II

TIME: *Later the same day.*

PLACE: *The living room of* KENNY's *home.* KENNY *and* UNCLE HARRY *are seated around the center table.* AUNT BESSIE *has on her hat and gloves, ready to leave the house.* KENNY *has school books on the table before him.* UNCLE HARRY *is reading the evening paper.*

AUNT BESSIE

Kenny, I simply don't see how we can afford to keep that donkey!

KENNY

Please let me keep him, Aunt Bessie! Please!

AUNT BESSIE

It's ridiculous, that's what it is! What *earthly* good is a donkey, I want to know.

UNCLE HARRY

Now, Bessie! A donkey is a good pet for a boy.

AUNT BESSIE

Pet, humph! A cat is just as good a pet and it doesn't eat as much. Now tell me, Harry, are you going to feed this pet?

UNCLE HARRY

Well, I'd like to, Bessie. But you know as well as I do that we can't afford to.

AUNT BESSIE

Just what I've been telling you. Kenny, we can't afford to keep a donkey.

KENNY

Aunt Bessie, you don't need to worry. We have it all figured out.

AUNT BESSIE

Who has it all figured out?

KENNY

The other boys and I. We made a plan today. I'm going to sell rides on Jocko and use the money to buy oats.

AUNT BESSIE

Humph! A lot of money *that* will bring in. Well, we'll wait and see. I'm going to the rehearsal at church now. I can't see why they didn't give you a part in the Easter pageant, Kenny. I hinted loud enough. But the mothers all got their say in, and before I knew it all the parts were given out.

KENNY

Oh, well. Don't feel bad about it, Aunt Bessie.

AUNT BESSIE

Well, I do! Land sakes, you're a good-looking boy, Kenny, and you'd have looked nice in a tableau. Yes, I had my heart set on you being in a tableau.

UNCLE HARRY

Kenny and I will enjoy seeing the Easter pageant from the audience, won't we, Kenny?

KENNY

Oh yes, sure. But I wish I could be in it too. Bill and Jimmy and Freddy are going to be in it. Bill is going to be Pilate.

AUNT BESSIE

Well, I think it's a shame, I do! Now I must hurry or I'll be late. Kenny, finish your lessons and get to bed.

KENNY

Yes ma'am.

   (AUNT BESSIE *goes out.*)

   (KENNY *heaves a big sigh.*)

UNCLE HARRY

Don't look so glum, my boy. There'll be other pageants!

KENNY

(*Sadly.*) It's not the pageant I'm worrying about.

UNCLE HARRY

What, then?

KENNY

It's Jocko. I'm afraid Aunt Bessie will make me give up Jocko.

UNCLE HARRY

We just don't have the money to pay for his feed, boy. If you can take care of your payments and buy the feed, Aunt Bessie won't say a word.

KENNY

I'll make out somehow! I've *got* to keep Jocko. He's a wonderful donkey and I love him.

curtain

ACT TWO

SCENE I

TIME: *One week later.*

PLACE: *Same as Act One, Scene I.* KENNY *and* BILL *are in the barn looking in at the donkey.*

KENNY

Gosh, Bill, I guess I'm going to have to give him up!

BILL

Jocko? Give up Jocko? Why, you can't, Kenny!

KENNY

What else can I do? Aunt Bessie's been against Jocko from the start.

BILL

How about your uncle?

KENNY

He likes Jocko. But he can't afford to help me keep him. And— well, I can't meet my payment to Mr. Burrows this week.

BILL

I thought you were going to give him the money you earn at Mr. Brown's store. Hasn't he paid you?

KENNY

Sure, he paid me. But I had to use it to buy oats for Jocko. Gosh, Bill, you don't think I can let Jocko starve, do you? Here, Jocko, eat your nice oats.

BILL

Thought you were going to buy the oats with the money from the rides?

KENNY

Huh, thirty cents! How much oats do you think that will buy?
(*Both boys stand looking sadly at the donkey in silence.*)

BILL

It's a shame to let a good donkey like this go! If I had the money or the place to keep him, bet I'd buy him in a hurry!

KENNY

No, I've got the place for him, and I've already paid ten dollars for him! It's up to me. I've got to think!

BILL

Mr. Burrows won't wait around while you think, Kenny. That tight-wad won't wait for his money. He'll take back the donkey!

KENNY

Bill, I've got to get to the store or Mr. Brown will be mad. Can't you come over here tonight after supper and help me think of a plan?

BILL

I'm sorry, Kenny, but I've got to go practice for the pageant.

KENNY

Oh, that old pageant!

curtain

SCENE II

TIME: *That night at nine o'clock.*

PLACE: *Same as Act Two, Scene I.* KENNY *is alone in the barn. A lighted lantern throws light on the donkey's stall.* KENNY *is seated on a keg, looking sadly into the stall at* JOCKO.

KENNY

Well, I guess this is your last night here, Jocko.

(*He goes to a bin and scoops out a bucket of oats and takes it into the stall. When he comes out he sits once more on the keg, rests his elbows on his knees and his head in his hands, and looks sadly at the floor. He heaves a great sigh.*)

KENNY

Aunt Bessie says you're good for nothing, Jocko. She says, "What earthly good is a donkey?" She says that all the time. I guess if you lived in Spain or some place you'd be of some use, Jocko. You could be a beast of burden, carry bags on your back, or whatever donkeys do over there! But here—well, Aunt Bessie thinks you have no *use.*

(*He stops and looks toward the stall. Then speaks hastily.*) But gosh, Jocko, don't think I agree with her! I didn't mean to hurt your feelings! *I* think you're the best little old donkey—the best donkey—(*His voice breaks and he turns his head away and wipes his eyes.*)

(AUNT BESSIE *enters.*)

AUNT BESSIE

Kenny! What in the world are you doing out here at this time of night? Do you know it is after nine o'clock?

KENNY

I—I came out to be with Jocko, Aunt Bessie. I came out to—to sort of say good-by to him.

AUNT BESSIE

Well, I'm glad you're going to be sensible, Kenny, and take him back to Mr. Burrows. Maybe Mr. Burrows will return the money you've paid on the donkey.

KENNY

Maybe. (*He hangs his head and looks at the floor.*)

AUNT BESSIE

I wish you wouldn't take this so hard, Kenny. You know we made a bargain. If you could keep up with the payments and buy the animal's food, you could keep him. Well, you haven't been able to do it.

KENNY

No'm. (*He still hangs his head and looks at his feet.*)

AUNT BESSIE

Kenny, I declare, I can't see why you are so attached to this animal! After all, he's just a stupid donkey! What good is he? Why, everybody knows that the ass is the most stupid of animals.

KENNY

Aunt Bessie, is a donkey the same as an ass?

AUNT BESSIE

Of course. In this country we call them donkeys.

KENNY

But it's the same thing, an ass and a donkey?

AUNT BESSIE

That's right.

KENNY

Well, listen, Aunt Bessie! Didn't Jesus ride into Jerusalem on an ass and that's why we celebrate Palm Sunday?

AUNT BESSIE

Well, we celebrate Palm Sunday the week before Easter to com-memorate Jesus's triumphant ride into Jerusalem, yes.

KENNY

(*Excitedly.*) Then don't you see, Aunt Bessie, that *that* makes the donkey important? Why, that makes him one of the most important animals in the world! Just think, it may have been a donkey just like Jocko!

AUNT BESSIE

Yes, I see what you mean. (*Pauses, then looks at* KENNY.) Kenny, this gives me an idea. Wait, I'm going to call the minister's wife. You just wait right here.

(AUNT BESSIE *hurries out. In a moment* UNCLE HARRY *enters.*)

UNCLE HARRY

Hello, Kenny. What are you and Aunt Bessie up to?

KENNY

Oh, we were just talking. Say, Uncle Harry, did you know that Jesus rode into Jerusalem on a donkey?

UNCLE HARRY

Why, yes. So He did, Kenny.

KENNY

Uncle Harry, I wonder if that donkey wasn't just like Jocko. Do you think he looked like Jocko?

UNCLE HARRY

It may well be, Kenny. (*He walks over to the stall and looks in at the donkey.*) Kenny, I've been thinking today about Jocko. And how much you want to keep him.

KENNY

I sure would like to keep him, Uncle Harry.

UNCLE HARRY

Well, maybe you can, boy. Maybe you can. There's that money in the bank your father left you that your aunt Bessie and I are keeping for you. Now, if we took enough of it from the bank to finish paying Mr. Burrows for Jocko—

KENNY

Oh, Uncle Harry!

UNCLE HARRY

If we got that paid off, I say, do you think you could pay for Jocko's feed from the money you earn at the store?

KENNY

Oh yes, Uncle Harry! (*He goes to the stall and speaks.*) Jocko, old fella, did you hear what Uncle Harry just said? Jocko, it looks as if maybe you can stay here after all!

(AUNT BESSIE *enters.*)

AUNT BESSIE

I called the minister's wife, and she thinks it's the most wonderful idea!

UNCLE HARRY

What's a wonderful idea?

AUNT BESSIE

About the donkey! That is, if you think Kenny could keep the donkey, Harry.

UNCLE HARRY

That's just what we've been talking about. I told Kenny I thought we could take a little of the money that his father left him and pay Mr. Burrows. What do you think, Bessie?

AUNT BESSIE

Well, my lands! I don't know why we didn't think of that before! That's just what we'll do. But listen to this, Kenny! The minister's wife was as thrilled as I am over my great idea.

KENNY

What idea, Aunt Bessie?

AUNT BESSIE

Why, to put you in the pageant, of course! It came to me when you said that about the Lord riding into Jerusalem on an ass. It came to me what a wonderful tableau that would make in our pageant! You, Kenny, riding on your donkey to represent Palm Sunday. Isn't it wonderful?

KENNY

Did she say I could? Did she say that Jocko and I could be in the pageant?

AUNT BESSIE

She certainly did. She's coming over in the morning to talk to me about it. So you see, Kenny, you will be in the Easter pageant after all.

KENNY

(*Looking at the donkey.*) Yes, and Jocko will be in it too! So Jocko will be of some use after all.

curtain

E.H.S.

The Great Tree Council

CHARACTERS

FATHER FOREST

RABBIT

DE SOTO OAK

SPANISH EXPLORERS

AMERICAN INDIANS

HENRY HUDSON TULIP TREE

DUTCH EXPLORERS

CHARTER OAK

COLONISTS

PENN TREATY ELM

INDIAN CHIEFS

WASHINGTON ELM

TWO BOYS WITH FIFE AND DRUM

REVOLUTIONARY SOLDIERS

LINCOLN OAK

YOUNG ABRAHAM LINCOLN

ALLEN GENTRY

JOYCE KILMER TREE

WHITTIER ELM

LOUISA MAY ALCOTT ELM

LITTLE WOMEN: MEG, JO, BETH
    AND AMY

APPLE TREES

FIRST BOY

SECOND BOY

JOHNNY APPLESEED

COSTUMES

FATHER FOREST, *tight-fitting suit of forest green, with short cape fastened at shoulders. Hat covered with evergreen boughs.*

RABBIT, *tight-fitting gray suit with cotton tail. Helmet-shaped cap with big ears.*

All trees, dressed alike in tight-fitting brown suits. CHARTER OAK *has large hole in side of his. Caps differ in that each one is covered with leaves of tree he represents. If real leaves cannot be used paper ones may be cut to pattern. Tulip and apple trees use real or paper blossoms to cover hats.*

SPANISH EXPLORERS, *short tunics, blouses with short puffed sleeves, sleeveless jackets belted at the waist. Helmet-shaped hats. They all carry spears.*

INDIANS, *conventional Indian dress.*

DUTCH EXPLORERS, *long sleeveless tunics worn over blouses. Waist-length capes hanging from shoulders. Ruffs around necks. Any felt hats with rounded crowns.*

COLONISTS, *New England Colonial dress. Both men and women wear long capes. The men wear broad-brimmed hats, the women close-fitting bonnets. Men carry muskets.*

REVOLUTIONARY SOLDIERS, *some wear blue coats, three-cornered hats and knee britches. Others wear the knee britches with ragged shirts and some have bandages around their heads.*

ABRAHAM LINCOLN, *trousers are a little short as though he had outgrown them. Ordinary colored shirt with sleeves rolled up. No hat.*

ALLEN GENTRY, *long frock coat. Wide-brimmed hat.*

MEG, JO, BETH, AMY: MEG *and* JO *in long full dresses belted tightly at waist.* JO'S *hair is arranged in a snood.* BETH *and* AMY *are in shorter dresses with pantalets showing.* AMY, *if possible, has curls.*

TWO BOYS, *dressed farmer-style in jeans.*

JOHNNY APPLESEED, *very ragged clothes. He is barefoot.*

PROPERTIES

Staff for FATHER FOREST; *spears for* SPANISH EXPLORERS; *muskets for* ENGLISH COLONISTS; *fife and drum for* REVOLUTIONARY BOYS; *basket of apples for two small boys; stick and bag of seeds for* JOHNNY APPLESEED.

PLACE: *A forest. Backdrop of tall trees, stage floor covered with green simulated moss with leaves scattered over it. Green footlights shed cool green light on stage. As the curtain goes up,* FATHER FOREST *stands straight and tall in center of stage, a long wooden staff in his hand. Bird whistles are heard in the background. With his head upraised toward the tall trees,* FATHER FOREST *speaks.*

FATHER FOREST

These stately trees are ancient things—
So strong and tall, and proud as kings!
Their heads I cannot even see,
And yet they all belong to me.

(*A large white* RABBIT *enters from right. He hops across stage and stops within few feet of* FATHER FOREST.)

RABBIT

Did I hear someone speaking?

FATHER FOREST

It was I.

RABBIT

Oh, I thought you were a tree.

FATHER FOREST

I am All Trees.

RABBIT

I beg your pardon.

FATHER FOREST

I represent All Trees. I am Father Forest.

RABBIT

Well, I've lived in these woods a long time and I've never seen you before.

FATHER FOREST

That is possible. You see, I'm really a spirit, and make myself visible only on special occasions.

The Spirit of All Trees am I,
And spirits never, never die.

RABBIT

Probably that's why I haven't seen you. You were invisible. But what is this special occasion, Father Forest?

FATHER FOREST

Oh, this is just our regular centennial. Every one hundred years we hold a council and review the happenings of the past century. Of course, sometimes we go back even more than a hundred years, because famous trees, like famous people, are often forgetful.

RABBIT

Famous trees, did you say?

FATHER FOREST

Of course. Trees can be just as famous as people. In fact, more so, because they live longer. I am expecting some of the oldest and most famous of our species to appear here today.

RABBIT

It certainly sounds interesting. I should very much like to see a famous tree. Are they—er,—spirits too?

FATHER FOREST

For this occasion, yes. Most of them are still living trees, but some of them have fallen. But their spirits live on.

RABBIT

Are they visible? And could I see them, do you suppose?

FATHER FOREST

Well, since you seem to be greatly interested, I see no reason why you should not be permitted to see them. (*A great twittering of birds is heard.* FATHER FOREST *assumes a listening attitude, then speaks.*) The birds tell me that most of our guests today will be historical. If you watch and listen you will learn a great deal about your country. You may stay if you wish.

RABBIT

Oh, thank you.

(*The birds are heard again.*)

FATHER FOREST

I think our tree guests are beginning to arrive.

(*The* DE SOTO OAK *enters from left followed by several* SPANISH EXPLORERS. *They approach* FATHER FOREST, *and* DE SOTO OAK *stands directly before him. Several* INDIANS *appear and stand in the background. The* RABBIT *hops back to far right and stands watching.*)

DE SOTO OAK

Greetings, Father Forest! I am De Soto Oak. Perhaps you may
remember me.

FATHER FOREST

Though you are very old, Sir Oak,
I knew you well before you spoke.
And if I've kept my facts in line,
You date from fifteen thirty-nine.

DE SOTO OAK

You have a remarkable memory, Father Forest.

FATHER FOREST

Then speak right up and tell your tale;
To entertain it cannot fail.

DE SOTO OAK

Though you've heard it before, I'll tell it again since you so kindly
ask me. Back in the earliest days of the Spanish settlement in
America, I knew the great De Soto. As a matter of fact, I knew
him so well that I was able to do a service for him. Hernando De
Soto at that time was governor of the Spanish Colony of Florida.
Even though he had come from the warm climate of sunny Spain,
De Soto could not get used to the hot Florida summers. He suffered
from the heat and found relief only when he came out to visit me.
He was fond of lying in my shade, and I held my great branches
above him and my many leaves whispered softly to him. Nearly
always he was lulled to sleep. He was most grateful for the rest he
found, and we became great friends.

FATHER FOREST

Now, if my memory serves me well,
There's also a story of Indians to tell.

DE SOTO OAK

Right! That's another time I was able to serve him. The settlers
were having trouble with the Seminole Indians. As governor of the
Spanish Colony, De Soto felt that he must do something to bring
peace between the Colonists and the tribes whose land they had
settled upon. So he drew up a fair peace treaty and arranged a

meeting with several of the chiefs of the tribes. It was an extremely warm day. When midday came, the time of the prearranged meeting, De Soto could think of only one place that would be comfortable. So he arranged to have the Indian chiefs meet him under the spreading boughs of his favorite oak. In the cool shade of my great branches this famous peace treaty was signed.

FATHER FOREST

Ah, that is a story I never tire of hearing. And I thank you for coming.

(*The* DE SOTO OAK, *the* SPANISH EXPLORERS, *and the* INDIANS *move off to a place at the back of the stage. At once the* HENRY HUDSON TULIP TREE *comes in from left. He moves toward* FATHER FOREST *while some* DUTCH EXPLORERS *follow and stand off a little from center. The* TULIP TREE *stands before* FATHER FOREST *and speaks.*)

TULIP TREE

Do you remember me, Father Forest?

FATHER FOREST

You ask if I remember you?
By Henry Hudson, sir, I do!
From Inwood Park, New York, you hail.
And now we'd like to hear your tale.

TULIP TREE

Though it is now one hundred years since last you saw me, you have not forgotten! Well, since I am the only living thing still remaining on Manhattan Island from the days of Henry Hudson, I suppose I *am* quite famous! The people who come to visit me at my shrine in the park always stop to read the inscription on my trunk. I will quote it for you. "Hendrick Hudson entered this inlet in 1609 and may have met the Indians here who used the place for a camp, as shown by the quantity of old broken oyster shells around this tree and nearby."

FATHER FOREST

Hmm. They seem to have been in some doubt about it. They say he *may* have camped at the spot mentioned.

TULIP TREE

But he did indeed, Father Forest. That was nearly three hundred and fifty years ago, but I remember it well. If Henry Hudson could see the island now, where he camped that day, I doubt if he would believe his eyes. Little did he think that spot would become a part of the greatest city in the world—New York!

FATHER FOREST

You're as right as you can be,

And thanks for coming, Tulip Tree!

(*The* HENRY HUDSON TULIP TREE *and the* DUTCH EXPLORERS *move to the rear of stage. A new group moves forward from left, preceded by another tree. These are* THE CHARTER OAK *and several* COLONISTS, *men and women, dressed in costumes of the period.* CHARTER OAK *stands before* FATHER FOREST.)

FATHER FOREST

There's none more famous than this tree,

For it's the Charter Oak, I see.

CHARTER OAK

You probably recognize me by this great hole in my trunk. (*He points to a large round hole in his side.*) Everyone knows that the famous Connecticut charter was hidden in my trunk.

FATHER FOREST

Yes, every school child has heard that story. But suppose you tell it to us anyway.

CHARTER OAK

Perhaps it may sound like boasting, Father Forest, to say that I was at one time the greatest hero of the Connecticut Colony! It happened in this way. Back in 1662, King Charles the Second of England granted a charter to the colony of Connecticut which served her for more than one hundred and fifty years. But if it had not been for me, that charter would have been destroyed in the year 1687.

FATHER FOREST

Pray, do not keep us in suspense!

How did you come to her defense?

CHARTER OAK

Well, I didn't exactly defend her, but I did save the charter. You see, the Connecticut Colony was founded in 1636. But it wasn't until some twenty years later that Governor Winthrop went to England to plead with King Charles for a charter. It was a wonderful document, sir. It gave the Colony complete self-government. There wasn't a more precious possession in all of Connecticut than that Charter. But there came a time when it was nearly taken from the people.

FATHER FOREST

How was that?

CHARTER OAK

A new king ruled England. When James the Second came into power, Connecticut's troubles began. King James appointed Sir Edmund Andros governor-general of all the New England Colonies. He believed that the Connecticut Charter gave the Colony too much freedom, and its surrender was demanded. But Andros never got his hands on it, for the valuable document was hidden in this hole in my trunk. I kept my precious secret well, sir, until such time as it was safe to give it back to the people of Connecticut.

FATHER FOREST

You were indeed a hero, Charter Oak;
We're grateful that you came today and spoke.

(CHARTER OAK *and* COLONISTS *move back to rear of stage. The* PENN TREATY ELM *and several* INDIAN CHIEFS *enter from left.* PENN TREATY ELM *moves up to stand before* FATHER FOREST.)

FATHER FOREST

We're highly honored, noble tree;
Penn Treaty Elm, we salute thee!

PENN TREATY ELM

I thank thee for thy courtesy, Father Forest, and for the invitation to speak with thee today.

FATHER FOREST

I'm sure you have a tale to tell
Of William Penn, whom you knew well.

PENN TREATY ELM

A tale all have heard before, so I shall make it short. I care little for idle chatter, as thee knows. I shall say only that I was privileged to extend my great leafy boughs above one of the greatest scenes in all history.

FATHER FOREST

That was Penn's treaty with the Indians?

PENN TREATY ELM

It was. As everyone knows, William Penn was a Quaker and a lover of peace. Therefore, his first wish was to bring about a peaceful settlement with the Indians in the Pennsylvania Colony. In the year 1662 he met with the chiefs of the Delaware tribes. That meeting was held beneath my branches. I am proud to have witnessed that famous treaty between the Christian, William Penn, and the heathen savages. It was a treaty that was not sworn to, for the Quakers do not believe in giving oath. But it was never broken.

FATHER FOREST

I am sure no other Colony could boast a finer relationship between settlers and Indians than that which existed in Pennsylvania.

Hail to Penn's Woods, especially

Our own beloved Penn Treaty Tree!

(PENN TREATY ELM *and* INDIANS *move off to rear of stage. Meanwhile a new group enters at left. First two boys with fife and drum, playing "Yankee Doodle."* WASHINGTON ELM *follows and stands before* FATHER FOREST, *while soldiers stand in background. Some are dressed in the uniform of the Continental Army but others are in ragged clothes. All on stage sing the first verse and chorus of "Yankee Doodle" after fife and drum have played the chorus alone.*)

"Father and I went down to camp,

  Along with Captain Gooding,

And there we saw the men and boys

  As thick as hasty pudding.

"Yankee Doodle, keep it up,

  Yankee Doodle, dandy,

Mind the music and the step
  And with the girls be handy."

FATHER FOREST

A merry tune that is, dear me,
But sober, too, as we shall see.
This tree approaching, I recall,
Is the most famous tree of all!

WASHINGTON ELM

Yes, probably I am. I am the great Washington Elm. Under my branches the Father of Our Country took command of the first Continental Army. I shall never forget that eventful and historic moment, Father Forest.

FATHER FOREST

I can well believe you. Please tell us about it, Washington Elm.

WASHINGTON ELM

The thing that made the greatest impression on me was the dignity of the occasion. There was George Washington, handsome and erect on his horse, taking part in one of the great moments of American history. This was his first command; this was the first army of the new nation, and now he was having his first glimpse of that army. It was an odd assortment of men, Father Forest. Few of them had uniforms, and many had no muskets. Some were in rags. But they had plenty of courage, and they stuck to General Washington until the war was won. It makes me proud to know that I was connected with them! As I said before, I'll never forget it.

FATHER FOREST

No red-blooded American son
Can ever forget George Washington!
(*The fife and drum again pick up the chorus of "Yankee Doodle" and march to rear of stage, followed by* WASHINGTON ELM *and group. Meanwhile,* LINCOLN OAK *enters at left with the young* ABRAHAM LINCOLN, *in shabby pants and shirt with rolled-up sleeves, and* ALLEN GENTRY, *similarly dressed.* LINCOLN OAK *approaches* FATHER FOREST.)

FATHER FOREST

This mighty oak I seem to know;
No stronger trees in forests grow.
Are you the symbol of the man,
Our best-loved, great American?

LINCOLN OAK

Yes, Father Forest, I am the Lincoln Oak. And what better symbol could there be to represent the strength of character of Abraham Lincoln?

FATHER FOREST

Tell us how you came to know Abraham Lincoln.

LINCOLN OAK

Abe Lincoln was only nineteen when I knew him, a tall homely man with the strength of many men. My home is on the banks of the Ohio River. It was back in 1840 and I had been growing in my wooded spot for years with no thought of fame when Lincoln entered my life.

FATHER FOREST

You saw him then?

LINCOLN OAK

Oh, yes, I saw Lincoln.

FATHER FOREST

Please tell us about it.

LINCOLN OAK

He had been working for a man by the name of Allen Gentry in Indiana. This Mr. Gentry wanted to take his produce down the river to New Orleans to sell it, but in those days transportation was not what it is today. "How shall we ever transport the food down the river?" Mr. Gentry asked. "I am not rich enough to think of boats." Abe was never one to give in to circumstance. He suggested a flatboat. "But I have no flatboat," said Mr. Gentry. Well, that presented no obstacle to Abe Lincoln. Splitting rails was a task in which he excelled. In no time he had the rails split and peeled, and a fine flatboat was built.

From my place along the river I saw them bring the flatboat to the water's edge and load it with produce. I saw Abe, with his long, strong arms, push the boat off the muddy shoreline and guide it skilfully along the rushing waters of the Ohio.

FATHER FOREST

Ah, I can imagine that scene myself! Is there not a symbolic meaning to it, think you, Lincoln Oak?

LINCOLN OAK

A symbol, yes, of the same manner in which this great man would one day guide a nation through the troubled waters of a terrible war.

FATHER FOREST

And did Abe conduct the cargo well upon the river?

LINCOLN OAK

Yes, very well, Father Forest. Even as he guided his country when it was placed in his keeping.

FATHER FOREST

It's just an incident you tell,
But one we understand full well.

(LINCOLN OAK *and the figures of the two men move back to rear. From left come the three Literature Trees, followed by the* LITTLE WOMEN: MEG, JO, BETH *and* AMY. *The* LITTLE WOMEN *stand in the background while the three trees approach* FATHER FOREST.)

FATHER FOREST

Our part in history you've seen,
Now let's recall another scene.
With government and wars we've dealt,
But what of how the people felt?
What did they think, what did they write?
Their literature should tell it right.

(*The* JOYCE KILMER TREE *steps forward and at the same time Oscar Rasbach's musical setting of Kilmer's "Trees" is heard.*)

JOYCE KILMER TREE

I am the Joyce Kilmer Tree, one of thousands growing in the Joyce Kilmer Memorial Forest in North Carolina. Our great forest is dedicated to the memory of that immortal poem, "Trees." We Joyce Kilmer trees cover a vast four thousand acres in the Nantahala National Forest. There we live in peace, our heads close to the sky, while beneath us the black bear and deer roam at will. We are truly a living memorial to the poet who wrote of us.

(*A voice off stage takes up the music of "Trees" and sings it to the end.*)

FATHER FOREST

Monuments are grand to see,
But none is like a living tree!

(JOYCE KILMER TREE *steps to rear of stage while* WHITTIER ELM *comes to center.*)

FATHER FOREST

Welcome! Are you not the Whittier Elm? Where do you come from?

WHITTIER ELM

My roots are in the ground near Haverhill, Massachusetts, upon which the great poet John Greenleaf Whittier often walked in his lifetime. But did you know, Father Forest, that at one time I was nearly cut down?

FATHER FOREST

Who would want to cut down such a healthy and flourishing tree?

WHITTIER ELM

After Whittier's death, his birthplace was sold and the new owner determined to have me felled. But fortunately one lover of Whittier's poetry appreciated the high regard Whittier had for me. He offered to pay rental for the ground upon which I stood so that I might continue as a memorial to the poet. My owners are now the Whittier Association. I have no more fears concerning my future.

FATHER FOREST

I am glad. No one loved trees more than Mr. Whittier. He showed this in those beautiful lines:

"With the calm patience of the woods I wait
For leaf and blossom when God gives us Spring!"*

(WHITTIER ELM *moves to rear of stage.*)

(*The* LOUISA MAY ALCOTT ELM *stands before* FATHER FOREST, *while the figures of the* LITTLE WOMEN *stand close behind the* ELM.)

*From "A Day" by John Greenleaf Whittier.

FATHER FOREST

Good day to you all. (*Turns to the* ELM.) May I ask how these four ladies happened to come to the Tree Council?

LOUISA MAY ALCOTT ELM

They seem to be so much a part of my story that I brought them along. I am one of the Louisa May Alcott elms which grow before her famous home in Concord, Massachusetts. We elms lived in an atmosphere of culture for many years, Father Forest. Perhaps nowhere else in our country have there been such distinguished gatherings as under our branches. Not only Miss Alcott walked and sat beneath us, but also her father Bronson Alcott, and Nathaniel Hawthorne, and his friend Henry David Thoreau!

FATHER FOREST

A venerable group, indeed.

LOUISA MAY ALCOTT ELM

And those were memorable days! Such brilliant conversation! Even though I was only an onlooker, I learned much from listening. I think I can safely say, Father Forest, that these dear departed friends of mine contributed so richly to American literature that their influence will be felt for many years. And of all the great writings to come from their pens, none is more beloved than Miss Alcott's book, *Little Women.*

(*He motions the four* LITTLE WOMEN *to step closer.*) May I introduce them to you, Father Forest?

FATHER FOREST

I should be happy to know them.

LITTLE WOMEN

(*In turn.*) I'm Meg.
I'm Jo.
I'm Beth.
I'm Amy.

FATHER FOREST

It is a great privilege to meet you, and I am grateful to you, Louisa May Alcott Elm, for bringing them here.

(ALCOTT *group steps to rear of stage.*)

FATHER FOREST

Well, I see that the tree guests have all been presented, so—

(*He is interrupted by the hurried entrance of several small apple trees, apple blossoms in their hair and on their clothes, tossing blossoms along their way. These are followed by two small boys carrying baskets of apples. Each is eating an apple. The small apple trees stand to one side of* FATHER FOREST. *The two boys stand in front of him. An old man in ragged clothes and carrying a stick in one hand and a large bag in the other enters last. As he walks he scatters seed, pokes it with his stick, and walks on, repeating the process.*)

FATHER FOREST

Whence came these little apple trees?

And who are all these others, please?

FIRST BOY

We've come to the Tree Council to tell you about Johnny Appleseed.

SECOND BOY

We have a real story to tell if you will listen.

FATHER FOREST

(*Laughing.*) Tell away, boys!

FIRST BOY

"Poor Johnny was bended well nigh double
With years of toil, and care, and trouble;
But his large old heart still felt the need
Of doing for others some kindly deed.

SECOND BOY

"He took ripe apples in pay for chores,
And carefully cut from them all the cores.
He filled a bag full, then wandered away,
And no man saw him for many a day.

FIRST BOY

"With pointed cane deep holes he bore,
And in every hole he placed a core;
Then covered them well, and left them there
In keeping of sunshine, rain, and air.

SECOND BOY

"Whenever he'd used the whole of his store,
He went into cities and worked for more;
Then he marched back to the wilds again,
And planted seed on hillside and plain.

FIRST BOY

"He knew that trees would soon abound
Where once a tree could not have been found;
And the little seeds his hands had spread
Would become ripe apples when he was dead.

SECOND BOY

"Weary travelers, journeying west,
In the shade of his trees find pleasant rest;
And they often start, with glad surprise,
At the rosy fruit that round them lies.

BOTH BOYS

"And if they inquire whence came such trees,
Where not a bough once swayed in the breeze,
The answer still comes, as they travel on:
'These trees were planted by Apple-Seed John.' "*

FATHER FOREST

Ah, now *there* is a story! How could anyone ever forget old Johnny
Appleseed? I am sure that we trees are grateful to you boys for
bringing his memory back to us today.

(*The* RABBIT *hops over to* FATHER FOREST.)

RABBIT

And I am grateful to everybody! I surely have learned a lot at this
Tree Council. And I've had a good time too!

(*All the characters on the stage step forward and form a close
semicircle about* FATHER FOREST. *The music of "Trees" is heard
from off stage as* FATHER FOREST *speaks.*)

FATHER FOREST

(*Slowly.*) And now, my friends, please gather near;
My last fond greeting you must hear.
For all your stories we are glad,

Adapted from "Apple-Seed John" by Lydia Maria Child.

And for this Council we have had.
But now the time has come at last
To say, "Adieu, farewell, dear Past!"
When God made Earth, it's good that He
Did not forget to make the Tree.

curtain

E.H.S.

Charlie's May Basket

CHARACTERS

MRS. MOORE

PENNY MOORE

DORIS MOORE

ANN EVANS

JAMES EVANS

DENNIS FARRELL

CHARLIE MOORE

COSTUMES

No special ones needed.

PROPERTIES

Living room furniture, card table for children to work on, six May baskets, paper, cardboard, scissors, bowl of violets or other spring flowers, plate of cookies.

TIME: *The afternoon before May Day.*

PLACE: *The living room of the* MOORE *home. When the scene opens,* MRS. MOORE *is showing* PENNY, DORIS, ANN, JAMES, *and* DENNIS *how to make May baskets.*

DENNIS

It sure was swell of you to invite us over, Mrs. Moore, to show us how to make May baskets.

MRS. MOORE

I'm so glad you could all come, Dennis. (*She pauses.*) I wonder where Charlie is.

PENNY

Oh, Mother, you're always worrying about Charlie.

DORIS

I should think he'd want to be here to help us.

MRS. MOORE

Charlie loves to make May baskets, and he's quite clever at it. (*She holds up an unfinished paper basket for all to see.*) This is the one he's been working on. He almost finished it last evening.

DORIS

Yes, and he said he would come *right* home from school today to work with us. Mother, I think you should scold him for not coming directly home.

JAMES

Doris, you sound as if *you* were his mother!

ANN

She's always picking on Charlie.

MRS. MOORE

Oh, don't quarrel, children, *please!* Charlie will be home soon, I'm sure.

DENNIS

I'll bet a cookie he's in trouble with Mr. Redding again!

MRS. MOORE

That reminds me. I have some cookies in the kitchen.

(MRS. MOORE *leaves the room.*)

PENNY

Why did you say that, Dennis?

DENNIS

Well, because he probably is! Charlie is always teasing Mr. Redding's cat and one of these days the old man is going to give him what he deserves.

PENNY

You stop talking about my brother that way, Dennis Farrell.

DORIS

But it's true, Penny. Charlie is big enough now to know better than to rile Mr. Redding. He *will* get into trouble, first thing you know.

PENNY

Mr. Redding is an old crank!

(MRS. MOORE *enters with plate of cookies.*)

MRS. MOORE

Who's an old crank, Penny? And what a thing to say!

JAMES

Penny said that Mr. Redding is a crank, and I agree!

ANN

Me, too.

MRS. MOORE

Mr. Redding is an old man and he just doesn't understand children. We should be more patient with him.

DORIS

Charlie isn't patient with anybody. Look, Mother! (*She holds up her May basket.*) Isn't this a pretty one?

MRS. MOORE

Indeed it is, dear. Tell me, children, did any of you see Charlie after school?

(*The children shake their heads.*)

DORIS

I'll just bet he's in some kind of mischief!

(*The door opens and a small boy of seven comes into the room crying. The children all exclaim "Charlie!"*)

MRS. MOORE

Oh, Charlie! What in the world has happened?

CHARLIE

He chased me! And I fell and hurt—hurt—hurt myself!

(CHARLIE *sits on the floor and cries. His mother goes over to him.*)

MRS. MOORE

Where did you hurt yourself, dear?

CHARLIE

My leg. Right here. And my arm, and, and—

DORIS

Crybaby!

MRS. MOORE

Now, Doris! Who chased you, Charlie?

CHARLIE

Mr. Redding, that's who! (*He sits up and stops crying.*) What are you all doing? Making May baskets?

DORIS

Don't change the subject, Charles Moore! Mother, don't let him change the subject!

MRS. MOORE

Why did Mr. Redding chase you, Charlie?

CHARLIE

Well, that old cat of his!

DENNIS

So you teased his cat again. Boy, no wonder he was mad. He thinks the world and all of that cat.

MRS. MOORE

If you teased his cat, Charlie, the fault was yours. I do wish you would try to make friends with Mr. Redding, dear. He's our new neighbor and we want him to like us.

CHARLIE

Well, I don't care whether he likes me or not. *I* don't like *him!*

MRS. MOORE

I think he's really a nice old man. Father and I called on him and we found him very interesting.

CHARLIE

Mother, let me finish my May basket.

DORIS

There he goes, changing the subject again, Mother!

PENNY

Mother, mayn't Charlie finish his May basket?

MRS. MOORE

Dear me! Here I thought we were going to have a nice little May-day gathering, and all we do is squabble. Come, Charlie, and get to work. (CHARLIE *joins the group at the table.*) Your basket is nearly finished, and it's very pretty.

(*They all work in silence for a moment.*)

ANN

I'm making my May basket for my mother. But I know who James is making his for!

DORIS

For his girl, I suppose.

JAMES

O.K., so what?

MRS. MOORE

(*Aside to* CHARLIE.) Charlie, as soon as you finish your basket, there's something you must do. You know what, don't you, dear?

(CHARLIE *squirms and says nothing.*)

MRS. MOORE

(*Continuing.*) How about it, Charlie?

CHARLIE

Do I have to apologize *again?*

MRS. MOORE

You teased the cat again.

PENNY

I don't think Mr. Redding wants Charlie coming over there to apologize all the time.

DENNIS

No, he just wants him to keep away from his place, I bet.

MRS. MOORE

Charlie will apologize to him.

CHARLIE

It's silly! I hate to do it, Mom!

DORIS

Then why don't you be good, then you won't *need* to be always saying you are sorry.

PENNY

Oh, Doris! There you go, scolding like an old woman.

MRS. MOORE

I have an idea, Charlie. (*She beckons him to a corner of the room and he rises and follows her. They whisper.*)

CHARLIE

(*Aloud.*) Oh Mom, that's silly. I can't do that! (*They whisper again.*) No, Mom, please don't make me!

MRS. MOORE

Well, come and finish your basket, anyway.

(*They go back to the table and lean over the basket, working together.*)

MRS. MOORE

Now, a little paste here, Charlie.

(*After a moment* CHARLIE *holds up his May basket.*)

CHARLIE

Say, this is a pretty one, all right!

MRS. MOORE

It surely is!

PENNY

The best one of the lot, Charlie!

ANN

What are you going to do with it, Charlie?

DENNIS

Haven't you got some girl in second grade to give it to, Charlie?

CHARLIE

I'm giving it to Mom.

MRS. MOORE

That's sweet of you, dear. But Doris is giving hers to me, and Penny is giving hers to Dad. Besides, how about our secret?

CHARLIE

Aw, Mom!

DORIS

What are you two up to, anyway?

CHARLIE

That's our secret, isn't it, Mom?

MRS. MOORE

Oh yes—a wonderful secret! If I were you I'd take it right over now, Charlie.

(CHARLIE *looks down at the basket in his hands, then sets it on the table.*)

CHARLIE

I can't. It's too silly!

MRS. MOORE

Nonsense! Wait until I put the violets in it. That's all it needs to make it perfect. I'm glad you children picked these flowers yesterday.

(MRS. MOORE *goes over to a large bowl of violets and removes some and places them in the May basket.*) There, now, how's that for a beautiful May basket? Here, dear. Now remember, hang it on the door and ring the bell. But wait until the door is answered and be sure to say *exactly* what I told you!

CHARLIE

Oh well, O.K.

(CHARLIE *goes out carrying the May basket.*)

DENNIS

What's all the mystery? Where is he taking it?

MRS. MOORE

Never mind, Dennis. Now children, while you finish making your baskets I have a little surprise. (*She goes over to the table and picks up several slips of paper.*) This morning I went through the children's poetry books looking for May-day poems. I thought it would be fun to copy some lines from the poems so that each of you might have one to pin to your May basket.

DORIS

Oh Mother, that's a wonderful idea!

PENNY

What do the poems say?

MRS. MOORE

I thought we could read them aloud and then you can copy them and fasten them to the baskets. I have one for each of you. Here, James, suppose you start. This is for your basket.

JAMES

"Good morning, lords and ladies, it is the first of May!
We hope you'll view our garlands, they are so sweet and gay."
What is a garland, Mrs. Moore?

PENNY

Flowers, silly! Mother, let me be next!

MRS. MOORE

Very well, Penny, here is one for you.

PENNY

"I love my little brother and sister every day,
But I seem to love them better in the merry month of May!"
Well, that's all right for me because I have a brother and sister.

DORIS

But I can't see why you should love us better in May than any other time.

PENNY

Oh well, it says that in the poem anyway. Who's next, Mom?

MRS. MOORE

Here is one for you, Ann.

ANN

"Spring is coming, spring is coming,
All around is fair;
Shimmer and quiver on the river,
Joy is everywhere.
 We wish you a happy May."*
Oh, I think that's a lovely one!

MRS. MOORE

Now yours, Dennis. (*She hands him the slip of paper. He reads.*)

DENNIS

"Little Kings and Queens of May,
If you want to be
Every one of you, very good,
In this beautiful, beautiful, beautiful wood,
Where the little birds' heads get so turned with delight
That some of them sing all night:

From "Oxfordshire May Song."

Wherever you look,
And whatever you find,
Leave something behind:
Some for the Naiads,
Some for the Dryads,
And a bit for the Nixies and Pixies!"*

PENNY

Nixies and Pixies and those other things are like the fairies, aren't they?

MRS. MOORE

Yes. You see, long ago it was thought that fairies roamed the earth on the eve of May Day.

DENNIS

Maybe that's where Charlie is now, out playing with the Nixies and Pixies!

DORIS

What do you have for me, Mother?

MRS. MOORE

Here it is, Doris. I'm sure you all know this one! I have copied just the first verse for you.

DORIS

"You must wake and call me early,
    call me early, mother dear;
Tomorrow'll be the happiest time of
    all the glad New-year.
Of all the glad New-year, mother, the
    maddest merriest day;
For I'm to be Queen o' the May, mother,
    I'm to be Queen o' the May."*

MRS. MOORE

Now you can all get busy and copy the verses on these pretty cards and fasten them to your baskets.

(*Heads are bent low over the table while the copying is done.* MRS. MOORE *moves nervously toward the window and looks out. Suddenly the door opens and* CHARLIE *appears.*)

*From "Good Luck" by Juliana Horatia Ewing.
*From "The May Queen" by Alfred Tennyson.

CHARLIE

(*Smiling broadly.*) Hi, Mom.

MRS. MOORE

Oh, Charlie, you're back already!

CHARLIE

Well, Mr. Redding just lives across the street.

(*All the children look up and exclaim in unison, "Mr. Red-ding?"*)

CHARLIE

Sure, Mr. Redding. Who else?

PENNY

You—you gave your May basket to Mr. Redding?

DENNIS

He's kidding.

CHARLIE

I am not! I gave it to him and he thanked me.

MRS. MOORE

Did he thank you, really, Charlie?

DORIS

What is all this?

MRS. MOORE

That was our secret, wasn't it, Charlie. Did you apologize, dear?

CHARLIE

Oh Mom, how could I apologize? I didn't have time! I rang the bell, and waited for him to come to the door, like you said. When he came I said, "Here's a May basket for you, and my mother and father want you to have May Day dinner at our house tomorrow, and we are going to have roast chicken."

PENNY

How did you dare?

DORIS

What did he say?

CHARLIE

He said he'd be glad to, and he looked at me sort of funny and invited me to come in.

MRS. MOORE

Oh, how nice! Did you go in, Charlie?

CHARLIE

Just for a minute. And—and guess what?

ALL

What?

CHARLIE

I played with his cat. She's all right, that cat!

DENNIS

Will wonders never cease! Charlie, my boy, you *must* have done it!

CHARLIE

I must have done what?

DENNIS

You must have played with the Pixies and the Nixies, and all the other fairies.

(*They all laugh.*)

MRS. MOORE

Well, now, I think the May baskets have done it, if you ask me! Charlie has made a good friend, and everybody's happy. Now we can all truthfully say "Happy May Day!"

ALL

HAPPY MAY DAY!

curtain

E.H.S.

Mother of the Town

CHARACTERS

JUDY

BARBARA

JOANNE

LINDA

DEBBIE, *Linda's little sister*

DR. BROTHERTON, *the minister*

MRS. O'REILLY

MRS. WILKINS, *a widow*

MRS. BROWN, *President of Parent Teacher Association*

COSTUMES

All the characters wear everyday clothes. The minister wears a clerical collar.

PROPERTIES

School books, pencil and paper, plate of cookies, and furniture for the living room.

TIME: *Thursday evening preceding Mother's Day.*

PLACE: *Living room of* MRS. WILKINS' *home. When the play opens* JUDY *is alone in the room. She is seated at a table writing with her school books open before her. With an impatient gesture she closes the books and jumps to her feet. She pushes the books to the back of the table.*

JUDY

Oh, lessons, lessons! I just can't keep my mind on them when I know the girls will be here any minute. I'd better get the cookies.

(JUDY *goes out and returns with a plate of cookies which she places on the table. She straightens the books on the table, gives the sofa cushions a pat, and samples a cookie. The doorbell rings.*)

JUDY

Oh, there they are!

(*She rushes to open the door, then says "Oh" in a disappointed tone when she sees it isn't the girls she expected.* DR. BROTHERTON, *a minister, steps into the room.*)

DR. BROTHERTON

Good evening, Judy. Is Mrs. Wilkins at home?

JUDY

Good evening, Dr. Brotherton. No, she isn't. She's over at the Jones' baby-sitting so that Mrs. Jones could go to the P.T.A. meeting. You know, the P.T.A.-ers are going to select the Mother of the Year tonight.

DR. BROTHERTON

Ah, yes, of course. Sunday is the day we shall honor mothers. A wonderful custom, Judy. Yes, a wonderful custom! Well, I must be on my way. I simply stopped by to tell Mrs. Wilkins something I'm sure she will be glad to hear.

JUDY

Could I give her a message?

DR. BROTHERTON

Why yes, Judy, you might do that. Just tell her that all final arrangements have been made now for her to become foster mother to a refugee child in Europe. Word came today that a little orphan boy will be adopted and cared for through her financial help. To-morrow, when I see her, I will give her all the details.

JUDY

Oh, isn't that wonderful? Mrs. Wilkins doesn't have any children of her own. But now she will be a foster mother.

DR. BROTHERTON

Yes. Through her great generosity she will make some child very happy. And now I must be going. Good night, Judy.

JUDY

Good night, Dr. Brotherton. I'll give Mrs. Wilkins your message.

(DR. BROTHERTON *goes out.* JUDY *walks thoughtfully back to center of room.*)

JUDY

Mrs. Wilkins is going to be foster mother to a poor hungry little boy in Europe she has never even seen.

(*She takes another cookie and nibbles on it. The doorbell rings and* JUDY *rushes again to the door and opens it.* BARBARA, JOANNE, LINDA, *and* DEBBIE *enter. All the girls are* JUDY's *age, about eleven or twelve, except* DEBBIE, *who is about seven.*)

ALL

(*As they enter.*) Hello, Judy!

JUDY

Hello! Goodness, I thought you'd never get here! Now we can have our meeting.

BARBARA

(*Looking at the plate of cookies.*) Umm, look at the cookies!

JUDY

(*Passing the cookie plate.*) Yes, and they're delicious! Mrs. Wil-kins made them 'specially for us this afternoon.

LINDA

How is it you are staying over here with Mrs. Wilkins, Judy?

JUDY

She invited me to stay here over the week end so Mother and Daddy could spend Mother's Day with Grandma. I *love* to stay with Mrs. Wilkins! She has so many wonderful ideas for things to do.

JOANNE

Was it Mrs. Wilkins idea for us to come over tonight?

JUDY

Yes, it was. She's baby-sitting for Mrs. Jones and she didn't want me to be alone, so she thought it would be fun for us to have a Mother's Day election here, the same as at the P.T.A. meeting.

BARBARA

And we'll select our own Mother of the Year. That *will* be fun. Wonder if we'll select the same mother they do at P.T.A. Are we going to vote?

JUDY

Yes, and then we'll make an award to the mother we choose. Here, Debbie, have some cookies.

LINDA

An award? What can *we* give as an award?

BARBARA

I know! Let's each of us donate a Saturday morning of our time to help her with her household chores. You know—help take care of the children and run errands and things like that.

LINDA

That's not much of an award!

JOANNE

Oh, but it is, *I* think! Especially if we choose some poor mother with loads of children. Think how grateful she'll be for our help.

DEBBIE

I want to help too.

JUDY

Well, let's get down to business. Shall I be the—the—

LINDA

You mean spokesman.

JUDY

I'll be the spokesman. Sit down, girls. We'll begin by having each one make a little speech. Barbara, you are the oldest so you may nominate the first candidate and tell why you are choosing her. Begin, please.

(BARBARA *rises, but at that moment the doorbell rings.*)

JUDY

(*Walking toward the door.*) Oh dear! (*Opens door.*)
    (*Enter* MRS. O'REILLY.)

MRS. O'REILLY

Is Mrs. Wilkins here?

JUDY

No, I'm sorry. She is out for the evening.

MRS. O'REILLY

I wanted to see her. I wanted to give her something. I don't know
when I can come back again. My little girl is sick.

JUDY

Perhaps I can give Mrs. Wilkins your message.

MRS. O'REILLY

Well, I don't know. (*She hesitates but finally hands Judy an envelope.*) Give her this. Tell her it's from Mrs. O'Reilly. Ten dollars, it is, saved from my husband's pay. Sure, and all the things
she sent us to eat these past weeks, it made it easier for me to put
the money by. Sure, and if it had not been for her, the angel, my
Katie could not have had the operation at all, at all! And tell her,
miss—tell her I said "God bless her!"
    (MRS. O'REILLY *goes out.*)

JUDY

(*Slowly walking toward the desk, where she places the envelope on
the blotter.*) That was Katie O'Reilly's mother. Mrs. Wilkins must
have paid for Katie's operation.

LINDA

And she gave them food. Mrs. Wilkins is just like a fairy godmother.

BARBARA

Well, girls, are you ever going to listen to my speech?

JUDY

Oh yes, Barbara. We're ready. Proceed.

BARBARA

(*Going to center of the room.*) Ladies and—I mean, ladies. I have
been thinking seriously and have considered the proposition.

DEBBIE

What?

JOANNE

Don't use such big words, Barbara, but get on with your nomination.

BARBARA

Don't interrupt me! Well, as I said, I have thought about the question seriously and I want to cast my vote for the woman in this town I consider the typical American mother. She is a good mother to two of my best friends, and she is a very good homemaker and good cook.

JUDY

(*Aside.*) My, she's really "good."

BARBARA

Besides, she is president of the P.T.A. I vote for Mrs. Brown as Mother of the Year!

DEBBIE

That's my mother!

LINDA

Oh Barbara! That's awfully nice of you to vote for Mother. But honestly, I don't think we should vote for our own mothers.

BARBARA

She's not *my* mother! And I'll cast my vote for her, no matter what you say.

LINDA

Judy, don't you think we should make a motion not to include any of our mothers in this election? It doesn't seem quite fair to—well, to the mothers of the rest.

JOANNE

You don't have to say that just to be polite, Linda.

JUDY

Barbara can vote for anyone she chooses. Remember, this election must be carried on fairly. Now it's your turn, Joanne.

JOANNE

(*Rising.*) I know who I'm going to vote for, all right! There's one woman in this town who really deserves it, and that is Mrs. Poppenoe. She's got twelve children, and I'd like to know who can qualify better to be Mother of the Year!

JUDY

That's true. Mrs. Poppenoe has the biggest family in town. And now it's your turn, Linda.

LINDA

(*Rising.*) I've been thinking very hard about my vote, and after careful consideration I want to nominate Mrs. Allen.

JOANNE

Why Mrs. Allen, of all people?

LINDA

Because I think she is just the kind of mother you read about in books! She's so pretty, and wears such lovely clothes!

BARBARA

As if that has a thing to do with being a good mother!

LINDA

Well, she has three children, and they just adore her. She sends them to camp in the summer and gives them wonderful gifts on their birthdays. And that garden party she gave last summer for Elaine was just like something out of a magazine!

BARBARA

I still say that doesn't qualify her! What *good* does she do?

LINDA

Why, she does lots of good! For one thing she's going to take a little girl from the Fresh Air Society for two weeks this summer!

JUDY

For goodness sake don't quarrel, girls! I think it's just grand Mrs. Allen is going to take a Fresh Air child.

BARBARA

Yes, and who persuaded her?

LINDA

What do you mean?

BARBARA

Why, Mrs. Wilkins did, that's who. She went all over town and talked to the mothers to get them interested. *She* takes two children every summer, Mrs. Wilkins does!

JOANNE

Judy, it's your turn.

JUDY

No, Debbie hasn't had her say yet.

ALL

Oh, Debbie.

(DEBBIE *rises, walks to the center of the room, and makes a bow.*)

DEBBIE

I vote for Mrs. Wilkins.

JOANNE

Mrs. Wilkins? Why, you silly goose, she isn't a mother!

LINDA

Debbie's too little to vote.

DEBBIE

I'm not either too little to vote! And I vote for Mrs. Wilkins.

BARBARA

Mrs. Wilkins hasn't any children!

LINDA

You can't vote for someone who isn't a mother, silly!

(DEBBIE *starts to cry.*)

DEBBIE

I can so! I will *so* vote for her, so there!

(*At that moment the doorbell rings.*)

JUDY

Oh, that *doorbell!*

(*She goes to the door, opens it, and exclaims, "Mrs. Wilkins!"*
MRS. WILKINS *enters smiling.*)

MRS. WILKINS

Well, girls, how is your meeting coming along?

JUDY

Oh, we were voting. (*She looks embarrassed.*) It was Debbie's turn
to vote, and—

DEBBIE

(*Running to* MRS. WILKINS.) I'm going to vote for you.

MRS. WILKINS

(*Laughing.*) Thank you, Debbie! (*Puts her arm around* DEBBIE.)
Girls, were there enough cookies?

JOANNE

Oh, yes.

BARBARA

They were delicious.

JUDY

Is the P.T.A. meeting over already?

MRS. WILKINS

Mr. Jones came home early and sent me home because he said
that I will soon be receiving a caller.
(*The doorbell rings.*)

JUDY

The doorbell again!
(MRS. WILKINS *opens the door.* MRS. BROWN *enters.*)

MRS. WILKINS

Mrs. Brown! Come right in. Did you stop for your girls?

MRS. BROWN

Hello, Mrs. Wilkins. Yes, I'll take my girls home, but that's not my
only reason for coming. Mrs. Wilkins, I came to tell you that by
a unanimous vote the members of the P.T.A. chose you tonight as
the Mother of the Year.

MRS. WILKINS

Chose *me?* Why, I'm not a mother at all.

JUDY

Debbie, do you hear that? Your vote wins!

MRS. BROWN

What do you mean?

JUDY

Debbie insisted upon voting for Mrs. Wilkins!

JOANNE

But—but Mrs. Wilkins isn't a mother, so how can she be Mother
of the Year?

MRS. BROWN

Mrs. Wilkins is Mother of the Town! And all the people in this town want to honor her.

MRS. WILKINS

(*Shyly.*) Oh, I don't know what to say. I don't deserve this.

ALL

Oh, you do, you do!

BARBARA

We know you deserve it, because we know that you are like a mother to all of us. And you mother the Fresh Air children in the summer.

JUDY

And she's going to be foster mother to a little orphan boy in Europe!

LINDA

And she's fairy godmother to Katie O'Reilly!

JUDY

Girls, I haven't put in my vote. So right now I nominate Mrs. Wilkins Mother of the Town. All in favor say "Aye."

ALL THE GIRLS

Aye!

MRS. BROWN

So you see, Mrs. Wilkins, the vote is really unanimous!

DEBBIE

(*Wistfully.*) I vote for Mrs. Wilkins!

curtain

E.H.S.

Each Star a State

PRODUCTION EXPLANATION

A huge outline map of the United States is the background. The boundaries of the states are indicated and the name of each is printed on it, but nothing more. Close to the front of the stage, a little to one side, is mounted a large drawing of the American flag. From the top point of each star a small hook projects so that each child can fasten his star in its proper place. As each child tells about his state the narrators shade that state in color on the map. The front of each star to be placed on the flag has the name of the state and its admission number. At the time of writing Hawaii and Alaska are not states. In the event of their admission speeches have been provided which can be used for them.

CHARACTERS

STATES (*Forty-eight boys and*   FIRST NARRATOR
girls. Each state may be rep-   SECOND NARRATOR
resented by a child or one   COLUMBIA
child may represent several
states.)

COSTUMES

No special costumes are needed except for COLUMBIA. *She is
dressed in a long white gown with a gold ribbon coming across one
shoulder and encircling her waist. She may also wear a gold crown.*

PROPERTIES

*Outline map of the United States and crayons for shading in
states; artist's drawing of the flag of the United States; a star for
each state; basket for* COLUMBIA; *the United States flag.*

SETTING: *When the curtain goes up the* NARRATORS *and other
children representing the states are all on the stage. The* NARRATORS
*stand near the map of the United States ready to shade in each
state as its star is added to the flag. The children who are to take
the parts of states are grouped together on the opposite side of the
stage. They are not standing in lines. The grouping is informal.*

FIRST NARRATOR

(*Stepping forward.*) Today we are going to tell you about the
making of The Star-Spangled Banner, the flag of The United States
of America. On June 14, 1777 the following resolution was adopted
by the Continental Congress: "Resolved, That the Flag of the
United States be thirteen stripes, alternate red and white; that the
Union be thirteen stars, white in a blue field representing a new
constellation."

SECOND NARRATOR

(*Stepping forward.*) These thirteen stars and stripes represented
the original states. But when Kentucky and Vermont were admitted

to the Union they wanted to be represented too. So the flag was changed to fifteen stripes and fifteen stars.

FIRST NARRATOR

As the number of states increased, Congress knew it couldn't go on increasing the size of the flag. So in 1818 it was decided to go back to thirteen stripes representing the original thirteen states, but a new star was to be added to the blue field for each additional state admitted to the Union.

SECOND NARRATOR

And now we are going to tell you about each one of our states. It has been said that each star is a state and each state is a star. We shall show you what that means.

(COLUMBIA *enters. She is carrying a basket which is held by a wide ribbon which goes around her neck. The stars are in this basket and are placed in order so that she can hand them to the children properly.*)

COLUMBIA

Delaware, the first star. December 7, 1787.

(*As* COLUMBIA *calls the name of each state, the child taking that part steps forward, takes the star from* COLUMBIA *and after telling about the state goes over and hangs the star in its place on the flag. While each speech is being made the* NARRATORS *take turns in shading in that state on the map.*)

DELAWARE

Delaware may be small—in fact it is next to the smallest of any state—but it can boast that it was the first state that adopted the Constitution of the United States. Delaware proudly claims the right to place the first star on the flag.

COLUMBIA

Pennsylvania, the second star. December 12, 1787.

PENNSYLVANIA

Pennsylvania is called "The Cradle of Liberty" because the Declaration of Independence was signed here. The state was founded by a Quaker, William Penn, who was noted for his fair treatment of the Indians. Two historic parks are in this state. They are Valley Forge, where Washington and his soldiers spent a terrible winter, and Gettysburg, where an important Civil War battle was fought. Pennsylvania is now known as a great manufacturing and mining state.

COLUMBIA

New Jersey, the third star. December 18, 1787.

NEW JERSEY

In Revolutionary War days New Jersey was important because of its location, and many battles were fought on its soil. Now it is known for its many large manufacturing cities and its large truck gardens. One of its most famous citizens was Thomas A. Edison who was known as "The Wizard of Menlo Park."

COLUMBIA

Georgia, the fourth star. January 2, 1788.

GEORGIA

Although Georgia was first explored by the Spaniard, De Soto, it was settled by the English, led by James Oglethorpe. He named this territory Georgia in honor of King George the Second of England. This state is sometimes called the Cracker State. Some people say it got this name because as the early settlers drove their wagons along they cracked their whips hard.

COLUMBIA

Connecticut, the fifth star. January 9, 1788.

CONNECTICUT

One of the famous stories about Connecticut is that of the Charter Oak. Charles the Second of England had been kind to the Colonists and had given them many rights which were all written down in what was called a charter. When his brother James came to the throne he was going to take it away from them. So the Colonists hid their charter in the trunk of an oak tree until it was again safe to take it out.

COLUMBIA

Massachusetts, the sixth star. February 6, 1788.

MASSACHUSETTS

Massachusetts holds high honors in the history of our country, for it was here the Pilgrims landed in 1620. Everyone knows their brave story and how they managed to survive the cold New England winter. They were the first to celebrate what is now our national Thanksgiving Day.

COLUMBIA

Maryland, the seventh star. April 28, 1788.

MARYLAND

Maryland, settled by Lord Baltimore, is interesting for many historical events. Chief among them is that Francis Scott Key wrote The Star-Spangled Banner during the siege of Fort McHenry in 1814. The United States Naval Academy is at Annapolis, Maryland and the famous Johns Hopkins University is located in Baltimore.

COLUMBIA

South Carolina, the eighth star. May 23, 1788.

SOUTH CAROLINA

South Carolina was once part of a huge territory which included what is now North Carolina and South Carolina. At that time it was called the Carolinas. It was at Charleston that the first guns of the Civil War were fired when South Carolina soldiers captured Fort Sumter, which was located in the harbor of that city.

COLUMBIA

New Hampshire, the ninth star. June 21, 1788.

NEW HAMPSHIRE

In the Colonial days New Hampshire was a dangerous place in which to live because of the Indian wars which were raging nearly all of the time. Now, people like to go to New Hampshire because it is such a quiet place to spend a vacation. Its mountains with their gorgeous scenery attract many visitors.

COLUMBIA

Virginia, the tenth star. June 26, 1788.

VIRGINIA

One of the best-loved stories of Virginia is that of the Indian maid, Pocahontas, who saved the life of Captain John Smith. But Virginia's favorite son and most famous citizen, of whom she is most proud, is George Washington, first President of the United States.

COLUMBIA

New York, the eleventh star. July 26, 1788.

NEW YORK

When Peter Minuit, the Dutch sailor, bought the Island of Manhattan for twenty-four dollars, he could never in his wildest imagination have seen what it would look like today with its skyscrapers. Although the state itself is not nearly so large in territory as some of the other states, it ranks first in the number of people that live within its borders.

COLUMBIA

North Carolina, the twelfth star. November 21, 1789.

NORTH CAROLINA

Between 1585 and 1587 the English made an attempt to settle on Roanoke Island and if that had been successful North Carolina would be known as the earliest Colony. But no trace of this Colony was ever found and what happened to it has always been a mystery. But North Carolina can claim to be first in something else. In 1903, the Wright Brothers at Kitty Hawk made the first successful airplane flight.

COLUMBIA

Rhode Island, the thirteenth star. May 29, 1790.

RHODE ISLAND

Rhode Island is the smallest state in the Union, it has the shortest motto, which is "Hope," and the smallest state flower, the violet. But though small it has always been noted for its courage. Roger Williams, its founder, believed in religious freedom and this state was a refuge for those who sought to worship in the manner they desired.

COLUMBIA

Vermont, the fourteenth star. March 4, 1791.

VERMONT

The name Vermont means Green Mountain and that is the name by which this state is known. Its people are noted for their dry humor. One day a visitor said to a Vermonter, "Why is it that in Vermont the railroad stations are always so far away from the towns?" The Vermonter replied, "Because in Vermont we would rather have the stations near the railroads."

COLUMBIA

Kentucky, the fifteenth star. June 1, 1792.

KENTUCKY

"The sun shines bright on my old Kentucky home." Everyone knows Stephen Foster's song and everyone knows, too, that Kentucky's hero is Daniel Boone. Kentucky used to be called "The Dark and Bloody Ground" because of all the Indian wars. Now it is known as the Blue Grass State, which certainly sounds a lot more pleasant. One of the most famous horse races in America is held here. It is called The Kentucky Derby.

COLUMBIA

Tennessee, the sixteenth star. June 1, 1796.

TENNESSEE

This state was settled by sturdy pioneers who were willing to risk their lives in order to seek new homes in the wilderness. Although Tennessee is remembered for many important historical events, it has become even more famous recently. It was at Oak Ridge that the atom bomb was developed.

COLUMBIA

Ohio, the seventeenth star. March 1, 1803.

OHIO

Ohio comes from an Indian word and means "Beautiful River." Its nickname, Buckeye State, refers to the buckeye trees which grow in large numbers. Besides this tree Ohio has many fruit trees and the first of these were planted by Johnny Appleseed. Ohio also has the honor of being the birthplace of seven Presidents of the United States.

COLUMBIA

Louisiana, the eighteenth star. April 30, 1812.

LOUISIANA

No one thinks of Louisiana without thinking of New Orleans, that gay city of the Mardi Gras. The Mardi Gras is a festival that takes place for three days, with singing and dancing in the streets. Most of the people wear fancy dress and masks. The Mardi Gras ends with a ball which is famous because of its splendor.

COLUMBIA

Indiana, the nineteenth star. December 11, 1816.

INDIANA

Indiana is known as the Hoosier State. One of its historic towns is Vincennes, which was at one time a fort. In 1799 George Rogers Clark, one of the heroes of the Revolution, captured it from the British and claimed it for the American Colonists. Nowadays Indiana is noted both for its manufacturing and its agriculture.

COLUMBIA

Mississippi, the twentieth star. December 10, 1817.

MISSISSIPPI

The name of the State of Mississippi is the same as that of the mighty river which forms its western border. The Mississippi river is called "Father of Waters." The beautiful magnolia which blossoms throughout the state is the official state flower. There are many beautiful gardens to see as well as cotton fields and these attract many visitors to the state.

COLUMBIA

Illinois, the twenty-first star. December 3, 1818.

ILLINOIS

Illinois, a great industrial state, manufactures practically everything. But its chief claim to fame in our history comes from the fact that it was for so long a time the home of one of our greatest national heroes—Abraham Lincoln. His former home and his burial place are in the Illinois state capital at Springfield.

COLUMBIA

Alabama, the twenty-second star. December 14, 1819.

ALABAMA

Alabama is known as the Cotton State and for many years cotton was its chief crop. But in 1910 the boll weevil destroyed most of the crop and many people lost all they had. So Alabama farmers learned it was safer to plant other crops too. At Enterprise there is a monument to the boll weevil, probably the only one to honor an insect.

COLUMBIA

Maine, the twenty-third star. March 15, 1820.

MAINE

Maine, the Pine Tree State, is one of the most popular summer places in the East. The inland lake region attracts those who like fishing or hunting. But those who love the ocean find the coast, with its rocky shore line and pounding surf, most exciting. New Englanders always speak of going "down east" to Maine.

COLUMBIA

Missouri, the twenty-fourth star. August 10, 1821.

MISSOURI

Missouri is known as the Show Me State. One day a Congressman from Missouri said in a public speech, "I'm from Missouri— you've got to show me." Since then when a person says, "I'm from Missouri" he means that he is not easily fooled.

COLUMBIA

Arkansas, the twenty-fifth star. June 15, 1836.

ARKANSAS

Arkansas is chiefly a farming state but many minerals are also found in its mountains. In fact, it is the leading state in producing the ore from which aluminum is made. When De Soto explored that part of the country he found the famous Hot Springs and even today many people go there to bathe in these mineral waters.

COLUMBIA

Michigan, the twenty-sixth star. January 26, 1837.

MICHIGAN

Once upon a time the wolverine, which is a fierce animal, ran wild in Michigan. Because of that Michigan is often called the Wolverine State. The football team of the University of Michigan is called The Wolverines and the name makes it sound as though the players were fierce and hard to beat. But people also call Michigan the Auto State because so many cars are manufactured there.

COLUMBIA

Florida, the twenty-seventh star. March 3, 1845.

FLORIDA

Every winter lots of people who don't like cold weather go to

Florida to enjoy the warm sunshine and ocean bathing. This state is the leading winter vacation land of the eastern states. Florida was discovered in 1513 by Ponce de Leon, who was looking for the Fountain of Youth which he believed was there.

COLUMBIA

Texas, the twenty-eighth star. December 29, 1845.

TEXAS

Texas people are very proud of their state and they have a lot to be proud of, for Texas is the largest state in the Union. It ranks first in beef production, sheep raising and wool. There are more farms in Texas than anywhere else in our country and it leads all other states in raising cotton and even spinach. Texas is the only state that was an independent republic before it was annexed to the United States.

COLUMBIA

Iowa, the twenty-ninth star. December 28, 1846.

IOWA

The name Iowa always makes people think of corn. If you traveled across this state you would understand why, for just about everywhere you can see huge fields of this tasseled crop. The first settlement in Iowa was made in 1788 by a Frenchman whose name was Dubuque. In later years, the citizens of the city which bears his name erected a statue in his honor.

COLUMBIA

Wisconsin, the thirtieth star. May 29, 1848.

WISCONSIN

If you like cheese Wisconsin is the place to go. This state is famous for its dairy products and also for its great iron and ore works. At one time it was an important lumbering region but now it has become more noted for its manufacturing.

COLUMBIA

California, the thirty-first star. September 9, 1850.

CALIFORNIA

When people think of California they think of sunshine, gold and moving pictures. The discovery of gold brought a great rush of settlers to that part of the country in the early days. Now there are many more reasons why this state attracts so many persons. Its fine climate, its crop production and its manufactures are some of them. San Francisco Chinese telephone operators have to have good memories. They have to memorize all the names and numbers of their subscribers because there is no Chinese alphabet.

COLUMBIA

Minnesota, the thirty-second star. May 11, 1858.

MINNESOTA

Minnesota has many things to be proud of. First of all it produces more iron ore than any other state. It is also an agricultural state and its huge flour mills are well known. One of its greatest claims to fame is the medical clinic at Rochester founded by the Mayo Brothers.

COLUMBIA

Oregon, the thirty-third star. February 14, 1859.

OREGON

Oregon likes to be known as the land of the empire builders, and it is true that the empire builders did have a lot to do with Oregon. The Lewis and Clark expedition first told people about this wonderful land that would someday become a wonderful state. One of the heroic stories of this state is that of Marcus and Narcissa Whitman, who founded a mission in the wilderness.

COLUMBIA

Kansas, the thirty-fourth star. January 29, 1861.

KANSAS

Just about everyone knows the answer to the question, "What is the Sunflower State?" Kansas, of course. Kansas, part of the Great Plains area, is in the exact center of the United States. The land is very flat there. When you look out across one of the vast prairies of grain waving in the breeze, you know what it is like to see as far as you can see, for there doesn't seem to be any limit to distance there.

COLUMBIA

West Virginia, the thirty-fifth star. June 20, 1863.

WEST VIRGINIA

West Virginia was really a part of Virginia until the people in the western part of the state disagreed about slavery with the people in the eastern part. So the west broke away from the east, and in 1863 it was formally admitted to the Union as a separate state. It is a mountainous country and visitors who drive along the mountain roads can look up and see cornfields on the steep hillsides. Sometimes they like to joke and wonder if a man would break his leg if he fell out of a cornfield.

COLUMBIA

Nevada, the thirty-sixth star. October 31, 1864.

NEVADA

The state of Nevada has three nicknames. The first is the Silver State because of the amount of silver mined in the mountains. The second is the Sagebrush State because of that desert shrub. And the third is the Battleground State because Nevada was admitted to the Union during the Civil War. Easterners like to go to Nevada to see the exciting rodeos the cowboys stage for visitors.

COLUMBIA

Nebraska, the thirty-seventh star. March 1, 1867.

NEBRASKA

Nebraska is another of our great farming states. But before it became famous for its farm products it was famous for its roads which linked the eastern states to the western states. Over these roads went stage coaches, the pony express, and the Conestoga wagons. Now when you travel on the Lincoln Highway from New York to San Francisco, you cross the State of Nebraska. And just outside of Omaha you pass Boys' Town, founded by Father Flanagan for homeless boys.

COLUMBIA

Colorado, the thirty-eighth star. August 1, 1876.

COLORADO

Colorado has many scenic wonders. One of these is Mesa Verde where you can visit the remains of the homes of the Cliff Dwellers who built their villages right on the steep faces of cliffs. Pike's Peak, Colorado's most famous mountain, is named after Zebulon Pike, an early explorer, who made a map of that region. In the pioneer days some of the covered wagons had signs painted on them, "Pike's Peak or bust."

COLUMBIA

North Dakota and South Dakota, the thirty-ninth and fortieth stars. (*Two children step forward hand in hand.*)

NORTH DAKOTA

At one time North and South Dakota were a territory known as The Dakotas. In 1889 it was divided into two states and both were admitted to the Union on the same day. The name of these states was taken from the Dakota Indians who lived here. Chief Sitting Bull was one of the famous chiefs of the tribe. Today North Dakota is known for being one of the greatest wheat-raising regions of the world.

SOUTH DAKOTA

South Dakota, known as the Sunshine State, while also famous for farm lands, is noted for its gold mines in the Black Hills. When gold was discovered there during the 1870's a regular stampede of miners followed. It was this gold rush that brought about trouble with the Indians which finally resulted in Custer's last stand. On the rocky side of Mount Rushmore in the Black Hills the famous sculptor, Gutzon Borglum, carved the heads of Washington, Jefferson, Lincoln and Theodore Roosevelt.

(*When South Dakota finishes speaking both children walk over to the flag together and hang up their stars.*)

COLUMBIA

Montana, the forty-first star. November 8, 1889.

MONTANA

One of the nation's great scenic parks is Glacier National Park in Montana. Montana, with its rugged scenery, dude ranches, and winter sports offers much to the visitor. It can also boast of having more copper mines than any other state. Helena is the capital but it was not always called by that name. When the first settlement was made there it was called Last Chance Gulch.

COLUMBIA

Washington, the forty-second star. November 11, 1889.

WASHINGTON

If you want to go to Alaska, one way would be to take a boat from Seattle or Tacoma in the state of Washington. These cities are located on Puget Sound, which is a great trading center. Washington leads the nation in its production of lumber. It is also noted for its fine apples. Mt. Rainier and Olympic State Parks are in Washington.

COLUMBIA

Idaho, the forty-third star. July 3, 1890.

IDAHO

Sportsmen like to go to Idaho because game is very plentiful there. Huge rainbow trout are also found in abundance. Years ago, people went there to find gold and precious gems in the mountains. Sun Valley, a very famous resort, is located in this state. Here one can enjoy swimming and skiing at the same time.

COLUMBIA

Wyoming, the forty-fourth star. July 10, 1890.

WYOMING

Old Faithful Geyser, which shoots hot water one hundred and twenty feet into the air every hour, is in Yellowstone National Park located in Wyoming. Wyoming boasts of something else besides its scenic parks and huge ranches. In 1869, when it was still a territory, it granted women the right to vote, the first place in the United States to do so.

COLUMBIA

Utah, the forty-fifth star. January 4, 1896.

UTAH

When the Mormons first settled in Utah they were faced by many hardships. Just as they were ready to harvest their first crops they had a plague of crickets. But the story is told that when the settlers had given up hope of saving their grain, snow-white gulls came from over Great Salt Lake and devoured the crickets. Today there is a monument to the gulls in the Mormon Temple grounds. Zion and Bryce National Parks are in Utah.

COLUMBIA

Oklahoma, the forty-sixth star. November 16, 1907.

OKLAHOMA

Oklahoma started out to be a farming state but something happened in 1901 to change all that. Oil was discovered and people became more excited about drilling oil wells than farming. Some of the best oil wells were drilled on Indian reservations so that the Indians living there are among the state's wealthiest people. Oil derricks can be seen everywhere. There is even one right in front of the state capitol building at Oklahoma City.

COLUMBIA

New Mexico, the forty-seventh star. January 6, 1912.

NEW MEXICO

Land of Enchantment is what the New Mexicans call their state, and it is a good description. For its Indian villages, its mesas and Pueblo ruins are most fascinating. Santa Fe, the capital, seems like a city of the old world and anyone who visits it never forgets its charm.

COLUMBIA

Arizona, the forty-eighth star. February 14, 1912.

ARIZONA

Arizona is the youngest state in the Union. (Substitute the following sentence if necessary, "Arizona was the youngest state for ————— years.") Its hot dry climate is particularly healthful. There are many interesting things to see in Arizona. Some of these are the Painted Desert, the Petrified Forest, and the greatest wonder of all, the Grand Canyon. Sometimes when people look at it for the first time they say in awed tones, "I just don't believe it!"

COLUMBIA

And now we welcome to our brotherhood of states (two) (a) newcomer(s). We are proud to add (these) (this) new star(s) to our flag. Hawaii (date to be added).

HAWAII

Hawaii, far off in the Pacific Ocean two thousand miles from San Francisco, consists of twenty islands. The largest of these is Hawaii, but the most important is Oahu. Honolulu, the capital and chief port, is located on this island and so is Pearl Harbor, our famous naval base. Besides being very important in a military way,

Hawaii furnishes us with many products we both need and enjoy. Sugar, pineapple and tuna fish are some of the chief ones. Its wonderful climate attracts many tourists each year. Hawaii is happy to add the (forty-ninth) (fiftieth) star.

COLUMBIA

Alaska (date to be filled in).

ALASKA

In 1867 the Territory of Alaska was purchased by the United States from Russia for seven million two hundred thousand dollars. Because the purchase was made by William Seward, who was Secretary of State under President Andrew Johnson, it was called Seward's Folly by those people who didn't approve. Now we know that this was a very wise purchase. Alaska has huge forests, it produces a great deal of gold and tin, and its fishing industry is very important. Although Alaska is far north, the Japanese Current helps keep the temperature along the coast to a sixty-degree average in the summer and it rarely goes below zero in the winter. However that is not the case in the interior. Sometimes in the winter there the temperature drops to seventy degrees below zero. No wonder people call Alaska "Uncle Sam's refrigerator." Alaska is proud to be the (forty-ninth) (fiftieth) star.

FIRST NARRATOR

We have shown you how the stars have been added to our flag and how our country has grown. And each star, representing a state, has brought with it something important that has made our country a wonderful place in which to live.

SECOND NARRATOR

Because the flag is its symbol we are asking each one of you to join with us in repeating the Pledge to the Flag and then in singing the first and last stanzas of "America the Beautiful."

(COLUMBIA *takes off her basket which held the stars and gets the flag.*)

CAST AND AUDIENCE (LED BY NARRATORS)

I pledge allegiance to the Flag of the United States of America and to the Republic for which it stands; one nation indivisible with liberty and justice for all.

(Everyone sings)
AMERICA THE BEAUTIFUL
O beautiful for spacious skies,
    For amber waves of grain,
For purple mountain majesties
    Above the fruited plain!
        America! America!
God shed His grace on thee
And crown thy good with brotherhood
    From sea to shining sea!

O beautiful for patriot dream
    That sees beyond the years
Thine alabaster cities gleam
Undimmed by human tears!
        America! America!
God shed His grace on thee
And crown thy good with brotherhood
From sea to shining sea!

               —*Katherine Lee Bates*

curtain

J.W.

A Picnic for Father

CHARACTERS

FATHER   BETH
MOTHER   TEDDY
PATSY   JEFFREY
MICHAEL   MRS. GRAY
                    SALLY

COSTUMES

No special ones needed. Children could wear jeans or shorts.

PROPERTIES

Acts One and Three: living room furniture, telephone; Act Two: something to resemble rocks, picnic basket, buns, bat, baseball.

ACT ONE

TIME: *The present.*

PLACE: *Living room of the Carters' home. As scene opens* MOTHER *is seen dusting.*

FATHER

(*Enters briskly.*) What a beautiful day! I couldn't have chosen a better time to take a day off from the office.

MOTHER

I'm glad for you, dear. Do you have any plans?

FATHER

I certainly do. We have a foursome all arranged at the Golf Club. By the way, don't plan on me for lunch. I'll eat at the Club.

MOTHER

It will do you good, dear. A day in the open is just what you need.

FATHER

Where are my clubs? I haven't seen them since last fall.

MOTHER

(*Laughing.*) Right in the hall closet where they always are. Honestly, Steve, you're as bad as the children. Always ask Mother— never look for yourself.

(FATHER *leaves as* MICHAEL *and* PATSY *come in.*)

PATSY

Mother, Michael and I have the most scrumptious plan. Haven't we, Michael?

MICHAEL

You bet we have. Just listen to this, Mother. Do you know what day tomorrow is?

MOTHER

Sunday, isn't it? At least Sunday always *has* come after Saturday.

PATSY

Oh Mother! Don't be silly. Of course it is Sunday, but it's a special day too. You haven't forgotten, have you? It's Father's Day!

MICHAEL

And Patsy and I have been talking it over. Of course we got Dad some presents but that isn't all we've planned, is it, Patsy?

PATSY

Just listen, Mother. Yesterday at our Brownie troop meeting we were discussing what we were giving our fathers for Father's Day and we all decided that we would do something special besides. I told Michael about it and he agrees with me. We're going to devote a *whole* day to our father.

MOTHER

You're going to do what? What do you mean, Patsy?

PATSY

Just that. I hope your feelings won't be hurt, Mother, but we've planned a picnic today just for Daddy.

MICHAEL

And we've invited Teddy, Sally, Jeffrey and Beth, too, because their fathers are working and they can't plan anything for them.

MOTHER

But—but—

PATSY

(*Interrupting.*) Listen to this, Mother. We pooled our allowances and we bought hot dogs and buns—and oh, boy, but it's going to be fun. Daddy will be *so* surprised when he hears about it.

MOTHER

I'm afraid he will!

FATHER

(*Enters with golf clubs.*) Hi, youngsters. What's going on? You both look mighty pleased about something.

PATSY AND MICHAEL

We are!

PATSY

We've planned a surprise picnic all for you, Daddy, because tomorrow is Father's Day.

MICHAEL

Some of the kids wanted to go fishing today. But I told them "No, sir. This day is to be my father's."

PATSY

Aren't you surprised, Daddy?

FATHER

I must admit that I am.

PATSY

Come on, Michael. Let's get the lunch packed.

(PATSY *and* MICHAEL *run out.*)

MOTHER

I'm sorry, Steve. I had no idea what was going on. What are you going to do?

FATHER

Do? Why there's only one thing to do. I'm going to call Tom and tell him he will have to find someone else for that foursome. (*Proudly.*) I shall explain to him that my children have planned a picnic for their father!

curtain

ACT TWO

TIME: *A little later.*

PLACE: *Picnic grounds.* FATHER, PATSY, MICHAEL, SALLY, BETH, TEDDY *and* JEFFREY *enter.* FATHER *is carrying lunch basket.*

TEDDY

That sure is a nice car, Mr. Carter.

JEFFREY

Boy, oh, boy! I want one just like it when I grow up.

FATHER

They will probably have much grander cars than that when you grow up, Jeffrey. But it got us here, didn't it? How does this place suit you, children?

PATSY

It's a wonderful place, Daddy. And look. There's a nice big rock. We can build our fire right alongside of it, can't we?

BETH

There's a lot of dried wood too.

FATHER

This place looks as though it were planned for picnics and waiting just for us.

SALLY

Yum! Yum! I can hardly wait for those hot dogs, Patsy. I'm hungry already.

PATSY

It makes me sick about the milk, though. If old smarty Michael hadn't tried to carry both bottles we'd still have some.

MICHAEL

I couldn't help it, could I, Daddy? How did I know I'd stumble over that stone?

FATHER

Now, Patsy, you know the old saying, "Don't cry over spilt milk." I'm just thankful Michael let go of the bottles. He might have fallen on them and gotten a nasty cut.

BETH

Oh, don't worry, Patsy. We have plenty to eat without having milk.

PATSY

What shall we do first?

MICHAEL

I know what we fellows are going to do. What do you think we brought that baseball and bat along for? Come on, Daddy. Play with us. You can be the first one up to bat. There's a swell level place over there.

SALLY

Come on, girls. Let's pick up some sticks and get them ready for the fire.

(*The boys and* FATHER *leave the stage. The girls begin to gather up sticks.* SALLY *goes over and looks in lunch basket.*)

SALLY

Hey, Pat. Where are the hot dogs? I don't see them.

PATSY

Why right there, silly. Let me look.

(PATSY *goes over and looks in lunch basket. Then she frantically begins to take things out.*)

PATSY

(*Slowly.*) They—aren't—here. I must have left them in the refrigerator. (*She begins to cry.*) Oh, dear. What shall we do now?

(FATHER *enters mopping his face.*)

FATHER

Whew! It certainly is a hot day. Guess I'll sit down a minute and look at my paper. (*Notices* PATSY, *who is wiping her eyes.*) Why Patsy! What is the matter? Did you hurt yourself?

PATSY

Oh, Daddy! I forgot the hot dogs! Now our picnic is all spoiled. What are we going to eat?

FATHER

(*Laughing.*) Let's not worry, Pat. We still have the buns, haven't we? Or did someone forget those too?

BETH

(*Peering in basket.*) No. They're here. And so are the oranges and marshmallows.

FATHER

Cheer up, Patsy. Why don't you girls go play ball a while with the boys? They could stand a few more players. And, Pat! Don't forget you may have to take a little teasing about this. After all, you were a little hard on Michael when he dropped the milk.

PATSY

I know, Daddy. It serves me right, doesn't it?

(*Girls leave stage and* FATHER *sits down against the rock and opens his paper. Suddenly he begins to move around—slaps himself vigorously and finally jumps up and looks down where he has been sitting.*)

FATHER

(*Disgustedly.*) I *would* have to pick an anthill to sit on!

(*He walks across stage to another rock, looks down and examines the ground carefully and then cautiously sits down. Just then* SALLY *runs on stage screaming, followed by* TEDDY, *who is obviously trying to put something down her neck.*)

SALLY

Mr. Carter! Mr. Carter! Make Teddy stop! Make him stop!

(FATHER *jumps up again.*)

FATHER

Now what?

TEDDY

(*In offhand tone.*) Oh, it's nothing, Mr. Carter.

SALLY

It is, too, something. He has a nasty old toad! That's what he has and he's trying to put it down my neck.

TEDDY

(*In singsong voice.*) Sally's a 'fraidy cat. Sally's a 'fraidy cat.

FATHER

Now, Teddy, behave. What happened to the ball game?

TEDDY

(*Disgustedly.*) Aw, girls can't play baseball. They ducked every time the ball came toward them.

SALLY

Well, you didn't have to throw the ball right at us. Suppose it had hit one of us.

TEDDY

For Pete's sake! See what I mean, Mr. Carter?

FATHER

(*Laughs and sits down.*) You'll learn, Teddy, you'll learn.

(BETH *runs in screaming.* FATHER *jumps up again and rushes to meet her.*)

FATHER

Beth! What's wrong? Tell me quickly. Is someone hurt?

BETH

N-no. But I went to pick a flower and there was an old bee sitting right in it and I almost didn't see it.

FATHER

Where did it sting you, Beth?

BETH

(*Looking a little ashamed.*) He didn't really sting me. (*Defensively.*) But he *might* have if I hadn't run.

TEDDY

(*Laughing loudly.*) You'll learn, Mr. Carter, you'll learn!

(MICHAEL, PATSY *and* JEFFREY *enter.* MICHAEL *is swinging the bat and* JEFFREY *is throwing the ball up in the air.*)

MICHAEL

I'm hungry. Let's eat—if there *is* anything to eat. (*He looks meaningly at* PATSY.)

PATSY

O.K. O.K. So I left the hot dogs at home. Well, we would at least have had some milk to wash down the buns if you hadn't been so clumsy.

FATHER

Come, come. Whose picnic is this anyway? We have buns, fruit and marshmallows. We'll eat what we have and on the way home we'll stop and have some ice cream. How does that sound?

ALL

Fine!

MICHAEL

Daddy, tell us about the time when you were a boy and you and Uncle Charlie were going fishing and the wasps chased you.

FATHER

That one again, Michael?

MICHAEL

Well, the other kids haven't heard it and it's exciting.

FATHER

All right, but let's sit down and we'll eat at the same time.

(*They all sit down and* PATSY *gets out the buns and passes them around.*)

FATHER

When I was about your age, boys, my brother Charlie and I decided to go fishing one Saturday. We were on our way to the creek and the path led us past an old deserted barn. There had been a farmhouse there at one time but it had burned down. Charlie and I had always wanted to explore the barn but our father had warned us it might be dangerous. But this day we thought we would take one peek inside.

SALLY

Ooh, Mr. Carter. Weren't you scared?

TEDDY

Of course he wasn't! Go on, Mr. Carter.

FATHER

Come to think of it, Sally, I guess we did think it looked a bit spooky. But we sort of sneaked up quietly to the door almost as though we expected someone to be in there. Just as we stepped inside—

(*Just at that moment there is a terrific crash of thunder. The children, who have been listening attentively, are obviously startled and the girls all scream.* FATHER *looks up and then jumps to his feet.*)

FATHER

Well—that black cloud certainly sneaked up on us when we weren't looking. But it means business, I'm sure of that. We don't have any time to lose. Run for the car, children, or we're all going to get soaked!

(*The children and* FATHER *all run off the stage but in a second* FATHER *returns and grabs the picnic basket. We hear the children all shouting off stage and* FATHER, *after another hasty look at the sky, runs off too.*)

curtain

ACT THREE

TIME: *Early evening of the same day.*

PLACE: *Same as Act One. As scene opens* MOTHER *is talking on the telephone. Pauses between each sentence as though listening to someone else talk.*

MOTHER

Yes, Mrs. Stevens . . . I know, Mrs. Stevens . . . No, I'm not worried . . . Why? Because I know my husband is an excellent driver. That's why . . . Oh I don't think it's necessary to call the police. I'm sure nothing has happened. We certainly would have been notified . . . Yes, I know Sally is a nervous child, but I'm sure everything is all right . . . Yes, I'll let you know if I hear anything. Good-by.

(MOTHER *hangs up receiver and as she does so the doorbell rings. She goes to the door, disappears for a moment and returns accompanied by* MRS. GRAY. *They are continuing a conversation started outside the room.*)

MRS. GRAY

Oh, stop worrying, Claire. You know that Lottie Stevens. She just *loves* to get upset and loves to get everyone else that way too.

MOTHER

Oh, I didn't let her know that I was worried. But, honestly, I can't help it either. After all, that was a terrific cloudburst we had this afternoon. And here it is seven o'clock and not a word from Steve. It isn't like him not to telephone if he had car trouble.

MRS. GRAY

Maybe he couldn't call. I heard over the radio that lots of telephone and electric wires are down all through the county.

MOTHER

I certainly hope that is the reason for no call, but *where* do you think they can be?

MRS. GRAY

I don't know but I'm sure they'll come walking in any minute. And now I must run back home. That Teddy of mine will be so full of talk when he gets home that he won't run down for a week.

MOTHER

You're a wonder, Janet Gray. You seem to take everything so calmly, and you make me feel better too. Good-by and thanks a lot for dropping in.

(MOTHER *and* MRS. GRAY *walk to the door together.* MOTHER *returns alone. She sits down, picks up a magazine and tries to read. Then she gets up and walks to the window. She comes back to her chair and sits down again. She crosses her feet one way, then crosses them the other. Suddenly she sits up straight as though listening intently. There is the sound of voices off stage.* MICHAEL *and* PATSY *are calling "Mother" and* FATHER *is calling "Claire."* MOTHER *runs toward the door and gets there as* FATHER *and children come in. She tries to hug them all and everyone seems to be talking at once.*)

MOTHER

Now wait a minute. One at a time, please. I can't get head nor tail out of what you are saying. Daddy first. Children, wait just a minute and then you may take your turn.

MOTHER
FATHER

What a day! Do you mind, dear, if I sit down? I'm really quite exhausted.

(*He sits down in chair and* MOTHER *pulls another up close by his. The children stretch out on the floor.*)

MOTHER

I know you are, Steve, but I can hardly wait to hear what happened. But first of all, are the other children all right?

FATHER

Of course they are. I'm the only one that's tired. And they're all safely delivered at their homes.

MICHAEL

Mother, did you ever see it rain so hard?

MOTHER

No, Michael, I never did. And I thought of you every minute too. Where were you during the storm? Hurry up, Steve. Can't you just see curiosity sticking out all over me?

FATHER

I never saw a storm come up as suddenly as that one did. If we had only had a little warning we could have gotten home hours ago. But the first thing we knew—bang!—crash! And there it was upon us. We had barely time to get into the car. Another minute and we all would have been drenched.

MOTHER

But I still don't see why you didn't get home sooner. After all, the storm has been over for three hours.

PATSY

We've been sitting parked in the car all that time.

FATHER

You see, I took the children to that spot where we had the picnic last year. You remember we had to cross a little brook on an old wooden bridge.

MOTHER

But that isn't far away. It can't take more than half an hour to get there.

FATHER

We might just as well have been in Timbuktu. By the time we got to the bridge it had rained so hard that the little stream had turned into a torrent and was pouring over the floor of the bridge. There was no chance of getting the car across. Even after the rain stopped it was some time before the water was down far enough to cross the bridge.

MOTHER

Weren't you afraid the bridge might give way after all that water?

FATHER

No. The farmer who lives up the road was waiting on the other side to cross too. He had a truck and he came over first. He assured me that it was perfectly safe and said that it often flooded that way when it rained hard.

MOTHER

Well, all I can say is that I am thankful to have you all safe at home.

MICHAEL

Hey, Mom! How about food? I'm starved. You know why, don't you?

PATSY

A glass of milk would have helped a lot.

FATHER

(*Laughing.*) Here we go again.

MOTHER

Skip upstairs and get cleaned up, children. Supper will be ready by the time you are downstairs again. And no hot dogs, either, even if there *are* plenty of them in the refrigerator.

(PATSY *and* MICHAEL *run off stage, each one calling* "*I'm first for the shower.*" MOTHER *and* FATHER *look at each other a second and then both laugh.*)

MOTHER

Was it pretty bad, dear?

FATHER

(*Straightening up in chair.*) Bad? I should say not. And wait until I tell the others at the office that my children planned a Father's Day picnic just for me. Why, I wouldn't have missed it for the world!

curtain

J.W.

This Dream Came True

CHARACTERS

CHRISTOPHER COLUMBUS
DOMENICO, *his father*
SIGNORA COLUMBUS, *his mother*
PEDRO, *his friend*

QUEEN ISABELLA
KING FERDINAND
PERSONS IN THE PROCESSION

COSTUMES

CHRISTOPHER COLUMBUS *the boy wears a knee-length tunic with flowing sleeves. It is belted at the waist and attached to the belt in the front is a leather coin purse.* COLUMBUS *the man wears a long, loose gown of rich-looking material. It is belted at waist with a scarf. From his shoulders hangs an ankle-length cape.*

PEDRO *is dressed similarly to* COLUMBUS, *the boy.* DOMENICO *wears same type of dress as* COLUMBUS, *the man.* SIGNORA COLUMBUS *wears a long, loose simple gown.*

PERSONS IN PROCESSION *wear same type of clothes as* COLUMBUS, *the man. Sailors wear white blouses, knee britches which hang loose, scarves with ends flying loose tied around their heads. Indians are in conventional Indian dress.*

QUEEN ISABELLA *and* KING FERDINAND *both wear long, flowing robes and have crowns on their heads.*

PROPERTIES

Act One: simple furnishings of a weaving room, including several chairs and a loom with cloth stretched over it, also a scroll. Act Two: kitchen furnishings, table and chairs, a letter. The back of the stage should be kept free of furniture so that the procession can move through easily. PERSONS IN PROCESSION *carry boxes and cages.*

ACT ONE

TIME: *The year 1465.*

PLACE: *The weaving room of* DOMENICO COLUMBUS *in Genoa, Italy. When the curtain rises, fourteen-year-old* CHRISTOPHER *is seen seated before the loom, but his hands are idle. He is reading from a scroll.*

(DOMENICO *enters the room.*)

DOMENICO

Cristoforo!

CHRISTOPHER

Yes, Father?

DOMENICO

You are reading again, though I told you to keep at your weaving. Have I not told you that this cloth must be ready before the week is passed?

CHRISTOPHER

Yes, Father. But . . . (*He hangs his head for a moment, then looks his father straight in the eye.*) I am tired of the weaving! I do not like to weave. But this tale, Father—it is wonderful! (*He rises, holding the scroll in his hands.*) This is what I like, what I want to be. Yes, I want to be like Marco Polo. You should read it, Father—all about the wonderful travels he embarked upon, and the strange sights he saw. *He* was afraid of nothing. Oh, if only *I* could be a sailor!

DOMENICO

What is this nonsense? Always the same, always this talk of becoming a sailor!

CHRISTOPHER

When I am grown I *shall* be a sailor. Not only that, a great navigator as well.

DOMENICO

You shall be nothing of the kind! My son shall be a weaver even as his father. And you must keep at your work, Cristoforo, and

stop this talk of sailing and navigating, I tell you. How can a lad
of fourteen know what he wants to be when he is a man?

CHRISTOPHER

I *know* what I want! When I am a man I shall follow in the foot-
steps of Marco Polo and travel over all the world. I shall have
ships that sail the seas, and I shall be their master!

DOMENICO

Let me hear no further talk of this kind. Now give me that scroll
and get back to your weaving at once! (*He takes the scroll from*
CHRISTOPHER'S *hands.*)

(DOMENICO *leaves and* PEDRO *enters.*)

PEDRO

What, Cristoforo! You sit at the weaving when even now a new
ship has come into port—a strange and wonderful ship—and you
not there to have seen her! All of Genoa was there to watch her
dock, and what a beautiful sight that was as she entered the harbor
with her white sails flying!

CHRISTOPHER

How could I be there when my father keeps me at the loom? Do
not bother me, Pedro. This cloth must be finished and sold. My
family can well use the money it will bring in.

PEDRO

Ah, well, there is still time for you to see her at the wharves. She
will be in dock for three days, then set forth once more.

CHRISTOPHER

Pedro, I wish that I might sail with her. With all my heart, I do.

PEDRO

What, *you* a sailor? (*He laughs.*) That's funny. You are little
more than a *bambino*. (*He cocks his head to one side and looks at*
CHRISTOPHER *appraisingly.*) Though I must say you are grown tall
for your age, Cristoforo.

CHRISTOPHER

I am just fourteen, but I know as much about ships and sailing and
charts and maps as many a grown man!

PEDRO

(*Taking a letter from his pocket.*) Here, I almost forgot my real reason for coming. I have a letter for your father. Strangely enough, Cristoforo, this letter was handed me by a sailor from the same ship I have been telling you about. Your father must be an important person to receive letters from foreign shores.

CHRISTOPHER

My father is not only a weaver, he is also a merchant of fine cloth and receives orders from many places. (*He goes to right of stage and calls to his father.*) Father, where are you? Come quickly— Pedro has brought an order for you.

(DOMENICO *enters.*)

DOMENICO

What is this?

PEDRO

A letter for you, *signor*. (*He hands the letter to* DOMENICO. DOMENICO *reads it.*)

DOMENICO

This is unfortunate.

CHRISTOPHER

Is something wrong, Father?

DOMENICO

Si, si. The very cloth you are working on, my son. Yes, most unfortunate, this. (*He sits at the table and puts his head in his hands.* CHRISTOPHER *moves closer to him.*)

CHRISTOPHER

Does the gentleman not want it after all?

DOMENICO

Well, yes. He wants it. But he was to have come to Genoa for it. Now he cannot come. He wants me to send it to him, all the way to Corsica.

PEDRO

Perhaps you could send it to him by the same sailor who carried the letter, *signor*.

DOMENICO

No, no! I do not know these sailors. This cloth is worth much money. Would the sailor bring back all of it, think you? I do not trust them.

CHRISTOPHER

Father. Ah, Father . . .

DOMENICO

Yes, yes, boy, speak up!

CHRISTOPHER

Father, let me take the cloth to the man!

PEDRO

(*Laughing.*) What, you, Christopher? Ha, ha, that is funny!

DOMENICO

Is it so funny? (*He looks at* CHRISTOPHER *for a moment without speaking. Then he rises and goes to* CHRISTOPHER, *placing his hands on his son's shoulders.*) My son, you have grown tall these past weeks.

CHRISTOPHER

Yes, Father. And I am strong. And I can take care of myself.

DOMENICO

May the saints be praised! I believe you could. Yes, Cristoforo, I believe you could make this journey. I shall try to sign you on as deck hand on the ship that even now rests in the harbor.

CHRISTOPHER

Then I may go? I may go on the ship? Pedro, do you hear? I shall sail on that very ship which you have just been begging me to go to see. It seems too good to be true.

DOMENICO

I shall go at once to see the ship's captain.

CHRISTOPHER

And I shall go with you.

DOMENICO

No. You are forgetting, Son, that there is still much work to be done on the cloth. You will stay here and work.

CHRISTOPHER

Oh yes, Father. (*He runs to the loom and seats himself before it.*) I shall waste no time, never fear!

curtain

ACT TWO

TIME: *Several weeks later.*

PLACE: *The kitchen of the* COLUMBUS *home.* DOMENICO *and* SIGNORA COLUMBUS *are seated at the table.*

SIGNORA COLUMBUS
It still seems strange in this house without our son Cristoforo. The other children miss him.

DOMENICO
And you, Susanna, you miss him too.

SIGNORA COLUMBUS
(*Sighing deeply.*) It is not just that I miss him, my husband. There is anxiety in my heart.

DOMENICO
He will come back safely, and he will bring the money which we sorely need to feed our children. Cristoforo is always to be relied upon.

SIGNORA COLUMBUS
Nor is that the extent of my fears.

DOMENICO
What is it, then, wife?

SIGNORA COLUMBUS
My fears are for the future. I know the lad better than anyone, for I am his mother. I know what is in his heart. The sea is in his heart and soul, Domenico! He talks of little else. He learns quickly, and when he returns from this, his first voyage, he will have learned much about the sea. But Cristoforo will want to know more!

DOMENICO
You are trying to say that from now on he will follow the sea, are you not?

SIGNORA COLUMBUS
Yes, our son will follow the sea.

DOMENICO
You are probably right, Mother. He has told me the same, and

always I have discouraged him. But—well, if it is in his heart and soul, as you say, I shall make no more complaints. And now I must go into the weaving room to see how the boy Bartholomew is making out. He is young yet and (*he laughs*) he is not Cristoforo!

(DOMENICO *goes out.*)

(SIGNORA COLUMBUS *puts her head down on the table and sleeps. The curtain falls for a brief moment. When it rises she is sitting up staring hard at left of stage, a strange expression on her face. Unseen by her,* QUEEN ISABELLA *and* KING FERDINAND *enter stage at right and stand a little in back of her. At the same moment* CHRISTOPHER COLUMBUS, *the man, enters from left. He is followed by other men in rich dress. These in turn are followed by sailors carrying baskets and boxes. Some of them carry cages. Behind them are six Indians with painted faces and feathered headdresses, carrying bows and arrows. The group walks slowly toward center.* SIGNORA COLUMBUS *rises but the group does not see her. She turns and gasps when she sees the king and queen standing near her. The procession approaches.* COLUMBUS *falls upon his knees and kisses the hand of* QUEEN ISABELLA.)

COLUMBUS

Your Majesties! (*He remains kneeling until* ISABELLA *motions him to his feet.*)

ISABELLA

Rise, Admiral of the Ocean Seas! You have brought us and our country great honor. It is we who should pay homage to thee, in all truth.

COLUMBUS

Without the support and aid of your Majesties I should never have made the voyage at all! What I bring here is only a small part of the wealth and vast treasures of the land I have discovered.

ISABELLA

We have waited eagerly to hear of this new country.

COLUMBUS

Strange lands they are, beyond the power of imagination, and filled with such great riches it is beyond my power to describe! All these, your Majesties, I was honored to take in the name of Spain and for her glory.

FERDINAND

You have been gone long, Columbus.

COLUMBUS

The voyage was long, and the hardships many. But now I am back, and I have only one further ambition. Your Majesties, I should like to return to the New World with many ships and men. Not only are there countless treasures there to be had for the taking, but also there are many souls to be saved. The country is inhabited by godless men. We must take to them the saving grace of Christianity. All of this I wish to do for our gracious Queen. (*He kneels once more before* ISABELLA *and kisses her hand.*)

ISABELLA

(*Motioning him to rise.*) The ships you shall have, Christopher Columbus. They shall be ready as soon as it can be made possible. Men, too, and priests shall go with you to take the word of God to those savages.

FERDINAND

All these things shall be made ready for your next voyage.

ISABELLA

Our Admiral is a hero this day, in all truth, and his name shall be famous throughout the world from this day forward.

curtain

(*When the curtain rises,* SIGNORA COLUMBUS *is seated at the table with her head on her arms. After a moment her husband enters.*)

DOMENICO

Do you sleep, my wife?
(*She raises her head and looks at him.*)

SIGNORA COLUMBUS

Domenico! I have just had the strangest dream.

DOMENICO

Ah, women are always dreaming.

SIGNORA COLUMBUS

But this was about our son Cristoforo.

DOMENICO

It is about Cristoforo that I have come to speak to you. We shall see him any moment. His ship is in the harbor!

SIGNORA COLUMBUS

That is good news! I wonder—I wonder if he is bringing treasures for the king and queen, or perhaps strange animals and painted savages.

DOMENICO

Don't talk nonsense, woman! He is bringing me the price of my cloth from Corsica, I hope!

SIGNORA COLUMBUS

But the dream was so real, Domenico! I must tell Cristoforo about it.

DOMENICO

Well, you may tell him now, for here is our son!
  (*Enter* CHRISTOPHER.)

CHRISTOPHER

You are right, Father. I am back, and here, safe and sound, is the money for the cloth. (*He hands a packet to* DOMENICO, *then turns toward his mother.*) And what is it you would tell me, Mother?

SIGNORA COLUMBUS

(*Kissing her son on his forehead.*) I am so filled with joy that you have returned, my son, that it has almost wiped the dream from my mind. Tell me, Cristoforo, have you brought back treasures from your voyage?

CHRISTOPHER

(*Laughing.*) No treasure, Mother. Just Father's payment for the cloth that I was able to deliver. Oh, yes, and something else too.

DOMENICO AND SIGNORA

(*Together.*) What is that?

CHRISTOPHER

An agreement with the captain to continue on his ship! And this next time we are to make an even longer voyage.

SIGNORA COLUMBUS

(*Looking at her husband.*) A longer voyage! You see, Domenico, he must follow the sea. Yes, he *must* follow the sea, for it is his destiny. Can you understand that, my husband? It will be as in my dream!

CHRISTOPHER

What is this dream?

SIGNORA COLUMBUS

While I slept just now, I had a strange dream of you, Cristoforo. In that dream I seemed to see you as you will be years hence, perhaps long after I have left this world. It was so real I cannot help but think that it was meant to show me what the future holds in store for you, my son!

CHRISTOPHER

Was I a sailor, Mother?

SIGNORA COLUMBUS

Oh, more than a mere sailor! The queen called you "Admiral of the Ocean Seas." You kissed her hand and spoke to both the king and queen as though they were your equals! It was a daring thing for you to do, Cristoforo!

DOMENICO

She is taking this dream seriously!

SIGNORA COLUMBUS

You spoke of foreign shores you had discovered, and great treasure. You asked for more ships to be put under your command, and they were promised you! You were a *very* great man in my dream, my son.

DOMENICO

Listen to her! She talks as though she believes all this nonsense of kings and queens and treasures. But it is very natural, I suppose. To any mother, her son is a hero.

SIGNORA COLUMBUS

Ah, yes, that is it! Cristoforo, the queen called you a hero, and said that your name would become famous over all the world!

DOMENICO

(*Laughing.*) Well, now that you have had a good sleep, wife, you may get us some supper. I am sure that Cristoforo could eat some of your good cooking.

(*They start to leave the room.* DOMENICO *goes off stage at right. When* CHRISTOPHER *and his mother approach the door, however, she stops him and takes his hand in hers.*)

SIGNORA COLUMBUS

Cristoforo, I have something to say to you.

CHRISTOPHER

Yes, Mother?

SIGNORA COLUMBUS

(*In a serious voice.*) This was no ordinary dream I had, nor half-waking fancy! It was too real for that. I am sure it was meant to reveal to me, your mother, the truth of what the future holds in store for you. Yes, my son, I believe with all my heart that this dream will one day come true! It is your destiny, Cristoforo Columbus, to become world famous. (*She places her hand over her heart.*) I feel it here, in my heart!

CHRISTOPHER

(*Dreamily and gazing off into space.*) Perhaps you are right, my mother. Who knows?

curtain

E.H.S.

The United Nations, the Hope of the World

CHARACTERS

GUIDE	DRUG TRADE
BOY	MINORITIES
GIRL	STATUS OF WOMEN
HOPE	HUMAN RIGHTS
VOICE (OFF STAGE)	REFUGEE
COURT OF JUSTICE	FOOD
SECURITY COUNCIL	HEALTH
ATOMIC ENERGY	LABOR
MILITARY STAFF	POSTAL
ARMED FORCES	COMMUNICATIONS
GENERAL ASSEMBLY	WEATHER
TRUSTEESHIP	AVIATION
SECRETARIAT	BANK
ECONOMIC AND SOCIAL COUNCIL	MONETARY FUND
POPULATION	EDUCATION
CHILDREN'S EMERGENCY FUND	

In the background is a riser made up of four tiers. The upper tier is wide enough for three people, the second tier for six people, the third tier for six people and the fourth tier for eleven people.

Plan of Platform

FLAGS OF THE UNITED NATIONS

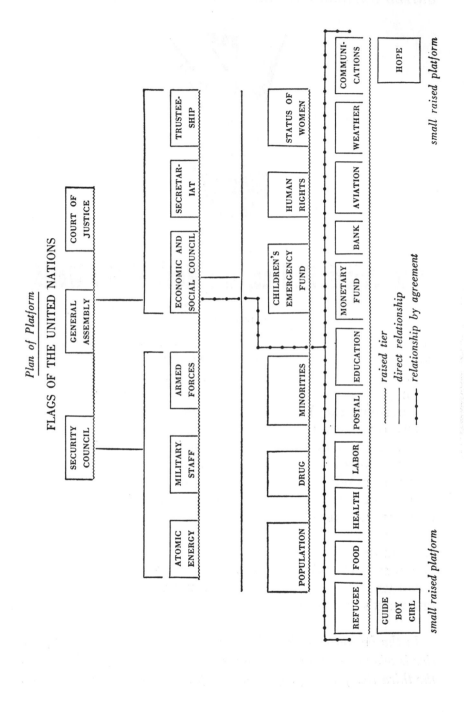

small raised platform

small raised platform

—— raised tier
—— direct relationship
•—•—• relationship by agreement

In back of the upper tier, arranged alphabetically, are the flags of the United Nations. Toward the front of the stage on either side is a raised platform. The one on the left is large enough for three persons and the one on the right for one.

COSTUMES

One boy is in a judge's robe, two are dressed as soldiers, one girl is a refugee with a shawl over her head. Several persons have bandages on them, some are in various national costumes. HOPE *is dressed in a white robe.*

PROPERTIES

Act One: doctor's bag, loaf of bread, bundle for the refugee.

Act Two: signs for each member of the United Nations. Signs are to follow the directions given in Act Two. They should be printed on white cardboard and mounted on a stick so that they may be held up for the audience to read easily. A scroll representing the Charter of the United Nations. Flags of all countries which are members of the United Nations and also the flag of the United Nations.

ACT ONE

The first act is meant to represent world confusion. When the curtains open twenty-six persons are on the stage running around aimlessly. They stop to quarrel with each other and each one is selfishly claiming his own right to be where he is and not be pushed around. In the crowd can be seen several with their arms in slings and bandages around their heads. One boy is carrying a doctor's bag, one is in a judge's robe. One boy has a loaf of bread under his arm. A girl with a bundle under her arm has a shawl around her head and is obviously a refugee. Two boys are dressed like soldiers and are acting particularly belligerent. The other boys and girls are dressed in the native costumes of several countries. Toward the front of the stage on the platform on the left are standing two boys and a girl. One of the boys is dressed in the costume of a guide who is conducting a tour through a public building. Finally the confusion dies down a little and the girl on the platform is heard speaking.

GIRL

But what is going on down there? Who are they and why are they quarreling?

GUIDE

Those, my dear child, are the people of the world.

BOY

But what is the matter? Can't they see that they are just going around in circles and not accomplishing a thing?

GUIDE

From up here looking down on them *we* are able to see it. But apparently they can't.

GIRL

But see those people over there who are bandaged. What has happened to them?

GUIDE

They are the victims of terrible wars. There will be many more persons looking like that unless something is done to make wars cease.

BOY

Who is that poor woman over there? (*He points.*) I mean the one with the shawl over her head and the bundle under her arm.

GIRL

Poor thing! She doesn't look as though she knew which way to turn.

GUIDE

And she doesn't know, either. She is a refugee, driven from her home by those who would enslave her. She is hoping to find some place where she will be free and able to live in peace.

BOY

Look! That is a doctor over there. Why doesn't he do something for those people who are suffering?

GUIDE

There are many fine doctors who would like to share their knowledge and to help in those countries where medical advice is practically unknown. But there doesn't seem to be any way for them to get started.

GIRL

And over there—look—there is someone with his arms full of food. See that poor woman stretching out her arms for some. Why doesn't he share with her?

GUIDE

He doesn't see her, my dear. He doesn't even realize she is hungry. I'm sure he *would* share his food with the starving if he knew who they were and how to get it to them.

BOY

I see a judge wandering around. Can't he advise people and help them solve their difficulties?

GUIDE

He could if they would agree to listen to his wisdom.

GIRL

You seem to know everything. Can't you do something about all this confusion in the world?

GUIDE

No. I am merely a guide. I am pointing out to you what needs to be done. You, as members of the world's family, will have to work out this problem yourselves.

BOY

There must be something we could do. If all the nations could only get together and talk their troubles over perhaps they could solve their difficulties without resorting to war.

GIRL

Listen! I hear something! It's growing louder and louder!

(*Off stage a gong is struck several times. And then a voice is heard intoning and the words get louder each time.*)

VOICE

San Francisco—1945. San Francisco—1945. San Francisco—1945.

curtain

ACT TWO

The same persons are on the stage as in Act One. They are dressed the same except that the ones that had bandages on have taken them off. They are quiet now and all eyes are on the platform at the right of the stage. HOPE *stands there dressed in a white robe; she has a scroll in her hand.*

VOICE FROM CROWD ON STAGE

Who are you?

HOPE

I am the Hope of the World and I have come to show you the road to peace and world understanding.

SECOND VOICE

Peace, did you say? That is a wonderful word, but how can we bring it about?

THIRD VOICE

We are the people of the world. We represent all nations. Our ideas are all different. How can we ever agree?

HOPE

I have in my hands the Charter of the United Nations, which was signed in San Francisco on June 26th, 1945. Fifty nations agreed to meet together as an organization to discuss world problems and the problems of individual nations which affect other nations.

FOURTH VOICE

But with so many nations taking part, and with so many problems to be discussed, how can it be done without a great deal of confusion?

HOPE

Each type of problem will be assigned to a commission which will be made up of experts on that particular subject.

FIFTH VOICE

Can you show us how it will work out?

HOPE

I certainly can. At the center of the organization are three principal organs. Will the Court of Justice please step forward?

(*The boy dressed in the judge's robe mounts to the upper tier and takes his place on the extreme right. He carries a sign which reads "INTERNATIONAL COURT OF JUSTICE."*)

JUSTICE

I am the International Court of Justice. Through my doors enter those nations who wish to have their disputes settled in a peaceful manner by means of international law.

SIXTH VOICE

And if we don't agree with your decisions?

JUSTICE

All members of the United Nations agree to abide by the decisions of my Court.

SEVENTH VOICE

And will this be the only way of keeping peace in the world?

HOPE

No, indeed. To watch over the peace we have chosen the Security Council.

(SECURITY COUNCIL *mounts to the upper tier and takes his place at the extreme left. His sign reads "SECURITY COUNCIL."*)

SECURITY COUNCIL

I am the Security Council. I am made up of eleven members. At all times there will be a representative of the United States, the United Kingdom, Russia, France and China on this Council. The other six members are elected by the General Assembly for two-year terms.

EIGHTH VOICE

And what means can *you* use to keep the peace?

SECURITY COUNCIL

I have three helpers; first the Atomic Energy Commission.

(ATOMIC ENERGY COMMISSION *takes his place on the second tier over at extreme left. His sign reads "ATOMIC ENERGY COMMISSION."*)

ATOMIC ENERGY

It is my duty to study all about atomic energy and to try to persuade the nations of the world to come to an agreement on how it
can best be controlled.

SECURITY COUNCIL

And then I have my Military Staff.

(*One of the soldiers takes his place on the second tier next to*
ATOMIC ENERGY. *His sign reads "MILITARY STAFF."*)

MILITARY STAFF

My Military Staff consists of the chiefs of staffs of the permanent
members of the Security Council. It is our duty to advise the
Council and to command any armed forces which are under orders
of the Security Council.

SECURITY COUNCIL

And lastly I have Armed Forces under my jurisdiction.

(*Other soldier takes his place on the second tier next to* MILITARY
STAFF. *His sign reads "ARMED FORCES."*)

ARMED FORCES

I am made up of the armed forces of all the United Nations which
may be called upon if necessary to maintain or restore international
peace.

BOY

Is there any provision made for a general discussion of world problems by *all* the nations?

HOPE

Oh, yes! And this is a very important part of the United Nations.
The General Assembly.

(GENERAL ASSEMBLY *mounts to the top tier and takes his place in
the middle between* SECURITY COUNCIL *and* COURT OF JUSTICE. *His
sign reads "GENERAL ASSEMBLY."*)

GENERAL ASSEMBLY

I represent all members of the United Nations. In our meetings we
can discuss any question which the Charter allows. We can at any
time consider any threat to the peace of the world.

GIRL

That sounds like a lot to do. Have *you* any helpers?

GENERAL ASSEMBLY

I certainly have. First I shall present my three main assistants. Trusteeship.

(TRUSTEESHIP *goes up to the second tier and stands at the extreme right. His sign reads "TRUSTEESHIP.")*

TRUSTEESHIP

I supervise the governing of those colonies which do not yet have self-government.

GENERAL ASSEMBLY

The Secretariat.

(SECRETARIAT *goes to second tier and stands next to* TRUSTEESHIP. *His sign reads "SECRETARIAT.")*

SECRETARIAT

I am the one who keeps everything in the United Nations running smoothly. It is my job to oversee all of the office force, have charge of the interpreters, prepare reports and keep records.

GENERAL ASSEMBLY

Economic and Social Council.

(ECONOMIC AND SOCIAL COUNCIL *takes his place on the second tier between* ARMED FORCES *and* SECRETARIAT. *His sign reads "ECONOMIC AND SOCIAL COUNCIL.")*

ECONOMIC AND SOCIAL COUNCIL

I am the one who has charge of the social well-being of people all over the world.

BOY

That sounds like a big undertaking. Surely *you* have some helpers too.

ECONOMIC AND SOCIAL COUNCIL

Of course I have, a good many. And I shall ask some of them to explain just what their duties are. Each one of these commissions or committees that you will hear from now is an expert in that particular field. And each one works toward benefiting, in some way, all of mankind.

(*The next six people take their places on the third tier without any introductions. They go up in the following order, each bearing a sign with the name of the commission printed on it: "POPU-*

LATION" at extreme left, *"DRUG TRADE"* next and then *"MINORITIES." "STATUS OF WOMEN"* goes to extreme right, *"HUMAN RIGHTS"* next and *"CHILDREN'S EMERGENCY FUND"* takes his place between MINORITIES and STATUS OF WOMEN. *When they are all in their places,* POPULATION *speaks.*)

POPULATION

I study the growth of population in various parts of the world to find out what effect it has on social conditions.

DRUG TRADE

I help to control the trade of narcotic drugs.

MINORITIES

I protect the rights of minority groups of people.

STATUS OF WOMEN

I try to see that women have equal rights in all countries.

HUMAN RIGHTS

I shall draft the Declaration of Human Rights which will recognize the right of all humans to have freedom, justice and peace in the world.

CHILDREN'S EMERGENCY FUND

I provide food, clothes and medical care for unfortunate children. I also build and operate children's hospitals and orphan homes. Anyone who is interested may contribute to my fund.

ECONOMIC AND SOCIAL COUNCIL

This next group of people will interest you, I am sure. They are agencies and some of them have been in existence a long time. Each one has its own charter and is related to me only by agreement. I try to help them coordinate their work so that each one will be a more effective organization. A nation does not have to be a member of the United Nations to belong to one of these agencies, but it does have to agree to the terms of the charter of the agency to which it belongs.

(*The next eleven people take their places on the fourth tier without any introductions. In this group we find the doctor, refugee woman, man with bread. They go up in the following order, each bearing a sign with the name of the agency:* "REFUGEE" *goes to extreme left,* "FOOD" *comes next, followed by* "HEALTH,"*

"LABOR," "POSTAL." "COMMUNICATIONS" goes to extreme right, "WEATHER" next to him, "AVIATION," "BANK," "MONETARY FUND," and finally "EDUCATION," who stands between POSTAL *and* MONETARY FUND. *When they are all in their places* REFUGEE *speaks.*)

REFUGEE
I bring relief and assistance to displaced persons.

FOOD
I study to see how more food can be raised, and how those people who do not have enough food can be better fed.

HEALTH
I am the World Health Organization and I work to fight disease. I respond to calls for help wherever disaster strikes.

LABOR
By my labor codes I help to raise the standards of workers and working conditions all over the world.

POSTAL
I continue the work which has been going on for many years which has resulted in a world-wide postal system.

COMMUNICATIONS
My work consists mainly of considering the problems of radio communication.

WEATHER
I continue work which was started years ago. I make weather forecasts available to persons all over the world.

AVIATION
I help to regulate air transportation and to provide weather stations along *flying* routes.

BANK
I am the International Bank and I help to provide loans to countries that need them to help develop their resources.

MONETARY FUND
I help trade by assisting countries to balance their foreign accounts.

EDUCATION
I am known as UNESCO and I have the job of restoring schools

and libraries that were destroyed in the war. I also encourage education in all countries.

(*After* EDUCATION *stops speaking the* BOY *and* GIRL *leave the platform where they have been standing and run across the stage to* HOPE.)

GIRL

Oh! You have given us HOPE. You really have! But tell us, is there anything we can do?

BOY

Yes, is there anything *we* can do to help in this plan for world peace?

HOPE

Yes, there is. You two represent the citizens of tomorrow. You are the ones who will make the future decisions. Peace will come only if everyone believes in it and will work toward making it possible. In your hands I now place this symbol of world understanding and peace—the flag of THE UNITED NATIONS.

(HOPE *gives the flag to the* BOY *and* GIRL. *They unfurl it and hold it in the center of the stage.*)

curtain

J.W.

The Witches' Complaint

(For string marionettes or hand puppets)

CHARACTERS

SUSAN	MALVOLIA, PRINCE SNEEZE'S
HER MOTHER	WITCH
HER FATHER	RAPUNZEL'S WITCH
SNOW WHITE'S WITCH	BABA YAGA
HANSEL AND GRETEL'S WITCH	TOM TIT TOT
SLEEPING BEAUTY'S WITCH	GHOST

COSTUMES

SUSAN *and her* MOTHER *and* FATHER *are dressed in modern every-day clothes. The* WITCHES *are all in conventional witch dress with black capes and black peaked caps.* TOM TIT TOT *is a grotesque animal-like figure with a very long tail. If string marionettes are used, attach a string to the tail so that it can be thrashed around.*

PROPERTIES

Scene I requires one chair and a table, while for Scene II a kettle suspended from three sticks over a fire of red paper suffices. Experimentation has shown that it is just as effective and far easier for the children if the scene is painted on a backdrop. Another advantage is that painting scenery affords more classroom participation in preparing for the production of the play. In Scene I a living room setting can be painted on ordinary wrapping paper such as is used for classroom friezes. This can be thumbtacked to the board used as a backdrop. For Scene II a forest scene with trees and a moon coming up over a hill should be used. This can be quickly tacked over the one used for Scene I and as quickly removed for Scene III. Do not turn on house lights between scenes. The music should create the atmosphere for Scene II and a flashlight will be enough to prepare the stage. A gong to be used off stage at the end of Scene II will also be needed. SNOW WHITE'S WITCH *should have a small doll's hand mirror attached to her hand so she can look in it frequently.* HANSEL AND GRETEL'S WITCH *should have a piece of ginger cookie in her hand so she can nibble on it occasionally.* SLEEPING BEAUTY'S WITCH *should have a spindle in her hand and* BABA YAGA *should have a broom in hers.*

SCENE I

TIME: *The present.*

PLACE: *Living room of* SUSAN'S *house. As curtain opens we find* SUSAN *standing near window crying.*

SUSAN

Oh dear, oh dear! Why does everything always have to happen to me? I wanted to go to Betty's Halloween party tonight, and now it is raining—and I have a cold, and—oh dear, oh dear!

(MOTHER *enters.*)

MOTHER

Come, come, Susan. It isn't as bad as all that! There are plenty of Halloweens coming and there will be lots of other Halloween parties.

SUSAN

But Mother, you don't understand! This is a special party. Betty told me all about it. She's going to have cornstalks all around and jack-o'-lanterns too. Her brother Tommy is going to be a ghost and her mother is going to dress up like a witch and tell fortunes.

MOTHER

That does sound like an exciting party, darling. Truly, I'm disappointed that you can't go! But we simply can't take a chance on that cold getting any worse. You know how sick you were last time.

SUSAN

I know. But I still want to go! Oh, Mother, they are going to have such fun. They are going to duck for apples 'n' everything.

MOTHER

Well, it's too bad. I am sorry, too, that Daddy had to work tonight. Maybe we could have had a party right here at home.

SUSAN

Mother, couldn't you tell me a story? You haven't done that for a long time; not since I've learned to read for myself.

MOTHER

It really has been a long time, hasn't it? Perhaps I have forgotten how. What kind do you want me to tell? (MOTHER *seats herself in chair.*)

SUSAN

(*Clapping her hands.*) Oh, a Halloween story, of course! About witches, Mother. Lots and lots of witches!

MOTHER

Witches? Well, let me see. I know, I'll tell you about—

SUSAN

Wait a minute, Mother. Let's turn out all the lights but one so it will be really spooky! (SUSAN *turns out lights. She then sits on floor close to her mother's knee. A dark cloth placed over stage lights gives the effect of dimness.*)

MOTHER

Are you ready, dear? (*Pauses and then speaks slowly.*) It was Halloween night just last year—(MOTHER's *voice fades away as curtains close and music begins. A recording of Saint-Saëns' "Danse Macabre" is suggested for the music to set the mood for Scene II.*)

SCENE II

PLACE: *The forest. Five* WITCHES *are grouped around a kettle. They peer in and mutter as they drop things in it while one witch stirs with big spoon. The sixth character is an odd little fellow whose distinguishing characteristic is a very long tail.*

WITCHES

(*Chanting.*) Witches' brew, Witches' brew,
　　　　　That gives us power our deeds to do.
　　　　　Drop in a worm, a giant's hair;
　　　　　Drop in a toad. Beware! Beware!
　　　　　For evil charms will be granted to
　　　　　All who drink our Witches' brew!

(*At this minute they are interrupted by* BABA YAGA, *who enters backward, sweeping with an old broom as she comes.*)

BABA YAGA

There, there! Old Baba Yaga has fooled them again. They'll never guess which path I took this time. (*Laughs a cackling laugh.*) I certainly am smart, I am! No one else would think of sweeping away her tracks as I do. Ha, ha, ha!

(SNOW WHITE's WITCH *looks up from kettle and then holds mirror close to her face and looks into it.*)

SNOW WHITE's WITCH

It's no use, I say. It's no use. It simply won't work any more. I can say:
　　　　Looking-glass, looking-glass, on the wall,
　　　　Who in this land is fairest of all?
and nothing ever happens. I can't understand it!

BABA YAGA

(*Walking to kettle and peering in.*) What's in it tonight? Do you have the right mixture, think you?

SLEEPING BEAUTY'S WITCH

All but the giant's hair. We haven't seen a giant for years! So the best we could do was to use one from a horse's tail.

HANSEL AND GRETEL'S WITCH

No, things aren't the same as they were in the good old days. How well I remember the day I got Hansel and Gretel to come to my house! There they were dancing around their kitchen in such a silly way—(*She dances and sings in an off-tune cackle.*)

Brother, come and dance with me,
Both my hands I give to thee.
First you twirl, then you turn;
Really, it's not hard to learn.

TOM TIT TOT

What happened then? I don't believe I ever heard your story.

SLEEPING BEAUTY'S WITCH

Oh, you must have heard that story! She's been bragging about it for years. Now, my charm was really a good one, Tom Tit Tot. Let me tell you—

HANSEL AND GRETEL'S WITCH

(*Interrupting.*) You see, I made Hansel knock against the table and spill all the milk. That made his mother so angry she sent them into the forest.

TOM TIT TOT

Oh, yes, I remember now. You were living in a gingerbread house, weren't you?

HANSEL AND GRETEL'S WITCH

Yes, and it was frosted all over too. And it had the most delicious clear sugar windows! Those children were certainly hungry after their night in the woods. It was just as I had planned it. "Yum, yum," they said after they had taken one bite of the roof. But they were really frightened when they heard me say,

"Nibble, nibble, like a mouse;
Who is nibbling at my house?"

RAPUNZEL'S WITCH

(*Turning toward* SLEEPING BEAUTY'S WITCH.) I notice she doesn't say anything about the way the story ended, though!

SLEEPING BEAUTY'S WITCH

Tom Tit Tot, don't you listen to that old braggart! She didn't do anything so wonderful. Just turned a little boy and girl into gingerbread. Why, almost anyone can work that charm! Now, it really takes some skill to make people go to sleep for a hundred years as I did Briar-rose and her family.

TOM TIT TOT

You know, this is the first time I've ever been to one of your meetings. Who is that over there? (*Points to* PRINCE SNEEZE'S WITCH.)

SNOW WHITE'S WITCH

Oh, she's a newcomer too. Her name is Malvolia. Tell Tom Tit Tot what a joke you played, Malvolia.

MALVOLIA

Oh, that was great fun! You see, I was invited to the christening of a young prince. And do you know what happened? At the feast after the christening the strawberry tarts gave out and they served me with an old chocolate éclair. But I fixed them, all right! I certainly got even with them! (*All the* WITCHES *laugh.*)

RAPUNZEL'S WITCH

That is funny! Tell him, Malvolia. We don't mind hearing your story again. After all, we haven't heard yours every year for the last hundred years or so, as we have the one about Hansel and Gretel. I'm certainly tired of that one, I can tell you!

HANSEL AND GRETEL'S WITCH

Oh, is that so! Well, how many times have we heard about you and that beautiful Princess whatever-her-name was that you kept locked up in a tower?

RAPUNZEL'S WITCH

That shows you haven't heard it very often or you would remember her name. Now, I'll never forget Hansel and Gretel! You won't let me. (*Turns to* TOM TIT TOT.) Her name was Rapunzel and you never saw such beautiful hair! They don't grow it like that nowadays. And when I'd say:

"Rapunzel, Rapunzel
Let down thy hair to me"
it was a sight to behold to see that long lovely hair come streaming
out of the tower window!

BABA YAGA

Why don't you two stop quarreling for a minute and let Malvolia
finish her story?

TOM TIT TOT

Yes, I want to know how you got your revenge for the insulting
way they treated you at the christening of the prince.

MALVOLIA

Oh, I just fixed it so that every time the little prince sneezed
something terrible would happen.

TOM TIT TOT

Such as—

MALVOLIA

One time I changed all the cats into dogs, and all the dogs into cats.
It was funny to see the cats running around trying to bark at
everyone, and the big old dogs trying to climb trees. Another time
I changed all the elderly gentlemen into elm trees, and the court
astrologer into an eight-day clock! His wife had to wind him up
every week.

(TOM TIT TOT *laughs and in his glee jumps around making his
tail go very fast.*)

TOM TIT TOT

What finally happened?

MALVOLIA

It was finally spoiled when he found a princess brave enough to
marry him. I was angry, of course, because everything changed
back again. But it was funny while it lasted!

SNOW WHITE'S WITCH

(*Who has been admiring herself in her glass during all the previ-
ous conversation.*) Was she as beautiful as I am?

MALVOLIA

(*Sarcastically.*) In the end she was much more beautiful! (*Turns to* TOM TIT TOT.) But who are you? If you don't mind such a personal question. You don't resemble any of us.

TOM TIT TOT

Oh, I'm Tom Tit Tot. Some people call me Rumpelstiltskin. But I'll answer to either one. Tom Tit Tot is just easier to say.

MALVOLIA

But what evil did you do?

TOM TIT TOT

Nothing very much. I just liked to worry queens. That was why I was never included in this group before; I hadn't really done anything bad enough! But witches are scarce now, so they asked me if I would help out this year.

MALVOLIA

Just what are we supposed to do, anyway?

BABA YAGA

Well, you see it's like this. People are queer nowadays. They say they don't believe in us any more, and yet once a year they insist that we get out our broomsticks. This is the night they have chosen. They call it Halloween.

SLEEPING BEAUTY'S WITCH

And I'm warning you—riding a broomstick is not as safe as it used to be.

RAPUNZEL'S WITCH

It certainly is not! There are huge monsters that fly about all over the place! They come swooping right at you from the clouds with the most terrible roar you ever heard in all your life. It's enough to frighten the wits out of a self-respecting witch!

SNOW WHITE'S WITCH

Well, *I* am getting mighty discouraged. There are so many beauty contests these days and so many beauty queens being chosen that I don't even stand a chance.

SLEEPING BEAUTY'S WITCH

How do you suppose I feel? Why, if a princess should prick her finger on a spindle now, she wouldn't stay in a swoon for a hundred years. Not she! She would simply run for the mercurochrome bottle.

HANSEL AND GRETEL'S WITCH

And my charms don't work very well, either. If you offer children candy now, most of them look at you in disgust and say, "I'm not allowed to eat candy between meals, thank you."

MALVOLIA

I suppose I shall have a hard time someday too. They will probably discover something to prevent people from getting colds, and then I won't be able to make anyone sneeze!

TOM TIT TOT

Yes, and queens don't care whether they can spin or not! They just go out and buy all their clothes.

RAPUNZEL'S WITCH

And this bobbed hair business makes me sick!

BABA YÁGA

Well, how do you think I feel with all these paved roads and cement sidewalks? I can't even see my tracks myself, so what is the use of sweeping and pretending that I am fooling someone!

(*A gong strikes twelve times. They all stand listening.* GHOST *enters, beckoning.*)

GHOST

(*In low, deep tones, very slowly and with deliberation.*) 'Tis time! 'Tis time!

(*All the* WITCHES *nod their heads.*)

HANSEL AND GRETEL'S WITCH

My rheumatism is so bad I dread to think of getting on that broomstick again!

GHOST

(*In same tones.*) 'Tis time! 'Tis time!

RAPUNZEL'S WITCH

(*Impatiently.*) Yes, yes, we're coming. (*Turning to others.*) Let's give it one more trial.

(*All stand around kettle as* RAPUNZEL'S WITCH *stirs.*)

WITCHES and TOM TIT TOT

(*Chanting.*) Witches' brew, Witches' brew,
        That gives us power our deeds to do.
        Drop in a worm, a giant's hair;

Drop in a toad. Beware! Beware!
For evil charms will be granted to
All who drink our Witches' brew!
(*Music begins again as curtains close.*)

SCENE III

PLACE: *Same as Scene I. As curtains open Susan and her mother are in the same positions as at the end of the first scene.*

SUSAN

Oh, Mother, that was a wonderful story! How did you ever think of anything like that?

MOTHER

Well, I've often wondered what witches would do if they had to live now. I'm afraid their evil charms wouldn't work as they did in fairy-tale times! Listen, isn't that Daddy coming?

(DADDY *enters.*)

DADDY

What is going on here? My goodness, I don't think I've ever seen it rain harder.

(SUSAN *jumps up and runs to meet him. He kisses her and then goes over to* MOTHER *and kisses her.*)

SUSAN

Oh, Daddy, Mother has been telling me a wonderful story! It was all about witches.

DADDY

Witches? That sounds like Halloween to me. Do you know what I was thinking about as I was driving home?

SUSAN

What, Daddy? What?

DADDY

About how good some popcorn and apples would taste.

SUSAN

(*Clapping hands.*) Goody, goody! Mother, may we please pop some corn right now?

MOTHER

I don't see why not. And maybe you could persuade Daddy to bob for apples with you. He used to be the champion bobber at parties when we were young. Do you remember, dear?

DADDY

(*Laughing.*) I certainly do. Come on, Susan! We'll bob for apples while Mother pops the corn.

MOTHER

And both of you tie aprons around your necks first. I know what bobbing for apples can do to clothes!

SUSAN

Come on, Mother! Come on, Daddy! Let's get started. Oh, boy! This is turning into a grand Halloween party after all.

curtain

J.W.

A Halloween Surprise Package

CHARACTERS

MISS WARDMAN, *the teacher*   TOMMY

PATSY BROWN   OTHER STUDENTS

JIMMY WEEKS   JANITOR

MARY LYNN   MR. WEEKS

COSTUMES

Ordinary school attire for Act One. In Act Two the children may wear masks and any costume they choose for the Halloween party.

PROPERTIES

Blackboard and erasers for the school room. Halloween decorations for the party. A box or carton large enough for JIMMY to hide in. The top must be easy to lift up so that he can pop up like a jack-in-the-box.

ACT ONE

TIME: *Afternoon one week before Halloween.*

PLACE: *School room.*

MISS WARDMAN

Before I dismiss the class this afternoon I have an announcement
to make. But first of all, who can tell me what special day will come
at the end of this month?

THE CLASS

(*In unison.*) Halloween!

MISS WARDMAN

That's right. Just one week from today will be Halloween. I thought
it would be fun if we celebrated with a real Halloween party.

VOICES FROM THE CLASS

Ooh, a party! Won't it be fun? . . . May we dress up? . . . And
wear masks?

MISS WARDMAN

Yes, indeed! The principal has given us permission to hold the
party in the gymnasium. We'll decorate it for the occasion. You
can all come disguised. I am sure your mothers will help with your
costumes. You must all tell your mothers when you go home today
so that you can begin at once to plan your costumes.

(*A buzz of voices is heard from the class.*)

MISS WARDMAN

I know you all like Halloween parties, and this one is going to be
extra special because there will be a prize.

(*More voices and cheers.*)

MISS WARDMAN

The boy or girl who comes to the party with the best disguise will
be given a prize of a big basket of groceries from Mr. Edwards'
store. And so you must be very clever and disguise yourselves so
that even Sherlock Holmes himself wouldn't know you! And now
the class is dismissed.

(*With excited chatter the class files from the room.* JIMMY
WEEKS *and* PATSY BROWN *remain.*)

PATSY

It's our turn to clean the blackboards, Miss Wardman.

MISS WARDMAN

Very well, Patsy. I have some arrangements to make with the

principal regarding the party. When you have finished cleaning the boards you may go.

(MISS WARDMAN *leaves*.)

(PATSY *and* JIMMY *take up erasers and start to clean the blackboards*.)

PATSY

I can hardly wait until we have the Halloween party! Won't it be fun, Jimmy?

JIMMY

I'm not coming.

PATSY

Not coming? Jimmy Weeks, you must be fooling. You wouldn't miss the fun!

JIMMY

Fun? Pooh, who wants to come to an old Halloween party! Just stand around and look at each other.

PATSY

Why, we won't, either. We'll play games, and the gym will be all decorated, and there will be food. And besides, there's to be a prize for the best disguise.

JIMMY

(*Rubbing the boards vigorously*.) Pooh, who wants to win any old prize!

PATSY

Oh, I think you're just talking. *You'd* like to win those groceries as well as anyone. And besides, with your father not working I bet you could use them.

JIMMY

(*Disagreeably*.) Is that any of your business? Just because your mother can afford to make you a costume, or even *buy* you one, you don't need to rub it in about my father being sick.

PATSY

Oh, Jimmy! I'm sorry, honestly I am. I didn't mean to hurt your feelings. Your father is so much better now that he'll probably be going back to work soon. Then your mother can get you a costume for the party.

JIMMY

(*Wistfully.*) It will be too late then.

PATSY

You *do* want to come to the party, don't you, Jimmy?

JIMMY

Of course I do. But how can I? I'm not even going to tell my folks about it, so there!

PATSY

(*As they clean the erasers.*) Jimmy, I think you're foolish. Tell your mother anyway. I bet she'll think of something for you to wear! Maybe you'll win the prize.

JIMMY

I wish I *could* win it, Patsy!

PATSY

Tell her, then, Jimmy. And I hope you do win!
(JIMMY *and* PATSY *leave and curtain falls.*)

ACT TWO

TIME: *One week later—Halloween.*

PLACE: *The school gymnasium. It is decorated with black and orange crepe paper and cats and witches. To right of stage there is a large cardboard carton against the wall. As the scene opens* MISS WARDMAN *is standing at the door greeting the children as they come in. The children are dressed in costumes representing many different characters—witches, ghosts, Indians, gypsies, fat men, babies, etc. All are masked.*

MISS WARDMAN

Oh, how can I guess all these strange people? Not one looks familiar to me. Wait, isn't this little gypsy Mary Lynn?

MARY LYNN

Oh, you guessed me! (*She removes her mask.*)

MISS WARDMAN

And isn't this Indian chief our Tommy?

TOMMY

Well, I guess *I* don't win that prize!

(MISS WARDMAN *continues to guess the identity of the children as they walk about. Soon all are unmasked. Now the boys begin to chant: "When do we eat? We're hungry. When do we eat . . . eat . . . eat!"*)

SEVERAL GIRLS

You boys aren't very polite!

MISS WARDMAN

I don't see Jimmy Weeks.

PATSY

He didn't come after all, then. Poor Jimmy, I guess he didn't . . .

MISS WARDMAN

Didn't what, Patsy?

PATSY

I guess he didn't have any costume to wear to the party.

(*The* JANITOR *enters.*)

JANITOR

Miss Wardman, Mr. Weeks is at the door.

MISS WARDMAN

Jimmy's father? Oh, tell him to come in, please.

(*The* JANITOR *goes out and returns with* MR. WEEKS.)

MR. WEEKS

I wonder if you've noticed that box, ma'am.

MISS WARDMAN

Why yes, but I thought it was some school supplies.

MR. WEEKS

No ma'am. I brought it here after supper tonight. Jimmy asked me to deliver it to you. He said to tell you that it is a surprise for the children.

MISS WARDMAN

Oh, how nice! Thank you very much, Mr. Weeks. I'm sorry, though, that Jimmy couldn't come to the party himself. I wonder what in the world this is he has sent us?

(MR. WEEKS *goes out quietly without replying.*)

MISS WARDMAN

Well, there is one way to find out. Please help me to open the box, boys.

(*The children crowd around the box exclaiming, "Open it!"*)

MISS WARDMAN

(*Bending over the box with her ear close to the top of it.*) Listen! There's something moving inside!

(*The children crowd in closer.*)

PATSY

Maybe it's a kitten. I think I can hear it purring!

TOMMY

Maybe it's a puppy.

OTHER BOYS AND GIRLS

Open it and see.

MISS WARDMAN

Be careful how you open it, boys. You may hurt whatever is inside!

(*The boys remove a rope from around the box and lift up the lid. The head of* JIMMY WEEKS *pops up like a jack-in-the-box, a big grin on his face.*)

MISS WARDMAN

Jimmy Weeks! It's our Jimmy! What a surprise!

JIMMY

(*Climbing from the box.*) Wasn't that a good disguise?

ALL

(*Cheering.*) Hurray for Jimmy! Jimmy wins the prize!

PATSY

How did you ever think of it, Jimmy?

JIMMY

I didn't. My mother had the idea. I told her about the party like you said, and she told me to hide in a box and to come as a jack-in-the-box!

MISS WARDMAN

Well, Jimmy, you certainly came to the party with the best disguise. None of us recognized you—that's certain!

PATSY

Does he win the prize, Miss Wardman?

ALL

Give Jimmy the prize. Hurray for Jimmy Weeks!

MISS WARDMAN

I guess the class is the best judge. The decision is unanimous. Everybody is voting for you, Jimmy. Hear them!

(*All cheer loudly for* JIMMY. *But suddenly the boys take up the chant again.*)

BOYS

Let's eat, let's eat! Eat, *eat*, EAT!

curtain

E.H.S.

Thanksgiving Proclamation—1863

CHARACTERS

ABRAHAM LINCOLN	SQUANTO
JOHN NICOLAY	GOVERNOR BRADFORD
MRS. SARAH HALE	PILGRIM WOMAN
CAPTAIN MILES STANDISH	OTHER PILGRIMS
MASSASOIT	OTHER INDIANS

COSTUMES

ABRAHAM LINCOLN *and* JOHN NICOLAY *should wear long frock coats. A portrait of* MRS. SARAH HALE *shows her dressed in black with a slightly bustled skirt. A small cape is around her shoulders. Her hair is parted in the middle and brushed slickly down ending in curls around her face. The back hair is pinned in a tight knot on the top of her head. Either a small plain bonnet or scarf is on her head and of course she wears gloves. The* PILGRIMS *and* INDIANS *are dressed in the conventional style.*

PROPERTIES

Table and two chairs.

TIME: *The year 1863.*

PLACE: *President Abraham Lincoln's office. When curtain opens* ABRAHAM LINCOLN *is seated at his desk working on some papers. The door opens and his secretary,* JOHN NICOLAY, *enters.*

NICOLAY

Mr. Lincoln, I am sorry to disturb you but Mrs. Sarah Hale is here to see you.

LINCOLN

That's all right, John. Mrs. Hale had an appointment. Bring her in.
(NICOLAY *goes out and returns immediately with* MRS. HALE. *He*

steps aside to allow her to enter first. LINCOLN *rises and extends his hand.*)

LINCOLN

Mrs. Hale, I am indeed honored that you have come from Philadelphia to Washington to see me. May I present my secretary, Mr. John Nicolay?

MRS. HALE

Thank you, Mr. Lincoln. I had the pleasure of meeting Mr. Nicolay a short time ago.

(*She curtsies slightly and* NICOLAY *bows low from the waist.*)

LINCOLN

That will be all, John. I shall ring for you if I need you later.

(NICOLAY *bows again to* MRS. HALE *and leaves the room.*)

LINCOLN

Will you sit down, madam?

(MRS. HALE *and* LINCOLN *both sit down.*)

MRS. HALE

Mr. Lincoln, it is very kind of you to take time to grant me this interview. I know what a trying time this year of 1863 is for you and how full your heart and hands are right now.

LINCOLN

I pray every day that this war which has so divided our country will come to an end. (*Slight pause, then he looks up and smiles at* MRS. HALE.) But madam, even if I were not happy to grant you an audience for your own sake, a letter from your son-in-law's brother, Major General David Hunter, would open any door to me.

MRS. HALE

General Hunter was extremely kind in offering to write seeking an interview for me.

LINCOLN

We have been friends for years. Perhaps you have never heard how much I owe him. On the way to Washington for my inaugural we stopped in Buffalo. The crowds got a little anxious and pressed pretty close to me. (*Humorously.*) I guess they wanted to see if I am really as ugly as my pictures make me out to be. Anyway,

David tried to protect me and got his arm broken for his pains. He really deserved a medal for being wounded in the line of duty!

MRS. HALE

General Hunter is a very modest man. I had not heard that version of his accident before.

LINCOLN

And now, madam, what can I do for you? I don't suppose you have come to ask me to pose as a model for one of the fashions for your *Godey's Lady's Book?*

MRS. HALE

(*Laughing.*) No, Mr. Lincoln. I assure you that is not the reason for my coming.

LINCOLN

Mrs. Hale, *Godey's Lady's Book* is very popular in my household. I consider it an honor that the editor of so famous a publication should ask to see me.

MRS. HALE

You flatter me, Mr. President.

LINCOLN

Mrs. Lincoln is really the person to whom you should be talking. She looks forward to each new issue and I am sure she follows your suggestions in every detail.

MRS. HALE

I should be very happy to meet Mrs. Lincoln.

LINCOLN

I must confess that while fashions don't interest me, I have listened to Mrs. Lincoln read your description of a New England Thanksgiving dinner and my mouth has watered at the very sound of the words—"ham soaked in cider three weeks, stuffed with sweet potatoes and baked in maple syrup." Tell me madam, do you make those recipes up out of your head?

MRS. HALE

(*Laughing.*) No, Mr. Lincoln. I assure you each one of those recipes has been very thoroughly tested. But, that, Mr. President, is not the reason I come to see you. It is to discuss Thanksgiving.

LINCOLN

Thanksgiving, Mrs. Hale?

MRS. HALE

Yes, Thanksgiving. For years, Mr. President, it has been my dream that Thanksgiving would be a national holiday. Ever since 1846 I have written thousands of letters to the governors of states and other important persons urging them to join together and make the last Thursday in November a universal Thanksgiving Day.

LINCOLN

I have read some of your articles on this subject. You feel very keenly about this, don't you Mrs. Hale?

MRS. HALE

Mr. Lincoln, can you not just see what this day would mean to generations to come? It would call to mind each year what sacrifices have gone into the making of our country. Every school child would be taught that the day is not only one of rejoicing, but also one of worship and prayer. Just picture that first band of brave settlers and what that first harvest meant to them.

(*The light goes out. The table where* MR. LINCOLN *sat can be pushed to one side. When the lights go on* MR. LINCOLN *and* MRS. HALE *have left the stage and in their place is a group of Pilgrim men and children. They are standing in a semicircle watching a group of Indians dance. This dance can be as long as is wished. After the dance is finished* CAPTAIN MILES STANDISH *steps forward and addresses one of the Indians.*)

CAPTAIN STANDISH

Thank Chief Massasoit and his warriors, Squanto. We all enjoyed your dance very much. Tell them, too, that we thank them for the fine deer they brought for our feast.

(*A group of Pilgrim women enter and one of them speaks to* CAPTAIN STANDISH.)

PILGRIM WOMAN

The feast is ready, Captain Standish. Let Squanto invite the warriors to join us.

(SQUANTO *motions to* MASSASOIT *and his warriors to follow him but they stop as* GOVERNOR BRADFORD *speaks to* CAPTAIN STANDISH.)

GOVERNOR BRADFORD

Captain Standish.

CAPTAIN STANDISH

Yes, Governor Bradford.

GOVERNOR BRADFORD

Before we partake of the feast of venison, geese and turkey and the other good things we have gathered from our harvest, I think we should give thanks to Almighty God for having brought us safely through this first year in a new land. It is through His mercy that we are at last delivered from the death that threatened us because of illness and starvation. In the midst of our rejoicing we should not forget the One to whom we owe these blessings.

(*The* PILGRIMS *all kneel reverently and the* INDIANS *stand by looking at them in amazement. The lights go out. When they come on again the* PILGRIMS *and* INDIANS *have left the stage. The desk has been pushed back in its place and* MRS. HALE *and* ABRAHAM LINCOLN *are seated as before.*)

LINCOLN

Mrs. Hale, I agree with you, Thanksgiving should be a national holiday. It should be a day for prayer and rejoicing that our country is a land where people may live and worship according to each one's own desire. And when this horrible war is over, may we once again be a united people. What is it you want *me* to do, madam?

MRS. HALE

When George Washington was President, he issued a Thanksgiving Proclamation. But since that time no President has followed his example.

LINCOLN

Then you would like me to issue a national proclamation?

MRS. HALE

Yes, Mr. Lincoln. If the President of the United States each year would do that I feel sure that the governor of each state would follow by issuing his own proclamation naming the same date.

LINCOLN

Mrs. Hale, you will have your Thanksgiving Proclamation.

MRS. HALE

Thank you, Mr. Lincoln. You have been most kind and patient
with me. I wish every person in this country could have the opportunity to talk to you and know you as I have. So many people
criticize you unjustly. Do you never resent the things that are
said about you?

LINCOLN

I am human, madam. Of course I do. And I have written many
letters to people telling them just what I think of them. I have a
good time doing it and I feel better when it is done. But I never
send those letters.

MRS. HALE

No?

LINCOLN

(*Simply.*) I burn them when they are finished. It does me good to
write them and they answer their purpose. But no one else ever sees
them.

(MRS. HALE *gets up and so does* LINCOLN.)

MRS. HALE

Thank you again, Mr. President, and good-by.

LINCOLN

Good-by Mrs. Hale. (*They shake hands.*) John will see you to
the door.

(MRS. HALE *goes out.* MR. LINCOLN *stands lost in thought.* JOHN
NICOLAY *enters.*)

NICOLAY

Do you want me now, Mr. President?

LINCOLN

Yes, John. Sit down. I want to dictate something to you.

(JOHN *seats himself at desk and takes a notebook and pencil.*
MR. LINCOLN *paces up and down and begins to speak very slowly.*)

LINCOLN

The year that is drawing to a close has been filled with the blessings
of fruitful fields and healthful skies. To these bounties which are
so constantly enjoyed that we are prone to forget the source from
which they come . . .

(*Lights go out for a moment and when they come on* LINCOLN *and* NICOLAY *have left the stage.* SARAH HALE *is standing at one side reading from a newspaper. She reads a continuation of what* MR. LINCOLN *had been dictating.*)

MRS. HALE

It has seemed to me fit and proper that they should be solemnly, reverently and gratefully acknowledged as with one heart and one voice by the American people. I do, therefore, invite my fellow citizens in every part of the United States and also those who are sojourning in foreign lands to set apart and observe the last Thursday of November next as a day of Thanksgiving and praise to our Beneficent Father who dwelleth in the heavens. (MRS. HALE *pauses and then clasps the paper close to her.*) Thank you, Mr. Lincoln, thank you!

curtain

J.W.

The Santa Claus Court

CHARACTERS

CAROL, *aged ten*

HER MOTHER

ST. NICHOLAS

SANTA CLAUS

CHRISTKINDLI, *from Switzerland and Germany*

KNECHT RUPRECHT, *from Germany*

PERE NOEL, *from France*

BOZHITCH, *from Serbia*

LA BEFANA, *from Italy*

CHRISTMAS OLD MAN, *from China*

HOTEIOSHO, *from Japan*

YULE NISSE, *from the Scandinavian Countries*

COSTUMES

CAROL *and her* MOTHER *in ordinary dress.* SAINT NICHOLAS, *bishop's robe and crown on head.* SANTA CLAUS, *traditional* SANTA CLAUS *suit.* CHRISTKINDLI, *an angel with white robe, silver or gold wings, crown on head; carries pack.*

KNECHT RUPRECHT, *a fur coat and fur cap; he has a long beard.* PERE NOEL, *dressed like* SANTA CLAUS. BOZHITCH, *dressed in white, his costume is either the tunic of a Serbian peasant or the white robe of a priest.*

LA BEFANA, *old woman dressed in Italian peasant costume; she carries a pack in one hand and a bell in the other.* CHRISTMAS OLD MAN, *costume of Chinese coolie; he wears a big straw hat and sandals and has a long white beard.*

HOTEIOSHO, *Japanese dress; he wears two masks, with face on both sides of his head.* YULE NISSE, *dressed like an elf with tight-fitting brown suit; he wears a red, pointed hat and has a long beard. He also carries a pack.*

PROPERTIES

Living room furniture. Christmas cards, candlestick, sleigh bells, packs for SANTA CLAUSES, *bag of ashes and bell for* LA BE-FANA, *and sprig of mistletoe. (If mantel is impractical the Christmas cards can be displayed on top of bookshelves or on the table.)*

ACT ONE

TIME: *Christmas Night.*

PLACE: CAROL'S *living room. Across the rear wall there is a mantel or shelf which holds a row of Christmas cards put there for display. The wall actually is a curtain which must be easy to move apart or raise. Behind this curtain are erected two large Christmas cards. These are simply large frames constructed of plywood or beaver board, large enough for the children who take the parts of* ST. NICHOLAS *and* SANTA CLAUS *to stand upright within, forming the pictures of the cards. The frames may be as simple or as elaborate as desired, but should be easily recognized as Christmas cards. The framework may be painted red or silver, covered with glittering stars, or entwined with tinsel. Their construction will depend upon the ingenuity of the children who are responsible for this project of the play. The living room itself should contain at least two armchairs, and a table standing at left of stage. When the curtain opens* CAROL *and* HER MOTHER *are seated in the armchairs talking.*

CAROL

Our Christmas cards look so pretty on the mantel, Mother, I think I'll take them down and look at them again.

(*She walks to the mantel and starts to remove the cards.*)

MOTHER

That's a good idea, Carol. It's always fun to take another look at the Christmas cards. And what better time to do it than on Christmas Night, after all the excitement is over? Wasn't this a nice Christmas, dear?

CAROL

(*Still taking down the cards.*) Oh, yes, Mother. And I do thank you and Daddy for all the wonderful gifts you gave me. And Santa Claus too. I think I'll leave this Santa Claus card here, it looks so—so appropriate! (*She takes away all the cards except the one with a picture of a big Santa on it, and stacks them on the table. Then from the stack she picks up the top card and studies it for a moment.*) This is a lovely picture of St. Nicholas. I think I'll put him up there beside Santa Claus.

(*She places the* ST. NICHOLAS *card on the mantel.*)

MOTHER

Well, *that's* appropriate too. Santa Claus and St. Nicholas are sort of related, you know.

CAROL

How do you mean, Mother?

MOTHER

Oh, I guess there wouldn't be any Santa Claus at all if it hadn't been for St. Nicholas. He started the whole thing.

CAROL

He did?

MOTHER

Yes, dear, you can thank him for the legend of Santa Claus, because St. Nicholas was the first patron saint of Christmas. He really lived, you know, a long, long time ago.

CAROL

Tell me about it, Mother.

MOTHER

St. Nicholas was a bishop in a place called Myra, in Asia Minor. That was way back in the fourth century. Everybody loved him because he was so generous. One story tells how he took pity on the family of a poor man and threw a bag of gold into their house through an open window. That, and other surprise gifts he made, gave him the reputation of gift-giving which has lasted all these many years.

CAROL

(*Looking fondly at the* ST. NICHOLAS *Christmas card.*) He must have been an awfully nice old man.

MOTHER

St. Nicholas was *the* Christmas saint for about fifteen hundred years and still is, in many nations. Our Santa Claus takes his place in this country.

CAROL

I wonder how he likes that! That someone else took his place, I mean.

MOTHER

(*Laughing.*) Well, he *could* be jealous, but such a kind understanding character as St. Nicholas surely must understand.

CAROL

I wonder! (*She picks up the pile of cards, goes over to the chair and sits down, then starts to go through them.*)

MOTHER

Well, while you look at your Christmas cards I will finish the dishes. Your father will be here soon with a client of his. They are going to discuss that case which comes up in court tomorrow. (MOTHER *goes out.*)

(CAROL *sits quietly for a moment going through her cards. They slide off her lap to the floor and she stoops to pick them up. While her head is bent, the curtain at rear of stage opens and the two giant cards are revealed. The life-sized figures of* ST. NICHOLAS *and* SANTA CLAUS *stand in tableau.* CAROL *sits back in the chair again, having retrieved the spilled cards.*)

CAROL

These cards are nice, but my favorites are St. Nicholas and—
and—and—

(*She doesn't finish her sentence. While she is speaking she
raises her eyes to the wall, and instead of the cards on the mantel
she sees the huge life-sized cards with* ST. NICHOLAS *and* SANTA
CLAUS *standing within their frames. She rushes over and stands
before them, her hand over her mouth in astonishment.*)

CAROL

I can't believe it! They look so lifelike! (*Stares at them.*) Almost
as though they would move.

(*The figure of* ST. NICHOLAS *stirs a little, then he slowly turns his
head and looks at* SANTA. SANTA *turns his head toward* ST. NICHO-
LAS. *The two continue to gaze at each other.*)

CAROL

They moved! (*She points her finger at them.*) *You moved!*

ST. NICHOLAS

Of course we moved. And why not? I'm *very* tired of being on
Christmas cards. My joints are getting stiff. (*He steps out of the
frame.*)

SANTA CLAUS

(*Laughing and holding his belly.*) Ho, ho! Guess I'll move about a bit myself.

(CAROL *is frightened and runs to her chair and tries to hide behind it. They both look at her.*)

SANTA CLAUS

Don't be afraid, little girl.

ST. NICHOLAS

What is she afraid of? I hope you don't think a good old saint would hurt a little girl.

CAROL

(*Coming from behind the chair and standing timidly in front of it.*) It's just that I didn't expect you to move and—and walk and talk.

ST. NICHOLAS

I don't know why we shouldn't! We are both real. At least I am! Don't you know that I am the patron saint of Christmas?

SANTA CLAUS

And so am I, Carol.

ST. NICHOLAS

Now, that statement I should like to have proved to me!

SANTA CLAUS

What do you mean by that? Do you doubt my word?

ST. NICHOLAS

Everyone who knows *anything* knows that *I* am the patron saint of Christmas. The original, the *only* St. Nicholas! You are an impostor, sir! (*He glares at* SANTA CLAUS.)

SANTA CLAUS

Oh come, now, St. Nicholas! I will admit that you were the first! But you ask any American child about Santa Claus! They will *all* vouch for me.

ST. NICHOLAS

I still say that you are an impostor! All others who claim to be patron saints of Christmas are impostors, frauds, and just plain fakes!

SANTA CLAUS

I am sorry that you have that attitude, St. Nicholas. You seem to forget that your counterpart, and mine, lives in the hearts of children all over the world, in some form or another, according to the children's interpretation! The name may not be similar, but the spirit is the same.

ST. NICHOLAS

I protest! Whatever the name, if it is not St. Nicholas, it is not I.

SANTA CLAUS

I don't want to quarrel with a saint. It seems irreverent. But I wish I could prove to you, sir, that your spirit lives on in many Santa Claus characters of different nations. I wish I could show you what I mean.

CAROL

I think I know what you mean, Santa Claus. My mother was explaining it to me a little while ago. But I wish you *could* prove it to St. Nicholas, so that he would understand.

SANTA CLAUS

I know what! I could call witnesses. I could ring my sleigh bells and summon the other Santa Clauses of the world to testify.

CAROL

Oh goody! That would be just like presenting a case in court! My daddy is a lawyer and attends court cases all the time! We could hold the trial right here, and I could be the judge because I know a good bit about it. That is, if you and St. Nicholas would like me to.

ST. NICHOLAS

I am a man of justice. I believe in giving this man (*pointing to* SANTA CLAUS) a fair hearing. When I lived on earth I was an important member of the Council of Nicaea. I think you are perfectly right, Carol. You may be the judge and we will present our cases to you.

CAROL

Then help me to set up the court. Here, we'll push this table over to the center of the room. It can be the bench. (*They push the table to stage center.* CAROL *picks up a candlestick from the table.*) This candlestick will be my gavel. Now, where are the witnesses?

ST. NICHOLAS

I need no witnesses! I shall present my case alone.

SANTA CLAUS

Well, since the important point in my case will be to present witnesses, I will call the other Santa Clauses of the world.

(*He shakes his sleigh bells and they ring out merrily for a moment.* CAROL *and* ST. NICHOLAS *wait.* SANTA CLAUS *shakes the bells again, louder. Suddenly the door opens and* CHRISTKINDLI, KNECHT RUPRECHT, PERE NOEL, BOZHITCH, LA BEFANA, CHRISTMAS OLD MAN, HOTEIOSHO, *and* YULE NISSE *enter. They stand at right and all on stage look toward* CAROL.)

CAROL

(*Rapping the candlestick on the table.*) Order in the court! (*She lays the candlestick down and turns timidly toward* ST. NICHOLAS *and* SANTA CLAUS.) I'm afraid I don't know the *exact* procedure! If only my father were here, he would make a better judge.

SANTA CLAUS

Nonsense! You are doing fine, Carol. I suggest that we hear St. Nicholas first.

CAROL

O.K. *Order in the court!* I call St. Nicholas to the chair. Present your case, St. Nicholas.

ST. NICHOLAS

Your Honor, it seems that Santa Claus, here, and all these other— other characters—are imitating my role of patron saint of Christmas! I wish to protest against this disrespectful mockery. My place in the observance of Christmas goes back for many hundreds of years! These others are only imitators! They have changed my entire character! They have even changed my name!

SANTA CLAUS

What's in a name?

CAROL

(*Rapping the gavel.*) Santa Claus, you must not interrupt! *Order in the court.* Proceed, St. Nicholas.

ST. NICHOLAS

Take this man who calls himself Santa Claus, for example. When

I was brought to the American Colonies by the Dutch, he stepped in and took over, with no authority from me whatsoever! Take the matter of my name. In Holland I was San Nik-o-laus. When I came to America the children began calling me San-o-claus, then Santa Claus!

SANTA CLAUS

Could I help that?

CAROL

Order in the court!

ST. NICHOLAS

And look how he changed my appearance! Look at him, your Honor! Compare those furs and silly red clothes and rubber boots he is wearing with my beautiful bishop's robes. I ask you, can you see any sense in such a ridiculous attire? Or in that big sack he's carrying on his back?

CAROL

Oh, that is because of the poem. You know, "A Visit from St. Nicholas." "He was dressed all in fur, from his head to his foot," it says. And in another line it tells about his bag: "A bundle of toys he had flung on his back . . ."

ST. NICHOLAS

Well, I can see it's useless to argue. I may as well give in.

CAROL

Have you anything further to say, St. Nicholas?

ST. NICHOLAS

I'm too old to be standing here arguing! I have my own personal opinion and I mean to abide by my original claim. *I* am the only true St. Nicholas—so there!

(*Very sadly he goes over to an armchair and sits down.*)

CAROL

We will now hear the other side of the case. I call Santa Claus to the chair.

SANTA CLAUS

Your Honor, I should like to present some witnesses who will prove my point.

CAROL

What *is* your point?

SANTA CLAUS

Resolved: That even though the character and name may differ as interpreted by peoples of the many nations of the world, the Spirit of Christmas is the same. First, before I call my witnesses, let me say this, your Honor. We feel no disrespect for the good saint who has just presented his case here. In fact, I believe when we have finished he will agree with me that the spirit of St. Nicholas is preserved and glorified by the work that is carried on by the characters I am going to introduce.

CAROL

Very well. Let us proceed.

SANTA CLAUS

I shall call eight witnesses who will tell you in what manner they endeavor to uphold the Christmas spirit each year. Furthermore, they will prove without a shadow of a doubt that millions of children the world over are made happy by them.

CAROL

Call your first witness.

SANTA CLAUS

I call my first witness, Christkindli.

(CHRISTKINDLI *comes forward and seats himself in the chair. He sets his white pack on the floor beside him.*)

CAROL

Do you swear to tell the whole truth and nothing but the truth?

CHRISTKINDLI

I do.

CAROL

What is your name?

CHRISTKINDLI

I am known as Christkindli, your Honor.

CAROL

Tell the court what you do.

CHRISTKINDLI

The best way to describe that would be to say that I am the Santa

Claus of Switzerland and southern Germany. In Switzerland I ride through the country in my sleigh on Christmas Eve, distributing gifts to one and all. My six reindeer pull my sleigh over the snow-covered streets. When the children hear the tinkling of the sleigh bells they come running to receive their gifts. You may be sure it takes a lot of work to see that each one receives his own special gift. My sleigh is filled to overflowing when I start out. My work is not finished until the sleigh is empty. But I can always tell by the shouts of joy and the many thanks I receive that all the boys and girls are happy when my task is done.

CAROL

You say this is in Switzerland?

CHRISTKINDLI

Yes, and also in the southern part of Germany. There I usually stop at each house. When I open the door and toss in the gifts, I call out "Yulklapp!" and there is a mad scramble by the children to get their gifts. This takes a great deal of time, but in northern Germany there is a different Santa to take some of the work off my shoulders.

CAROL

A different Santa? Who is he?

CHRISTKINDLI

He is known as Knecht Ruprecht.
(*An old man with a long beard, dressed all in fur, comes forward.*)

KNECHT RUPRECHT

Did someone call Knecht Ruprecht?

CAROL

Are you Knecht Ruprecht?

KNECHT RUPRECHT

I am. Who else?

CAROL

Then you may step down, Christkindli, and let this old gentleman have the chair.

(CHRISTKINDLI *picks up his bag and steps back while* KNECHT RUPRECHT *takes his place.*)

CAROL

(*Continuing.*) Do you swear to tell the whole truth and nothing but the truth, Knecht Ruprecht?

KNECHT RUPRECHT

Well of course! Knecht Ruprecht never tells anything but the truth.
(*The others giggle.*)

CAROL

Order in the court! Will you please say "I do."

KNECHT RUPRECHT

You do.
(*More giggles.*)

CAROL

I realize that you are a very old man so I will overlook your un— un—unusual answers. Let us proceed. Tell us in your own words, Knecht Ruprecht, what you do in Germany at Christmas.

KNECHT RUPRECHT

Ach, *mein liebes kind,* it is not just what I do at Christmas! Throughout the entire year I am working and planning, and planning and working. Nowhere in all the world is so much made of Christmas as in Germany. It's the greatest nation in the world for toys, Germany is! And I must never disappoint a single child. My great sack is so full when I start out on Christmas Eve that it is no wonder I look so ancient! Look here, I have some in my pack to show you. (*He dips into his pack and brings out several toys and places them on the table.*) There, have you ever seen such toys?

CAROL

Oh, they are wonderful! It must be fun to be a German child at Christmas time.

(*A stir is heard and* PERE NOEL, *a small old man resembling our* SANTA CLAUS, *drags a pack as big as himself over to the table and stands beside* KNECHT RUPRECHT. *He shakes his finger in* KNECHT RUPRECHT'S *face.*)

PERE NOEL

Your toys are not better zan ze ones of France, mon ami!

CAROL

Order in the court! Who are you?

PERE NOEL

I am Papa Noel!

CAROL

I can't listen to all of you at once! Order in the court! (*She raps the gavel sharply on the table.*)

SANTA CLAUS

Hear! Hear! Let us hear from Pere Noel of France.

KNECHT RUPRECHT

Ach, vell, let him speak. I am through speaking, anyway. (*He steps down.*)

CAROL

Very well, but we *must have order* here.

(PERE NOEL *seats himself in the chair, then takes a beautiful French doll from his heavy pack.*)

PERE NOEL

You see, *ma cherie?* To speak of toys, ah—no one can make ze dolls like ze French. (*He holds up the doll for her to see.* CAROL *takes it in her hands.*)

CAROL

Oh! Oh! It is the most beautiful doll I have ever seen! How I envy the little French girl who will find this in her stocking next Christmas!

PERE NOEL

Oh, *non, non!* It is not ze stocking that is hung on Christmas Eve as in your country. In France ze shoe is left out for Pere Noel to fill with ze gifts. (*While he is speaking he brings up two more dolls and places them in front of* CAROL.)

CAROL

Oh, this baby doll is adorable. Oh, they are all so lovely!

PERE NOEL

Papa Noel cannot give these away. Already they are marked with some child's name for next year. (*He reaches into his bag a third time, then holds a branch of mistletoe toward* CAROL.) But here is a gift from France, *ma cherie*. It is ze mistletoe. Hang it in ze room and good luck will come. And now Papa Noel must be packing up ze Christmas bag. (*He puts the dolls back in his pack, drags the huge bag after him, and withdraws.*)

CAROL

What a sweet Santa Claus! It makes me wish I lived in France. (*Raps the table with her gavel.*) Who's next?

(BOZHITCH, *the little white Christmas god of Serbia, comes before her.*)

BOZHITCH

(*Speaking gently.*) May I please be next?

CAROL

Oh yes! Just sit down in that chair, please. Do you swear to tell the whole truth and nothing but the truth?

BOZHITCH

I do. Oh yes, indeed I do.

CAROL

What is your name?

BOZHITCH

I am Bozhitch, the little white god of Christmas in the country of Serbia.

CAROL

Can you tell us what part you play in the Serbian Christmas?

BOZHITCH

I am very important to the people of Serbia at Christmas time. The boys and girls and their parents, too, think of me as the Spirit of Christmas. They sing of me in their Colleda songs, and I am sure they all love me, though they have never seen me. I must admit, your honor, that I am somewhat different from the usual Santa Claus.

CAROL

In what way?

BOZHITCH

I am more of a religious character. The Serbian people are deeply religious. They have many important customs connected with their Christmas, all of a reverent significance. These customs are very dear to the families of Serbia.

CAROL

Can you take time to tell us of just one of their customs?

BOZHITCH

The one the boys and girls like best, I think, is the custom of sitting on the floor to eat supper on Christmas Eve.

CAROL

That sounds very strange. Why do they do that?

BOZHITCH

The mother of the family scatters straw on the kitchen floor to represent the stable where the Child Jesus was born. After the father has prayed for Christmas to come to all parts of the earth, the whole family settles down on the straw and eats the good Christmas Eve supper. It is only one of the many customs of the Serbs at Christmas time.

CAROL

That is an interesting story. Thank you for coming. (BOZHITCH *leaves the chair.*) Who is your next witness, Santa Claus?

SANTA CLAUS

Let us hear from La Befana.

CAROL

La—who? I've never heard of *her!*

(LA BEFANA *comes forward. She carries a pack in one hand and a bell in the other.*)

LA BEFANA

Well, what are we waiting for? I have no time to tarry! I've waited around long enough. I want to get this over! (*Sits in chair.*)

CAROL

Do you swear to—

LA BEFANA

Never swear! So you can just skip that part. Tell me what you want to know, *now*.

CAROL

Pardon me! It seems we are taking up your precious time.

LA BEFANA

That's right, *signorina,* you are! My time is valuable. I must get back to work. Here it is Christmas Night, and only 364 more days until Christmas Eve!

CAROL

Perhaps you can tell us why you are carrying a bell, to begin with.

LA BEFANA

That's just what it's for, to begin with! I never enter a house without ringing this bell first. Then I jump down the chimney and fill up the shoes that I find on the hearth. Good boys and girls get toys and sweets in their shoes. Want to know what the bad ones get in theirs?

CAROL

(*Timidly.*) Wh—what?

LA BEFANA

Ashes, that's what! (*She reaches down into her bag and brings out a handful of ashes which she scatters on the floor.*)

CAROL

Goodness! Aren't the children terribly disappointed?

LA BEFANA

(*Suddenly smiling.*) Well, just between you and me, I usually have a nice toy for them too. The ashes are just to *remind* them to be good or next year they will get nothing but ashes.

CAROL

I'm glad they get some toys.

(LA BEFANA *picks up her bag in one hand, rings her bell vigorously with the other, and moves off chuckling to herself.*)

CAROL

Are there any other witnesses, Santa Claus? Why, what have we here?

(CHRISTMAS OLD MAN *from China, and* HOTEIOSHO *from Japan have approached her. Both old men carry packs.*)

SANTA CLAUS

Your honor, these Santa Clauses have come clear across the world to speak for us.

CAROL

Are they Santa Clauses, really?

CHRISTMAS OLD MAN

(*Stepping closer.*) I am Chinese—Christmas Old Man. Boys and girls of China look for me Christmas Eve to bring them gifts. Call me Christmas Old Man, some places. Other places, call me Nice Old Father.

CAROL

I didn't know the Chinese children knew about Santa Claus.

CHRISTMAS OLD MAN

Missionaries tell Chinese people about Little Jesus born in manger where cows are. Tell about Santa Claus too.

HOTEIOSHO

(*Stepping closer.*) Missionaries tell Japanese people also about Baby Jesus. Little Japanese girls love babies. Also like dolls. They ask Hoteiosho for baby dolls for Christmas.

CAROL

Do you give them dolls?

HOTEIOSHO

If they are good. I watch to see if they are good. (*He turns around and* CAROL *sees that he has two faces. She screams.*)

HOTEIOSHO

(*Smiling.*) Japanese children know that I watch them. That makes them good! Then they receive gifts at Christmas time.

CAROL

Aren't the little children afraid of you?

HOTEIOSHO

Mothers tell little children, "If you are bad, Hoteiosho will see you. He never misses anything—has two faces! You be good children, he will see you being good and bring you presents." So little Japanese children are very good. I give them many toys at Christmas time.

CAROL

Well, I guess all the children all over the world try to be good around Christmas time. (*She turns to* SANTA CLAUS.) Santa, are there any more witnesses?

SANTA CLAUS

Yes, Carol; I mean, your Honor. There is one more witness. I call the Yule Nisse to the chair.

(*The* YULE NISSE *of Scandinavia comes before the judge. He, too, carries a pack.*)

YULE NISSE

I am the Yule Nisse. I am the Santa Claus of the Scandinavian countries of Norway, Sweden, and Denmark. Unlike other Santa Clauses, I do not live at the North Pole.

CAROL

You don't?

YULE NISSE

No. You see, our countries have a cool climate which just suits me all year round. So I live under the houses, and sometimes even under the tables and chairs in the house. I guess you might call me the most surprising of all the Santa Clauses.

CAROL

How is that?

YULE NISSE

Oh, I am always causing the boys and girls to be surprised. They call me their good little old Christmas elf. While they are sleeping I do many chores for them. To show me their gratitude they leave a dish of goodies on the table for me to eat. Especially around Christmas time. That is when the mothers and their daughters cook delicacies of all kinds for the Christmas feast. It keeps them so busy that they claim they'd never be ready in time for Christmas if it weren't for me!

CAROL

You must be very helpful to them.

YULE NISSE

Yes, but as I say, they are very good to me too, and never forget to feed me. On Christmas Eve, when they know I shall be tired and hungry from all the work I have to do filling their stockings, they leave me the very best of their Christmas dainties. The Scandinavian people are very, very kind. They remember even the birds at Yule time. A Scandinavian family never sits down to eat Christmas dinner without first feeding the birds.

CAROL

That's a very thoughtful thing to do. I think I should like to live up there in one of those northern countries, especially at Christmas. And it's nice to know that they have such a wonderful Yuletide elf to share their fun at Christmas.

(YULE NISSE *withdraws.*)

SANTA CLAUS

Your Honor, you have now heard all of my witnesses. If it please your Honor, I will sum up my case.

LA BEFANA

(*From the rear of stage, where she is standing with the others.*) Be brief, please. Remember, it is only 364 days to Christmas!

CAROL

Yes, Santa Claus, you had better be brief.

SANTA CLAUS

You have heard these witnesses tell of their Christmas roles in such faraway lands as Switzerland, Germany, France, Serbia, Italy, China, Japan, Norway, Sweden, and Denmark. Some of them take the form of a jolly old man with whiskers, like me; some are elves, and some are angels. Some of them fill the children's stockings and some fill their shoes and others deliver the gifts in person. But I think you will all agree that every one fulfills the original role of St. Nicholas, that of a generous gift-giver. And all are in existence for the sole purpose of keeping alive the spirit of St. Nicholas, the patron saint of children.

ALL

Hurrah! Three cheers for St. Nicholas!

SANTA CLAUS

I think we will all agree that St. Nicholas is the originator of all true Santa Clauses the world around. And we all honor and love him.

ALL

Good old St. Nick!

CAROL

St. Nicholas, have you anything to say before we dismiss the court?

ST. NICHOLAS

(*Coming slowly forward, his head bent.*) Only this, your Honor. I wish to say that I feel very much ashamed. And I also want to say that what I have seen here tonight has more than convinced me that all these Santa Clauses here, and others from other parts of the world, are my friends. They have kept my legend alive throughout the centuries. I thank you, my friends, one and all. And to you, Santa Claus, (*bows to him*) my greatest thanks are due.

(*At this moment the sound of sleigh bells is heard off stage and all stand at attention, listening.*)

SANTA CLAUS

You know that sound, my friends?

ALL

(*Except* CAROL.) Yes!

CAROL

What is it?

SANTA CLAUS

They are ringing the sleigh bells! All the Christmas workers around the world are calling for the Santas to come back and get to work. It is only—

LA BEFANA

Three hundred and sixty-four days until Christmas!

(*They all run off stage, leaving* CAROL, SANTA CLAUS, *and* ST. NICHOLAS.)

CAROL

Well, now that the court is dismissed I must put this room to rights. Daddy will be bringing company in. I'll just put this table back in place. (*While she is pushing the table,* SANTA CLAUS *and* ST. NICHOLAS *have returned to their positions in the large frames of the Christmas cards, where they remain motionless.*) There! That looks better. (*She notices that she is alone in the room.*) Why, where did Santa Claus and St. Nicholas go? (*She sees the large cards with the motionless figures of* SANTA CLAUS *and* ST. NICHOLAS.) Oh! So there you are, back on your Christmas cards! (*She walks over to them.*) Please come out. Don't just stand there! Say something!

(*The figures remain still. At that moment* CAROL'S *mother's voice is heard off stage.*)

MOTHER

Carol! Carol, where are you?

(CAROL *turns toward the door, and while her back is toward the rear of stage, the curtain or backdrop falls and there is only the wall with a mantel shelf. There are no Christmas cards on the mantel.*)

CAROL

I'm in here, Mother. In the living room where I've been all the time.

(MOTHER *enters.*)

MOTHER

I thought I heard the men's voices. Has your father come home?

CAROL

No, Mother. That was the Santa Clauses you heard. (*She turns about and sees the blank wall.*) My goodness, they've gone!

MOTHER

Who has gone?

CAROL

Why, St. Nicholas. And Santa Claus. They were here just a second ago.

MOTHER

Perhaps you dropped them, dear. (*She stoops and picks up two cards from the very spot on which* ST. NICHOLAS *and* SANTA CLAUS *had been standing during the court scene.*) Here they are, right where you must have dropped them, Carol. See! (*She holds them toward* CAROL *and* CAROL *takes them in her hand, a dazed expression on her face.*) Here is the Santa Claus card, and here's St. Nicholas.

CAROL

These are just the cards.

MOTHER

Just cards? Honey, you talk as though they ought to be something else!

CAROL

Y-yes. Yes, Mother, I thought they were. I wonder if I could have been dreaming. It certainly all *seemed* real enough!

MOTHER

Did you fall asleep, dear? Well, that's nice. (*She goes to the table and picks up the piece of mistletoe.*) I wonder where this piece of mistletoe came from! You know how I looked and looked for mistletoe for Christmas and couldn't find a single piece.

CAROL

Mistletoe? Oh, Mother! (*She rushes over and looks at it.*)

MOTHER

Carol, just look at this floor! Where in the world did all those ashes come from?

CAROL

Ashes? OH, MOTHER!

MOTHER

Yes, ashes! And your father and his guest will be here any minute! I'll run and get the sweeper. But for the very life of me I can't imagine where they came from.

CAROL

(*Laughing and seizing her mother in a big hug.*) Mother, those ashes came all the way from Italy and that mistletoe came from France! (*She whirls her mother around the floor until her mother gasps for breath.*)

MOTHER

Carol, I do declare, I sometimes think you're possessed by the elves!

CAROL

Yes, Mother—Christmas elves!

curtain

E.H.S.

The Good Old Days

CHARACTERS

PHYLLIS	PETER
DAVEY	SAMUEL
TEACHER	JOAN
FAITH	DORIS
DAN	SEVERAL OTHER CHILDREN

COSTUMES

PHYLLIS, DAVEY *and* JOAN *in modern clothes. Other boys in knee pants, long stockings, tight short coats. Girls in fairly long gingham dresses and plain gingham aprons.* TEACHER'S *coat should be long to look like a frock coat. His tie should be long and flowing.*

PROPERTIES

Act One: sign with two arrows pointing in opposite directions and reading "Forward" and "Backward."

Act Two: two long benches; the desks should be two wide boards fastened on an angle to standards and should be the same length as the benches. A desk and chair for the TEACHER, *a dunce stool, and dunce cap. Several old battered books, a ruler, a bell, pencil and paper or slates.*

ACT ONE

TIME: *The present.*

PLACE: *This scene takes place in front of the curtain. Near side of stage where* DAVEY *and* PHYLLIS *make their entrance is a sign that has an arrow pointing in one direction that reads "Backward" and another arrow pointing in the opposite direction that reads "Forward."* DAVEY *enters first, walking very slowly and scuffing his feet.* PHYLLIS *enters and catches up with him.*

DAVEY

Oh, hi, Phyllis.

PHYLLIS

Hi, Davey. You'd better hurry. You'll be late to school if you don't walk any faster than that.

DAVEY

I don't care if I am. I have just a good notion not to go to school anyway.

PHYLLIS

Why, Davey Carter. Something *awful* will happen to you if you don't go to school.

DAVEY

I'll bet it won't. School's no fun. I wish I had lived long ago. That must have been when the kids really had a good time. They could go huntin' or fishin' when they wanted to and no one to say, "Have you practiced your music lesson, Davey?" "Do you have your homework finished, Davey?" "Don't forget to mow the lawn, Davey." "Be sure to shovel the walk, Davey." "Do this, Davey." "Do that, Davey." Honestly I'm sick and tired of all of it.

PHYLLIS

Well, maybe you are right. But my Daddy says that people who are always wishing for the "good old days" would be awfully thankful to get back to today if they had to live like people did then.

DAVEY

I'd like to try it once anyway. Look, Phyl. I never saw that sign before, did you? (*He points to the sign.*)

PHYLLIS

No, I never did. That's funny isn't it? We've walked this way to school every day.

DAVEY

I have an idea! Let's skip school today and take that road that says "Backward." It would be something different to do for once and it might be fun.

PHYLLIS

Oh, Davey. I don't dare. And anyway that road looks sort of scary. It goes back through that woods. It's dark in there and you can't see *where* it goes. No, I'm sure I don't want to go.

DAVEY

Please, Phyllis. There's nothing to hurt us. I've been in those woods before. Just for once it will be fun.

PHYLLIS

Well, all right. But somehow I have a feeling that we may be sorry.

(DAVEY *and* PHYLLIS *take hands and walk off stage in the direction of "Backward."*)

ACT TWO

PLACE: *The interior of an old-fashioned school. A slanting board is fixed to standards which run along two sides of the room. In front of this desk is a bench on which the pupils sit. This means of course that they have their backs to the center of the room. There is a desk for the* TEACHER *and a stool in one corner for the dunce to sit on. This particular scene does not portray any one period of our history but is rather a telescoping of the different types of old-fashioned schools and is intended to show the contrast between them and the schools of today. When the scene opens the only one in the room is the* TEACHER. *He is writing at his desk. Suddenly he looks up with a start and, picking up a bell from his desk, goes over to the door and rings it briskly. Immediately the children file in two by two. Among them are* PHYLLIS *and* DAVEY, *looking very much out of place in their modern clothes. The boys go to their seats at one side of the room and the girls take their places on the bench on the opposite side.* PHYLLIS *and* DAVEY *stand looking around rather awkwardly, not knowing exactly what to do.*

TEACHER

Who are you? Speak up! Speak up! Don't stand there like that.

DAVEY

I'm Davey Carter and this is Phyllis Lawson.

TEACHER

Say "sir" when you speak to me. Haven't you been taught any manners?

DAVEY

Yes, sir.

TEACHER

That's better. I suppose you have just moved into this neighborhood. It's strange I haven't heard anything about two new families. What does your father do, Davey?

DAVEY

Oh, he's a television engineer, (*pauses*) sir.

TEACHER

Young man, I won't stand for any impudence. You know very well that there is no such word. Even if it is your first day in school I must insist that you have respect and answer truthfully when you are asked a question.

DAVEY

Please, sir, I didn't mean any disrespect and I *did* answer truthfully.

TEACHER

Don't make a bad matter worse, if you please. And now we shall drop the subject for the moment. After school you will remain and answer the questions which I shall ask you about your family. And now you may take a seat with the other boys. I shall hear you read presently and decide what reader you will have.

DAVEY

Yes, sir. Thank you, sir.

(*He takes his seat in a relieved manner but looks a little apprehensive at the small space allotted to him on the end of the bench. The boy sitting next to him doesn't move an inch and* DAVEY *can hardly manage to squeeze on to the end.*)

TEACHER

And now, Phyllis. I shall question you after school too. You may sit over there with the girls. I shall listen to you read later. Faith will share her book with you for the present.

(PHYLLIS *sits down beside* FAITH *and pretends interest in the book* FAITH *offers to share. All during the preceding conversation the other boys and girls have looked around furtively at* DAVEY *and* PHYLLIS, *trying not to be detected by the* TEACHER. *There has also been a lot of nudging one another.*)

TEACHER

The primer class will please come forward.

(*Several boys and girls come up and carefully toe a crack on the floor. They stand with their hands behind their backs and look at the* TEACHER, *waiting for his cue to begin their recitation.*)

TEACHER

You may begin by reciting the syllables through L.

(*During the following recitation, which should be done by all the children in the primer class in unison, there may be mistakes by one or two. At each error the* TEACHER *points his ruler sternly at the culprit but the children continue without stopping. The recitation should be done as fast as possible and in a loud tone.*)

PRIMER CLASS

Ba be bi bo bu; Ca ce ci co cu; Da de di do du; Fa fe fi fo fu;
Ga ge gi go gu; Ha he hi ho hu; Ja je ji jo ju; Ka ke ki ko ku;
La le li lo lu.

TEACHER

That will do. You will now recite your arithmetic lesson.

PRIMER CLASS

One and one are two. Two and two are four. Three and three are six.
Four and four are eight. Five and five are ten. Six and six are
twelve. Seven and seven are fourteen. Eight and eight are sixteen.
Nine and nine are eighteen. Ten and ten are twenty. Twenty is a
score and five scores are a hundred.

TEACHER

You may take your seats. Be prepared to know the rest of the
syllables tomorrow. The fifth class will come forward to recite.

(*The primer class returns to their seats and* FAITH, PHYLLIS,
DAVEY *and* DAN *come forward.*)

TEACHER

I shall now prepare to examine you, Phyllis and Davey, and then
we shall decide with which class you will recite.

PHYLLIS

I know. I am in the fifth grade.

DAVEY

So am I. I've passed every year.

TEACHER

Well, we shall soon find out. First you will spell the new words
in your lesson. You will also give the definition of each word.
Faith, alacrity.

FAITH

(*Quickly.*) Alacrity. A-lac-ri-ty. Alacrity. It means a cheerful
readiness.

TEACHER

Phyllis, career.

PHYLLIS

(*Breathlessly.*) Career. C-a-r-e-e-r. It means something you decide
to do.

TEACHER

Dan, integrity.

DAN

Integrity. In-teg-ri-ty. Integrity. Its meaning is honesty of purpose.

TEACHER

Davey, vicissitude.

DAVEY

Wh-what? (*Pauses.*) Sir?

TEACHER

Vicissitude.

DAVEY

I—I never heard that word before, (*pause*) sir.

TEACHER

Nonsense. That simply means that you haven't studied your lesson. It is right here in your reading lesson for today. If you are in the fifth reader as you say, you should have studied it. Faith, you may spell it.

FAITH

(*Smugly.*) Vicissitude. Vi-cis-si-tude. A change or revolution.

TEACHER

(*Sarcastically to* DAVEY.) Do you think you can read the lesson or have you never heard of the *McGuffey Reader* either?

DAVEY

(*Miserably.*) I never heard of it, sir. It's not the one we use in our school but I'll try.

TEACHER

Very kind of you, I'm sure. (*Claps his hands.*) Children, you may all listen. Davey will honor us by reading to us.

(DAN *hands* DAVEY *the book opened to the right place. This next speech of* DAVEY'S *may be typed and placed in the book so he will not have to memorize it. As he comes to the underscored words he hesitates and stumbles until prompted in a stage whisper by* DAN. *During the whole reading* DAVEY *acts most uncomfortable. The other children at the desks look around as he reads the passage, trying not to laugh aloud, but many snickers are audible. The*

TEACHER *says nothing until* DAVEY *is through, but he looks very stern and unamused.*)

DAVEY

"The man who is <u>conscious</u> of the <u>rectitude</u> of his intentions, as to be willing to open his bosom to the <u>inspection</u> of the world, is in possession of one of the strongest <u>pillars</u> of a decided character. The course of such a man will be firm and steady, because he has nothing to fear from the world, and is sure of the <u>approbation</u> and support of heaven."

TEACHER

(*More sarcastically than before.*) Excellent! Excellent! So excellent in fact that we shall let you have the seat of honor so we can all admire you.

(*He takes* DAVEY *by the arm and leads him to the high stool. After* DAVEY *has climbed up on it he is given the tall dunce cap to put on and the book to study. All the other children, with the exception of* PHYLLIS, *laugh.* TEACHER *takes his seat at his desk again.*)

TEACHER

You children may sit down again. I'm afraid we have taken all the reading time we have. (*A little girl raises her hand.*) Yes, Doris, what do you want?

DORIS

Please, teacher. May I say my piece for you?

TEACHER

The one you have learned for next Friday? Yes, you may.

(DORIS *comes up and toes the crack in the floor. As she says her verse she twists one corner of her apron.*)

DORIS

"How doth the little busy bee
  Improve each shining hour,
  And gather honey all the day
  From every opening flow'r!"*

  (*As she finishes she curtsies and runs back to her seat.*)

*From "How Doth the Little Busy Bee" by Isaac Watts.

TEACHER

Very good, Doris. I hope you will do that well on Friday when we have our entertainment.

(*While* DORIS *has been reciting her piece, two boys on the bench have been pushing each other. Just as she takes her place with the girls again, one of the boys manages to push the other off the bench. The* TEACHER *goes grimly over to the bench and takes both culprits by the ear and leads them to the front of the room. There he takes his ruler and pretends to whip them soundly. Then he leads them back to the bench.*)

TEACHER

(*Sternly.*) Peter Johnson and Samuel Miller, you will each write this sentence five hundred times. "Foolishness is bound up in the heart of a child but the rod of correction shall drive it from him."

(PHYLLIS *raises her hand timidly.*)

TEACHER

And now, Phyllis, what do you want?

PHYLLIS

Please, sir, I think this geography book I am reading is very much out of date. It says here that roads will be cut across the Rocky Mountains ere long and that lines of stages will convey travelers from the shores of the Atlantic to the Pacific.

TEACHER

And what, pray, is wrong with that statement?

PHYLLIS

(*In amazement.*) Why everyone knows we don't use stagecoaches any more. My daddy flies back and forth to California often on business. It only takes him a few hours.

(*The* TEACHER *walks quickly over to* PHYLLIS *and puts his hand on her forehead.*)

TEACHER

Yes, it does feel a trifle hot. Phyllis, are you sure you feel well? I'm afraid you may be coming down with a dreadful fever. You are talking very strangely.

(*At this point the other girls on the bench all shove as far away from* PHYLLIS *as possible. She puts her head down on her arms and begins to cry. The* TEACHER *looks at her for a moment and then shakes his head. He walks back to his desk.*)

TEACHER

It is time for recess, children. Lay aside your books. Davey, you will have to stay in and study your lesson some more. Phyllis, I think you probably have a touch of the sun. You had better stay in too. The others form in twos and leave quietly.

   (*The children and* TEACHER *all leave the room. As soon as they are gone* DAVEY *jumps down from the stool and runs over to where* PHYLLIS *is sitting with her head still buried on her arms.*)

DAVEY

Aw, Phyl, don't cry, please. I'm awfully sorry I got us into this mess. Honestly I am. But we'll get out some way.

PHYLLIS

(*Raising her head.*) Davey, let's leave right away. I'm scared. And I don't like this school one bit. I like ours a lot better.

DAVEY

I do too. And would Miss Phillips look good after *this* old cross-patch! Wait a minute until I look and see if the coast is clear.

   (*He goes over to the door and takes a quick look outside.*)

DAVEY

Come on. I don't see anyone. I guess they must all be around on the other side of the building.

PHYLLIS

Oh, Davey. Do you suppose we can find our way back through the woods?

DAVEY

(*Stoutly.*) Sure we can. We got here, didn't we? All we have to do is follow that same road back the other way.

   (*They tiptoe over to the door, look around and then run out. In a second* DAVEY *runs back in, snatches the dunce cap off his head, and tries to kick it across the room. Then he runs out again.*)

curtain

ACT THREE

PLACE: *The scene is again outside the curtain only this time there is no sign.* PHYLLIS *and* DAVEY *come running in. They are panting and out of breath.*

DAVEY

Here we are again, Phyllis.

PHYLLIS

And am I glad! But what do you suppose Miss Phillips will say to us for being so late?

(JOAN *enters carrying some books.*)

JOAN

Hi, Phyllis. Hi, Davey. Better hurry. It's almost nine o'clock.

(JOAN *runs off.* DAVEY *and* PHYLLIS *stand looking at each other in amazement.*)

PHYLLIS

Did you hear what she said, Davey? It isn't nine o'clock yet!

DAVEY

I can't understand it. Why, we were gone almost all morning.

PHYLLIS

And look. The sign is gone too.

DAVEY

We couldn't *both* have dreamed the same thing.

PHYLLIS

(*Excitedly.*) I know! If we went backward in time, the time just couldn't have gone forward. So it's no later than when we went through the woods the first time. Do you see, Davey?

(DAVEY *shakes his head in bewilderment.*)

DAVEY

No, I don't.

PHYLLIS

You *are* stupid. Maybe you should have kept that dunce cap after all.

(*She starts to run and* DAVEY *follows after.*)

DAVEY

You just wait, Phyllis Lawson. I'll get you for that one!

(*They both stop and begin to laugh. Taking hands, they run off the stage.*)

curtain

J.W.

Mother Goose Gives Advice

CHARACTERS

MOTHER GOOSE
ANNOUNCER

FROM EIGHT TO TWELVE CHIL-
DREN

COSTUMES

The only costume needed is for MOTHER GOOSE. *She can wear a blouse and a long full skirt, a little shoulder cape, and a tall peaked hat.*

PROPERTIES

A chair for Mother Goose.

SETTING: *When the curtain rises* MOTHER GOOSE *is seated, surrounded by six or more of the children. They are all pointing at one little boy who stands apart from the rest. The* ANNOUNCER, *who is standing near the side of the stage, speaks first.*

ANNOUNCER

Old Mother Goose was sitting one day
Watching her little book children at play.
She was shaking her head and looking so sad,
Because one little boy had been acting bad.

FIRST BOY

Ding, dong, bell,
Pussy's in the well!
Who put her in?
Little Tommy Green.
Who pulled her out?
Little Johnny Stout.

What a naughty boy was that
To try to drown poor pussy-cat,
Who never did him any harm
But killed the mice in his father's barn.

ANNOUNCER

But she smiled very proudly and nodded with pride,
At one little girl standing close by her side.

FIRST GIRL

I love little pussy.
Her coat is so warm,
And if I don't hurt her,
She'll do me no harm.
So I'll not pull her tail,
Nor drive her away,
But pussy and I
Very gently will play.
(*Little boy enters crying.*)

MOTHER GOOSE

Why, what is the matter, dear little lad?
Come dry your tears now, don't be so sad.

LITTLE BOY

I had a little pony,
His name was Dapple Gray,
I lent him to a lady,
To ride a mile away.
She whipped him, she slashed him,
She rode him through the mire;
I would not lend my pony now
For all the lady's hire.

MOTHER GOOSE

I cannot understand it,
Why one could be so cruel!

SECOND GIRL

And have you heard, dear Mother Goose
What happened at our school?

ONE OR MORE CHILDREN

Mary had a little lamb,
Its fleece was white as snow;
And everywhere that Mary went,
The lamb was sure to go.

He followed her to school one day,
Which was against the rule;
It made the children laugh and play
To see a lamb at school.

And so the teacher turned him out,
But still he lingered near,
And waited patiently about
Till Mary did appear.

Then he ran to her, and laid
His head upon her arm,
As if he said, "I'm not afraid—
You'll keep me from all harm."

"What makes the lamb love Mary so?"
The eager children cry.
"Oh, Mary loves the lamb, you know,"
The teacher did reply.

And you each gentle animal
In confidence may bind,
And make them follow at your call
If you are always kind.

MOTHER GOOSE

And now although it's very sad,
I'm sure you'll all agree,
That people careful in some things,
Can in others thoughtless be.
So don't forget, but keep in mind,
We profit more by being kind!

THIRD BOY

Far want of a nail, the shoe was lost;
For want of the shoe, the horse was lost;
For want of the horse, the rider was lost;
For want of the rider, the battle was lost;
For want of the battle, the kingdom was lost;
And all for the want of a horseshoe nail.

ANNOUNCER

Dear Mother Goose, our thanks to you,
In rhymes you've told us what to do.
We'll try to do just as you say,
"Be kind to animals" every day!

J.W.

The Wonder World of Books

CHARACTERS

MISS LANE, *librarian*	DOMESTIC SCIENCE	TRAVEL
PAUL	AIRPLANES	HOLLAND
EDDIE	HISTORY	SWITZERLAND
CATHY	BIOGRAPHY	HAWAII
NATURE	INDIAN	SCANDINAVIA
SPORTS	ARTIST	AFRICA
HEALTH	SCIENCE	PAN AMERICA
SAFETY	TWO HANDBOOKS	FICTION

COSTUMES

SPORTS, *helmet and jacket;* DOMESTIC SCIENCE, *apron;* HISTORY *and* BIOGRAPHY, *costumes of any historical period;* INDIAN, *an Indian suit;* ARTIST, *a smock. Countries should be dressed in proper costumes or carry a symbolic article such as toy wooden shoes for* HOLLAND, *an alpine stick for* SWITZERLAND, *a lei for* HAWAII, *a bicycle for* SCANDINAVIA, *pottery for* AFRICA *and a gay shawl for* PAN AMERICA.

PROPERTIES

Desk, table, chairs, bookshelf, books, pencil, cards, flower, magnifying glass, football, mixing bowl, spoon, model plane, palette, brush, marionettes.

TIME: *The present.*

PLACE: *The librarian's office.* MISS LANE *is seated at her desk. Two boys and a girl hesitate at the door. They finally enter with one of the boys dragging the others, who seem reluctant to come in.*

PAUL

Aw, come on. Nobody's going to hurt you.
    (MISS LANE *looks up as they approach the desk.*)

MISS LANE

Good afternoon, Paul. I didn't think I would have any visitors on such a rainy afternoon, so I came in my office to do a little work. Are these some friends of yours?

PAUL

This is Eddie Lawrence and his sister Cathy, Miss Lane. They just moved into the house next door to me and I brought them over to see the library.

MISS LANE

That was nice of you, Paul. I am glad to know you, Cathy and Eddie. Do you each want a library card?

EDDIE

Naw. Paul made us come.

PAUL

But Miss Lane, they don't know anything about a library. Eddie says books are for sissies and I know they're not. Can't you explain to him what kinds of books there are? He won't believe me.

MISS LANE

Paul is right, Eddie. There are all kinds of books to suit all kinds of people. It would be silly to say that everyone should like the same kind of book.

CATHY

That's like saying everyone should like the same color, isn't it, Miss Lane? My mother likes pink and she is always buying me a pink dress. (*Vehemently.*) I *hate* pink.

MISS LANE

Exactly the way it is, Cathy. The room you just came through where all the books are is a very important place. Those books tell us of all the events which have taken place in this world of ours— and of the sacrifices that men have made to make this a better world to live in. Suppose that books could tell us about themselves. Let's imagine what they might say.

(*Enter* NATURE *carrying a magnifying glass and pretending to study a flower which he is carrying.*)

NATURE

If you are a person that people call
A nature lover true,
You'll find the shelves are filled with books
To give you lots to do.
Can you identify every shrub,
The wildflowers and the trees?
Do you know the habits of animals
And how honey is made by bees?
Can you tell the different bird calls,
The sound each insect makes?
Do you know which are the harmless,
And which the poisonous snakes?

(*After each succeeding book gives his speech he goes to rear of the stage and stays there until the end of the play.*)

CATHY

Miss Lane, I have been asked to join the Girl Scouts. Books like that would certainly help me, wouldn't they?

MISS LANE

You could earn your badges in nature study in a short time. The Girl Scouts borrow a number of books for that very purpose every summer when they go to camp. But who is this coming?

(*Enter* SPORTS. *He is in football uniform and carries a foot-*

ball. He runs around as though he were running down the field, zigzagging back and forth.)

SPORTS

I represent all kinds of sports
I'm 'specially meant for beginners.
Just study me and perhaps someday
You may be one of the winners.

EDDIE

Now you're talking, Paul. Books like that make sense. Do you suppose there's one that explains the T formation? My dad and I were watching a game on television last Saturday and boy—did we have an argument! I'll bet I could prove I was right if I could just show him in a book.

PAUL

See, didn't I say they weren't just for sissies? Hey! (*He points to door and begins to laugh.*) Look at this!

(HEALTH *and* SAFETY *enter. They are dressed just alike, Tweedledum and Tweedledee fashion, and have their arms locked together. They dance in sideways as they approach the center of the stage.*)

HEALTH

I can tell you about your body,
How to keep well and strong.
If you listen to me carefully,
You really can't go wrong.

SAFETY

I'm the twin of my brother, Health;
Safety is my theme song.
Stop, and look and listen always
If you want to live long.

(*The twins do a tap dance before they go to the back of the stage. When they finish,* MISS LANE, CATHY, PAUL *and* EDDIE *applaud.*)

(*Enter* DOMESTIC SCIENCE. *This is a little girl and she wears a big apron. She is carrying a mixing bowl and spoon and stirring vigorously as she approaches.*)

DOMESTIC SCIENCE

I'm read by the girl who wants to lead
A happy domestic life.
And when she has learned to cook and sew,
She'll make a splendid wife.

CATHY

(*To* MISS LANE, *shyly.*) Could I get one of those books?

EDDIE

(*In singsong voice, pointing at* CATHY.) Cathy wants to get married!
Cathy wants to get married!

CATHY

You hush up, Eddie Lawrence. He isn't a bit nice, is he Miss Lane?

MISS LANE

Now, Eddie! Of course Cathy will want to know how to cook and
sew whether she gets married or not. And by the way—did you
know the high school has a special cooking class for boys? Evi-
dently boys want to learn too.

EDDIE

Not me! Here's one that suits me better.

(*Enter* AIRPLANES. *He is wearing a leather jacket and helmet
and is carrying a model plane.*)

AIRPLANES

I represent the modern age
Of radar, rockets, jets.
My books are full of wonders
That no one ever forgets.

PAUL

I heard a jet the other day but I couldn't see it. (*Makes a swoop
with his arm to show how fast they go.*) Whissssssh. Boy! Can they
travel!

(*Enter boy and girl hand in hand. They are* HISTORY *and*
BIOGRAPHY *and are dressed in historical costumes.*)

HISTORY

History and Biography
Come marching hand in hand.

In our pages you will find
Brave deeds from every land.
					BIOGRAPHY
We tell you of the dauntless men
Who helped to build our nation.
The sacrifices made for us
Should be your inspiration.
					EDDIE
Miss Lane, in the school I just left our teacher was reading *Abe Lincoln Grows Up.* Do you have that book here? I'd like to finish it.
					MISS LANE
Yes, we do have it, Eddie. It's one of the finest books Carl Sandburg ever wrote. I'll lay it aside for you when it is returned. But look who's here! I hope he isn't as ferocious as he looks.

(INDIAN *enters. He does a dance before and after his speech. Children and* MISS LANE *applaud heartily.*)

					INDIAN
I'm the one who provides excitement
In all the stories of the West.
You won't be able to put me down;
Lots of readers vote me best.
You can read of Custer and Sitting Bull,
George Rogers Clark and Buffalo Bill,
Pioneers, Indians, cowboys too,
These tales will thrill you through and through.
					EDDIE
Yea! Man! Now that's something like it. But will you look at this!

(EDDIE *laughs and points at the entrance where* ARTIST *is just coming in. This is a boy dressed in a smock and carrying a palette and brush.*)

					ARTIST
Music, Poetry and Art
Play quite a different role.
The Indian (*points brush at Indian*) may provide the thrills,
I satisfy the soul!

(ARTIST *pretends to paint on an imaginary canvas. He backs away and studies it and then steps up and adds another touch.*)

MISS LANE

Don't make fun of him, Eddie. This world would be a dreary place to live in if we didn't have beautiful paintings to look at, wonderful music to hear, and poetry to point out in words the beauty there is around us.

EDDIE

I'm sorry, Miss Lane. I didn't intend to be rude. My uncle is an artist and our family is awfully proud of him.

CATHY

Eddie is like that Miss Lane. He just hates to practice his music lesson. (*Virtuously.*) I *like* to practice but Mother has to nag and nag Eddie.

PAUL

I'm taking lessons too. I want to be able to play the piano and tap dance at the same time. (*Demonstrates.*) I saw a fellow do it on television one night and was he keen!

MISS LANE

Here comes someone who is so interested in his reading he doesn't even see where he's going.

(SCIENCE *enters. He is wearing glasses and is reading as he walks slowly in. He is holding the book up in front of him and the cover has "SCIENCE" printed on it in big letters. He stumbles and this makes him look up.*)

SCIENCE

Perhaps I look a little serious
But there's a reason why,
For Science makes such rapid strides,
It's apt to pass one by.
This study of the molecule,
And of atomic energy,
Demands a lot of concentration
So please don't bother me!

(*He walks slowly to the back of the stage and sits at the table completely engrossed in his book.*)

EDDIE

(*Wonderingly.*) Do you have books on atomic energy in *this* room? I didn't know they had *children's* books about that!

MISS LANE

(*Laughing.*) I guess there isn't much they *don't* have in children's books, Eddie.

(*Enter two* HANDBOOKS, *a boy and a girl. They each have a marionette and they make them do a little dance together.*)

HANDBOOKS

(*Together.*) We are the Handbooks who tell you how
To make things like model jets,
Toys and party favors,
And even marionettes.

CATHY

Oh, Eddie. Make me a marionette, won't you please? (*To* MISS LANE.) Eddie's awfully good at making things.

EDDIE

(*Modestly.*) I don't know how *good* I am but I sort of like to fool around with tools.

PAUL

(*Excitedly.*) Here comes a whole delegation.

(*Enter* TRAVEL, HOLLAND, SWITZERLAND, SCANDINAVIA, HAWAII, AFRICA, PAN AMERICA.)

TRAVEL

Perhaps you are not able
To travel by air or sea,
But you can take an armchair journey
If you come along with me.

(*He holds up a sign which has "TRAVEL" printed on it. Then he acts as master of ceremonies, beckoning to each of the others to step forward in turn.*)

HOLLAND

I'm from the land of windmills
Of tulips and wooden shoes.

SWITZERLAND

You can climb the highest Alp with me,
I specialize in views.

HAWAII

The jewel of the Pacific, Hawaii
Is a pleasant place to be.
You can visit the place made famous in song,
The beach at Waikiki.

SCANDINAVIA

In Scandinavia there are many things
You'll be interested to see,
Fjords and mountain saeters
And fishing fleets out at sea.

AFRICA

The Sphinx, the pyramids and ancient tombs,
You'll find throughout my land,
Gold mines and deepest jungles,
High waterfalls, long rivers,
Huge desert lands of sand.

PAN AMERICA

I represent those other states
You'll find south of the U. S. A.
You can call me Pan America
It's what most people say.
My people like to dance and sing,
We're colorful and gay,
"Good Neighbors" is our policy,
It's the all-American way.

TRAVEL

I could tell of many other lands
If time were not so short,
But you can see what fun you can have
From this very brief report.
Though our clothes and customs differ
And may seem strange and new,

People the whole world over
Are really the same as you.

CATHY

My, that was nice, wasn't it?

(*The others agree enthusiastically.*)

(*Enter* FICTION. *He carries an armful of books and he gives them to* CATHY *and* EDDIE *as he speaks.*)

FICTION

If some days you feel out of sorts
And don't know what to do,
Just pick me up and I'll guarantee
You'll forget you were ever blue.

Cathy, I can tell you tales
Of peasant boys and kings,
Of princesses enchanted
Of dragons who fly on wings.
Or if you like your stories true,
Here's one about a girl like you.

For Eddie who likes them excitement packed,
How about *The Lost Battalion?*
Are you a lover of horses wild?
Here's a thriller about a stallion.
There's basketball, football, baseball,
If sport stories are more your line—
Or how about one of pioneer life?
I know you'll think it's fine.

And oh, I almost forgot
To tell you what my name is,
I'm Fiction, and now you know
That stories are my business!

EDDIE

(*Excitedly as he looks at books in his hands.*) How can I get a library card, Miss Lane? I'd like to read all of these.

MISS LANE

I'll show you, Eddie. (*She gives* CATHY *and* EDDIE *each a card.*)
Sign right here.

(PAUL, CATHY *and* EDDIE *stand close together as* EDDIE *signs.*
MISS LANE *goes quietly over to Book People and thanks them.*)

curtain

J.W.

Radios Versus Doughnuts

CHARACTERS

MAC	FRED	KEN
JOHN	CHUCK	RANDY
BILL	JOE	LARRY
LES	HANK	SCOOP
DON	PETE	MR. SANDERS

COSTUMES

All the boys except RANDY *and* MR. SANDERS *are in Scout uniforms.*

PROPERTIES

Rope, bandages, map, crayons, picture (preferably landscape), feeding tray, bird seed, wooden stool, polishing cloth, Indian moccasins, headdress and other Indian craftwork. The room is simply furnished with tables, chairs and a divan if possible.

TIME: *The present.*

PLACE: *Boy Scout room. A group of boys are busily engaged in getting various exhibits ready for an open house to take place the next night, February 8th, which is the first day of Boy Scout Week.* MAC *is busy splicing a rope.* JOHN *is watching* BILL, *who is trying to bandage his finger.* LES *and* DON *are working on a map of the town.* FRED *is trying to hang a picture while* CHUCK, *sprawled comfortably in a chair, is offering all kinds of advice.* JOE *is scattering bird seed on a feeding tray.* HANK *is polishing a little wooden stool.* PETE *is arranging an exhibit of Indian handcraft.*

MAC

Let's see—the eye should be turned toward me—like this. The strands and standing part are therefore away from me—so—

JOHN

Hey, Mac. Can you come here just a minute?

MAC

Wait a second.

(*He lays rope down carefully and goes over to* JOHN *and* BILL.
BILL *is trying to bandage his own finger and* JOHN *is watching.*)

JOHN

Mac, you've taken the first-aid test. What is Bill doing that is
wrong? It doesn't work.

BILL

It's awkward to try and work with my left hand and bandage my
right. Why can't I bandage my left hand?

MAC

Because if you are as right-handed as all that you would surely
hurt your right hand and not your left. See?

BILL

Sure, I see. But if I ever hurt my right hand I'd certainly be mighty
helpless.

(MAC *has been looking at* BILL's *struggles with the bandage.*)

MAC

Look here, Bill. Your trouble is that you are not leaving a long
enough end to bring up over your finger tip. It's that first end that
has to be used for that.

BILL

Oh! Now I see. Thanks a lot.

(MAC *goes back and begins again on his rope splicing.*)

CHUCK

A little more to the left, Fred. Oops! Not that much. Now the left
side is higher than the other. No—you went too far. Back the other
way.

FRED

(*Turning around.*) For Pete's sake! Look at you. You're sitting
crooked, that's what is wrong. How can you tell whether a picture
is straight or not from that angle?

(*Door opens and* MR. SANDERS, *Boy Scout Leader, walks in.*)

MR. SANDERS

Good afternoon, boys. How is everything coming along? Will you all be ready for the big night?

PETE

Oh, hello, Mr. Sanders. Everything is under control. Say, how do you think these moccasins turned out? I just finished them at home last night.

(*He holds up a pair of moccasins.* MR. SANDERS *goes over and examines them closely.*)

MR. SANDERS

Pete, they look great. You did a good job on them. (*He looks around at the other boys.*) Where are Ken, Larry and Scoop? They seem to be missing. I thought everyone agreed to be on hand today to see that everything is in shape for our open house tomorrow night. Boy Scout Week comes just once a year, you know, and we want this February 8th to be a good one.

CHUCK

Haven't seen Ken, but Scoop and Larry went down to see about the radio. We wanted to be sure to have it here tomorrow night so our parents can see what we did with all that hard-earned cash.

(*Door opens and* KEN *and* RANDY *enter.*)

KEN

Hi—everybody! Meet Randy Towers. He's visiting me right now but his folks are moving here as soon as they find a house.

(MR. SANDERS *goes over and shakes hands with* RANDY.)

MR. SANDERS

Glad to know you, Randy. So you are moving to Grandport.

RANDY

Thank you, sir. I'm glad to know you too. (*Looks around admiringly.*) Boy! What a swell Boy Scout room you have. We don't have anything nearly as nice as this.

KEN

Come on, Randy. Meet the other fellows. I won't bother with their last names. This is Mac. He's *good,* he is. Anything you want to know, just ask him.

MAC

Don't believe a word of it, Randy. But it's nice to know you even if you *did* arrive in such poor company!

(KEN *gives* MAC'S *hair a ruffle as they walk on over to* FRED.)

KEN

This is Fred. He's our artist. He not only framed that picture he's hanging, he painted it too.

RANDY

Bro-ther! Honestly, did you?

FRED

(*Modestly.*) Oh, this one is not so much. I have one at home that's a lot better but Mother won't give it up.

CHUCK

Hi, Randy. I'm Chuck. No artist—no good—just nothing.

KEN

Don't say that. You're good and you know it. Good and lazy!

(*The others all laugh.* CHUCK *does too.*)

MR. SANDERS

And he's good something else too. Good-natured!

CHUCK

Thanks, Mr. Sanders. Glad *someone* appreciates my fine qualities.

(RANDY *and* KEN *walk over to where* HANK *is industriously polishing the seat of a small stool.*)

KEN

This is Hank. Say! That's a beauty. (*He picks up stool and looks earnestly at seat* HANK *has been working on.*) Sorry, I still can't see if my hair is parted straight. You'll have to give it a better polish than that!

HANK

Oh, is that so? Well, let me warn you all. This may be a footstool but woe unto the person I catch setting a foot on it!

MR. SANDERS

(*Laughing.*) What are you going to do with it, Hank?

CHUCK

Haven't you heard? His mother has a special place reserved for it in the center of the fireplace mantel.

RANDY

(*Walks over to* JOE.) What is it?

JOE

A bird feeder. I'm Joe. And this fellow who looks as if he's just home from the hospital is Bill. The one offering him the bad advice is John.

JOHN

How soon are you going to move here, Randy?

RANDY

I'm not just sure. But Ken's dad and my dad are good friends and we're staying with them until we find a house.

BILL

Are you a Boy Scout?

RANDY

Yes, but I haven't been one very long. Just since September.

KEN

You should see Randy tap dance. Boy! Is he keen!

JOE

Honest? Teach me, will you, Randy?

RANDY

Sure. And say, I'm awfully interested in that feeder. How does it work?

JOE

You just fasten it to your window sill and put the food on it. They say it doesn't take too long before birds that use it get really tame.

MAC

In the Merit Badge book it tells about a man in West Virginia who feeds them from his hand.

JOE

Yes, I read that too. He got them used to it by making a scarecrow. He put food in its hand and after they ate from that he stood with his hand outstretched the same way, and they would come and take food from him.

MAC

Not only that but he put food in the scarecrow's hat and when they got used to that he put food on his own hat, and now they come and perch on his head to eat.

KEN

Now *that* I'd like to see.

LES

Say, isn't anyone going to introduce Don and me?

KEN

Patience, sonny, patience. (*To* RANDY.) Les. (*Points to* LES.) Don. (*He points to* DON.) They are making a map of our city. We'll be over to see your handiwork as soon as we get the birds fed. And one more, Randy, this is "Injun Pete."

(PETE *grabs up an Indian headdress, puts it on and goes into an Indian war dance ending up in front of* RANDY. *He puts his hand up in Indian salute.*)

PETE

How!

RANDY

(*Salutes.*) How, yourself!

(KEN *walks over and begins talking to* MAC.)

RANDY

(*To* PETE.) Did I understand Ken to say that there are still two others in your troop?

PETE

Yes, Larry and Scoop. They went down to buy our radio and recorder.

FRED

You should see it. It's a honey. It's a little portable but it's good— really good!

CHUCK

It had better be! My hands are all calluses from shoveling snow so I could add my contribution.

(*He looks doleful. The others all laugh.*)

HANK

You see, Randy, we wanted a radio and record combination so we could have some music whenever we had parties. We earned the money for it ourselves.

KEN

And don't let Chuck work on your sympathy. We *all* have calluses!
Larry and Scoop have gone down to get the radio. They ought to
be here any minute now.

LES

You mean they *should* be here soon. But only if Larry is able to
drag that Scoop past the *Courier* office.

RANDY

What do you mean?

BILL

Oh, Scoop is crazy about newspapers. He has a paper route but
even outside of that he hangs around that office every chance he
gets.

HANK

My dad works there and he says Scoop sweeps the floor, runs
errands—anything just to be there.

PETE

Scoop says he thinks the smell of that newspaper office is the
sweetest smell in the whole world. He's always telling us the latest
news and that's why we call him Scoop.

LES

I thought you fellows were coming over here to look at our map.
    (RANDY *and* KEN *walk over to* LES *and* DON *and peer over their
shoulders.*)

RANDY

Say, this is interesting. I'll bet even I could find my way around
town if I had this map.

CHUCK

Don't forget to put the police station in. We might need to get there
in a hurry if riots broke out here sometime.

DON

That's a laugh. I see you going any place in a hurry. (*To* RANDY.)
Chuck is the pride and joy of the fire department. He always obeys
their rule, "Walk, don't run, to the nearest exit."

CHUCK

(*Laughing.*) I'd get you for that one if it wasn't so much trouble to get out of this chair.

(*Just then the door opens and* LARRY *and* SCOOP *rush in.*)

SCOOP

Fellows! What do you think?

MAC

We think you don't have our radio, that's what we think. What happened?

LARRY

Well, Scoop just happened to drop by the *Courier* office on our way down.

(*All the boys groan.*)

SCOOP

Now, wait a minute. You'll be glad I did.

KEN

Come on, Scoop. Tell us. It must be something important to make you forget our radio.

SCOOP

It's something important, all right. But I didn't forget the radio. Did any of you hear the fire alarm last night?

CHUCK

Sure, but it was the out-of-town signal so I just turned over and went back to sleep.

FRED

I did too. With the temperature down almost to zero I knew I couldn't persuade my father to take me even if it had been right in the next block.

MR. SANDERS

(*Quietly.*) Tell the boys where it was, Scoop.

SCOOP

Do you know, Mr. Sanders?

(MR. SANDERS *nods his head.*)

SCOOP

Do you fellows remember last summer when we went on that all-day hike? Remember the place we stopped to fill our canteens?

BILL

Remember? I'll say *I* remember. Who could ever forget those doughnuts?

KEN

(*To* RANDY.) We stopped for water at a farmhouse and the nicest people lived there. The lady had just made fresh doughnuts and she insisted that we take all we wanted.

CHUCK

Not *all* we wanted. Politeness kept us from that.

KEN

Well anyway, she and her husband were as friendly as could be. They invited us to come back some other time and she said that she would like to fix a *real* meal for us.

LES

Don't say anything happened to them, Scoop?

SCOOP

(*Slowly.*) Yes, it was their house. It burned to the ground. They lost practically everything that was in it. Fortunately the wind was right and the barn and stock are safe.

JOE

But what are they going to do?

SCOOP

Already the neighbors have offered to rebuild their house. It seems everyone around likes them. They have always shared whatever they had with others and now people are all eager to help them.

LARRY

The *Courier* is printing a big story about it and asking people who have anything they can spare to give it, like a chair, bed clothing—in fact, anything at all.

SCOOP

And I thought—

MAC

Sure. I think so too. How about it fellows?

BILL

Count me in.

OTHERS

And me—and me—and me.

SCOOP

(*Putting his hand in pocket.*) Here it is, Mr. Sanders, our radio money. I sure am glad I stopped in at the office before I went to the radio store. Will you take care of it?

MR. SANDERS

No, Scoop. It was your idea. I think you should turn it over to the *Courier* yourself. What do you think, boys?

KEN

That's what we all think.

ALL

You bet. Sure.

(CHUCK *gets up out of his chair and goes over and picks up his hat and coat and puts them on.*)

BILL

Where are you going, Chuck?

(CHUCK *looks at his hands carefully.*)

CHUCK

I see I missed a place. There's room for one more callus. (*He walks toward door, turns and smiles.*) They sure were mighty good doughnuts! (*He leaves.*)

FRED

Chuck is right. They sure *were* good doughnuts. What do you say fellows? Let's show those folks we appreciated them.

RANDY

Count me in too. Maybe I'll get to try one next summer.

curtain

J.W.

Mars Calling!

CHARACTERS

BILL	SU YUNG LEE
BOB	CHRISTINA SANTOS
JOE	THE MAYOR
TOM	BILL'S MOTHER
PAT	BILL'S FATHER
MAX	TOM'S FATHER
MR. MORLEY	THE VOICE
JOHN CORN TASSEL	

COSTUMES

All the characters wear everyday dress. In Act One the boys could wear blue jeans. In Act Two they should be dressed more formally with trousers and sport shirts or sweaters.

PROPERTIES

An improvised radio transmitter with microphone, many tubes and wires. A table for the radio set, small tables, chairs, set of chessmen, ukulele, tools, and for Act Two some books and papers.

TIME: *The present.*

PLACE: *A Boys' Club room in any average-sized town in the United States. When the curtains open six boys are seated about the room at various occupations.* PAT *and* MAX *are seated at a small table playing chess.* JOE *is strumming idly on a ukulele.* TOM *is sitting cross-legged on the floor mending a pair of ice skates. But the center of interest is* BILL, *who is seated with his back to audience before a ham radio transmitter, tinkering with the dials, and every so often speaking into a microphone, "CQ, CQ," then repeating call letters and repeating "CQ, CQ." For the first two or three minutes no other words are spoken on stage. The boy strumming the ukulele starts to sing a popular song and the other boys hum it, but each is occupied with his own interests. Finally* BILL *turns, facing the others, and speaks.*

BILL

I can't get Altoona. That guy must have overslept. I can't get anybody this morning. *Everybody* must have overslept.

BOB

Saturday morning is a good time to oversleep. It's only nuts like us that get up this early in the morning.

BILL

It's eight o'clock, and that's when he said he'd be on the air. Oh well, I'll keep trying for a while.

(BILL *busies himself at the dials again, calling repeatedly "CQ" in low tones. The others in the room pay no attention.*)

BOB

Say, fellows, Mr. Morley's coming over here sometime this morning to talk to us about that Brotherhood Week program.

JOE

What about a Brotherhood program?

BOB

The Rotary Club asked him to put on a program at their meeting next Thursday because it's Brotherhood Week. He wants us to help him.

TOM

What do we know about it, anyway? And gosh, next *Thursday!*

BOB

Yes, it doesn't give him much time. Or us, either, for that matter.

TOM

You mean we're going to help him?

BOB

Why shouldn't we? Gee whiz, didn't he help us to get this club started? And doesn't he give us this big office room, rent-free?

JOE

I say let's help him.

BILL

W3BXAU calling W3TKAU. Over please. (*He turns and addresses the boys excitedly.*) Listen to this, fellows!

(*A voice is heard coming through the loud-speaker in low tones at first then clear and loud.*)

THE VOICE

Calling W3BXAU. Can you hear me? Can you hear me? This is Mars calling U.S.A. Mars calling. Mars calling. Can you hear me? Over.

(*All the boys rush over to the set and stand beside* BILL.)

TOM

It's a joke. Somebody's kidding us. Pretty corny too.

BILL

(*Fiercely.*) Quiet, fellows! (*Into microphone.*) This is W3BXAU. W3BXAU here. Can you hear me? Over.

THE VOICE

I can hear you, W3BXAU. Note your point of reception, please. Note your point of reception. Don't lose contact, W3BXAU. Over.

BILL

This is W3BXAU. I am receiving you on 122 megacycles. Give your location, please. Over.

THE VOICE

Sorry, W3BXAU, I can't give you my point of contact. You wouldn't understand. This is an entirely different system. Our wave band is not the same as yours. That is the reason we have never before been able to make you hear us. Can you hear me now? Am I coming through clearly?

BILL

(*Laughing.*) Just as clearly as though you were in the next room. And I'd bet a dollar you *aren't* far away from here. Where are you? Over.

THE VOICE

This is Mars calling. You don't know what a relief it is to us that you are finally able to hear us. We have been trying for many years . . .

(THE VOICE *goes on but there is such a hubbub in the room that it cannot be heard.*)

JOE

Mars? MARS? Holy smoke!

TOM

I don't believe it!

BOB, PAT, and MAX

Mars? Does he mean MARS?

BILL

Be quiet, fellows! I can't hear!

THE VOICE

(*Continuing.*) And our most brilliant men have been trying for many years to contact the Earth. So you can understand that reaching you is a big event on our planet. W3BXAU, are you there? Over.

BILL

(*In a shaky voice.*) Yes. I mean, yes, sir! Are you really from Mars?

TOM

Ask him how he can understand English if he's really from Mars?

OTHERS

Yes, ask him that.

BILL

If you are really from Mars, how is it you can understand me? Over.

THE VOICE

You forget that we have been listening to your radio for many years. Though you have not heard us, we have heard you. We have learned your languages. Over.

(BILL *shakes his head in a bewildered manner and speaks to the other boys.*)

BILL

I don't know what to think. (*The boys confer with heads close together. After a moment* THE VOICE *comes over the loud-speaker once more.*)

THE VOICE

This is Mars calling. Mars calling W3BXAU. Are you there? Over.

BILL

Y-Yes, we're here. What did you want from us, Mars? We are just boys. We think we had better not talk any more until we get our fathers here. Over.

THE VOICE

I understand. You are naturally concerned as to whether I am friend or enemy. Is that right?

BILL

Oh, we don't think you are an enemy. We'd just like to wait and talk to you later. My name is Bill. You can call us later.

THE VOICE

Wait one minute, Bill. Don't go off the air yet, please! We have one request to make. Can you hear me?

BILL

We can hear you.

THE VOICE

Before you go off the air, promise me that you will tune us in again later today. You must not wait until tomorrow. You see, atmospheric conditions might change any moment and cut us off from you again, perhaps forever. Do you understand? It is very important that we talk together again this very day. Over.

BILL

(*To the other boys.*) What shall I tell him?

BOB

Mr. Morley's coming after a while. We'll ask him what to do.

JOE

Tell Mr. Mars to call us again in a few hours.

BILL

(*Into the microphone.*) This is Bill. O.K., Mr. Mars, we'll contact you later today. How about four o'clock this afternoon? Over.

THE VOICE

That is well. But first let me say this, my friend. We have waited many years to reach you, and now that we have, there are many things we wish to know. Most of all, we want to know how the earth people live.

BILL

What do you mean, how we live?

THE VOICE

We know from what we have heard that there are many kinds of people on earth. What we are eager to learn is this: How do you all get along together? That is what we wish to know, and when we speak with you later on today we hope you will tell us. Over.

BILL

Oh, is *that* all you want to know! Well, we'll think it over, Mr. Mars. And we'll talk to you again at four o'clock this afternoon. This is W3BXAU, signing off!

(*For a half minute there is dead silence.*)

JOE

Well, *what* do you know about that!

(*The curtain closes for one minute. When it opens the boys are all huddled around the table on which the radio transmitter stands mute. They have their heads together as though planning something. They are all looking at* BILL.)

BILL

We can't really get started until Mr. Morley gets here, but fellows, *my* idea is this . . .

curtain

ACT TWO

TIME: *Four o'clock the same day.*

PLACE: *The Boys' Club room. It is crowded with people. Besides* MR. MORLEY, *and the* MAYOR *of the town, several of the boys' parents are present, as well as the boys from Act One and several other boys and girls. Among them are a Filipino girl, an Indian boy, a Korean girl, and Joe, a Negro boy. The adults are seated in chairs forming a semicircle around the radio set, while most of the boys and girls sit on the floor, or stand. Over the room there is an air of expectancy as the curtains open.*

BILL'S MOTHER

This is the most amazing thing I ever heard of!

BILL'S FATHER

I still don't believe it!

MR. MORLEY

Now, boys and girls, do you think you all know your parts? It's five minutes of four. I want you to be all ready as soon as Bill has tuned in on Mars.

TOM

Mr. Morley, do you *really* think that was Mars calling?

SEVERAL VOICES

Of course it was!

THE MAYOR

I'm biding my time.

TOM'S FATHER

I'm from Missouri!

BOB

Oh, give Bill a chance! He'll prove it to you.

MR. MORLEY

Quiet everybody, please. I want to make a short speech.

JOE

Quiet, please.

MR. MORLEY

The boys have explained to you why you were asked to come here. When they told me what had happened, it was hard for me to decide what was best to do. But after the boys and I had talked it over, we decided not to let the rest of the world in on our secret until after this second contact was made. We have now met together to learn the truth. The outcome of this contact with Mars may revolutionize the world.

(*Voices are heard saying, "I'll say!" "What will the President say to this!" and "Won't the papers love to get this news!"*)

MR. MORLEY

(*Continuing.*) On the other hand, it is possible that today may be the only time in our lifetimes when the Earth and Mars are in contact, because of certain atmospheric conditions. So the boys have decided that they would like to comply with the wishes of the Martians. That is, to try to explain to them how we, on our planet, live and work and get along together. You all know your parts. We have worked hard getting ready for this broadcast. And now, Bill (*turning to* BILL, *who is seated at the controls*), I think we are all ready. Will you try to get through?

(*There is complete silence in the room as all eyes are turned on* BILL. *He works at the dials and then speaks into the microphone.*)

BILL

Calling Mars. Calling Mars. This is W3BXAU calling Mars! (*He listens and repeats the same call. Listens again. The people in the room squirm with impatience.*)

MR. MORLEY

Just keep trying, Bill.

BILL

I'm sure this is where they came through this morning. W3BXAU calling Mars. Calling Mars. Can you hear me?

THE VOICE

(*Clear and loud.*) This is Mars calling W3BXAU. Mars calling. W3BXAU, can you hear me? Mars calling. Can you hear me, W3BXAU?

(*Every person in the room has leaned forward tensely, watching the transmitter and* BILL.)

BILL

O.K., Mars. This is W3BXAU. I can hear you. Go ahead. Over.

THE VOICE

That is well. We got through to you again. Is this Bill? Over.

BILL

Yes, Mr. Mars. This is Bill. And my dad and mother and many of my friends are here with me. We weren't sure—well, we weren't sure it really happened! Over.

THE VOICE

You were not sure it was Mars? Let me tell you something, Bill. We were not sure you were really Earth! We had tried for so long.

This may never happen again. Did you think over our request? Over.

BILL

Oh yes. We talked it over with Mr. Morley. He's our club sponsor. Then we talked it over with our parents. We are going to try to tell you something about ourselves. Over.

THE VOICE

That is well, Bill. We have learned some things from listening to broadcasts. But we wish to know more of your relationships with each other as nations, and of how you live together.

BILL

I think I know what you mean. We've prepared a sort of broadcast program to try to explain these things. (*At this moment* MR. MOR-LEY, *who has been standing close to* BILL *with a sheaf of papers in his hands, gives* BILL *some of the papers and points with his finger to the place where* BILL *is to read.*) My friends are going to help me. But first I will explain that there are many different kinds of people on our planet Earth. Now, it so happens that we have a number of them represented here today, and I am going to have them speak to you. First I will introduce Mr. Morley.

(MR. MORLEY *steps to the microphone.*)

MR. MORLEY

I will speak for the Caucasian race. This part of the world which you have contacted is inhabited for the most part by white men. We have settled in this western part of the world and made it our home. But there was a time only a few hundred years ago when the Western Hemisphere was inhabited by the red man, or Indians as we call them. I am going to introduce you to John Corn Tassel, who is a full-blooded American Indian. He looks very much like the other boys in this room except that his eyes are sharp and black. Come, John.

(JOHN *steps to the microphone.*)

JOHN

I guess I inherit my sharp eyes from my ancestors, who were great hunters. I like to hunt, too, and go camping with the other boys. But music is what I like best. When I grow up I'd like to become a band leader. But you take Joe, now—(*he touches* JOE *on the shoulder*) he's the real musician. He can sing like an angel and dance too. Joe is a good student. Meet Joe!

(JOE *steps to microphone.*)

JOE

I sure like music, all right. Many of my people have made a name for themselves in music. But when I'm through high school I want to go on to college to learn to become a doctor. And now I think I should introduce you to two unusual girls we have here. They are Su Yung Lee and Christina Santos.

SU YUNG LEE

I am a Korean girl. Most of my people live on the continent of Asia. I have been permitted to come to America to finish my education. When I have finished high school I shall go to college to learn to become a teacher. Then I can go back to my native country to teach what I have learned.

BILL

(*Interrupting.*) Just a moment while I check. This is W3BXAU. Can you hear us, Mars? Over.

THE VOICE

We can hear clearly. I should like to ask the Korean girl what she has learned, please.

SU YUNG LEE

Oh, I have learned many things from books. But the most important is not learned from books. I have learned the true meaning of democracy. I have learned that there is really a country which practices it. The nations that sent soldiers to save my country have stretched out a helping hand to *all* our people. The democracies of the world are our only hope. We feel that we must survive to prove that our hopes have not been in vain. But I have spoken long enough. My roommate at the school I am attending is my dear friend, Christina Santos of the Philippine Islands.

(CHRISTINA *steps to microphone.*)

CHRISTINA

I am so happy to speak over the radio. My native islands were settled hundreds of years ago by the brown people from Malaya.

In the years from that time the Filipino has developed from an intermingling of various races and nationalities. And we know that today all races of men are greatly intermixed, as also are the nationalities of the world. Mr. Morley can explain this much better than I can.

MR. MORLEY

I am glad you brought that up, Christina. There are, indeed, many different kinds of people inhabiting our world. These differences are not just in physical appearance alone. They are differences of customs, languages, religions, and governments. Our friends from Mars may well ask, "How can they all get along together on one planet, these various peoples? If they do not look alike, live in the same way, or even understand each other's speech, how can they ever hope to think alike?"

THE MAYOR

I guess that brings us right down to the big sixty-four dollar question, doesn't it, Mr. Morley?

MR. MORLEY

That's right, Mr. Mayor. And that big question is this: On what common ground can the peoples of the world learn to understand each other? And, is there not some great purpose in the minds of us all, some common hope that will make us brothers under the skin? We believe there is, my friends. We think that what the world is seeking is freedom. Freedom brings peace, for no nation can remain in peace without freedom.

First of all, we would like to tell you the part that freedom has played in the founding of our own country, the United States of America. Bob, will you tell why men and women came to the New World to live, some of them more than three hundred years ago?

BOB

You see the countries of Europe were having some pretty hard times. Men and their whole families were being thrown into prison for debts they couldn't pay. The prisons were crowded. In fact, the countries were crowded. Many people wanted to come over here to be free of the hardships of their old countries. But of course one of the main reasons people came to America was so they could worship as they pleased. From the rugged coasts of New England down to the Carolinas and Georgia, men and women came and braved the strange and lonely wilderness so they could worship God as they chose.

MR. MORLEY

No wonder our country has always been known as "the land of the free!" It was settled by people from all walks of life who were seeking that one thing—freedom. Now, Tom, will you tell us how a nation developed from all these new settlements?

TOM

You might say that the new nation developed because of that very same thing—the desire for freedom. When the Colonies began to resent the heavy burden of taxes that were levied by the mother country, they longed to break away. The Colonies joined together in rebellion. They founded our country, the United States of America, so that all who lived here would have liberty and freedom.

BILL

And that brings us down to our own Declaration of Independence. Everything that we believe about liberty was written right there by our founding fathers in 1776. If they had written it yesterday they couldn't have said it better. I'll read you the part about liberty. "We hold these truths to be self-evident, that all men are created equal, that they are endowed by their Creator with certain unalienable Rights, that among these are Life, Liberty, and the pursuit of Happiness."

MR. MORLEY

Thomas Jefferson was the author of those words, for it was he who drafted our Declaration of Independence. Jefferson also wrote this: "The God who gave us life, gave us liberty at the same time." That helps us to understand those words in the Declaration "that they are endowed by *their Creator* with certain . . . Rights." Thomas Jefferson and others who founded our nation felt that every man, by the grace of God, had the natural right to be free. It

is on this great truth our country was founded and for this that we
have fought and died, and worked and lived, and prospered.

BILL

I'd better check on the reception, Mr. Morley. W3BXAU calling
Mars. Can you hear us? Over.

THE VOICE

Yes, we can hear you clearly. We are very much interested. We
can understand about the importance of liberty. But we wish to
know what your prescription is for getting along together, not only
in your country, but also with other nations of the world. Over.

BILL

We have more to say, Mr. Mars. We hope that when we have
finished you will understand.

MR. MORLEY

(*Laughing.*) We *hope* that you will! Sometimes we have trouble
understanding these things ourselves. Perhaps we have taken our
birthrights too much for granted. What our fathers and grandfathers and their grandfathers have stood for has become so much
a part of us!

BILL

Like what, Mr. Morley?

MR. MORLEY

Well, like public schools and public playgrounds, and Boy Scouts
and YW's and Sunday school and all that.

JOE

I know what you mean, Mr. Morley! Like my being able to work
my way through college and getting a scholarship to help me.
That's what you call opportunity, isn't it?

SU YUNG LEE

And Christina and I, we are girls, but we have that same opportunity to get an education. Here in America, women have the same
chance as men.

CHRISTINA

Another thing! It is not just for the Americans, this opportunity.
That is why we have this chance in the United States. When I was
in New York, I went to see the Statue of Liberty. That beautiful

goddess stands in New York harbor to greet newcomers to these shores. Mr. Morley, while I was there I wrote down the words that are written on the Statue of Liberty.

MR. MORLEY

Can you tell us what they are, Christina?

CHRISTINA

(*Assuming pose of the statue, with one hand upraised.*)

. . . "Give me your tired, your poor,
Your huddled masses yearning to breathe free,
The wretched refuse of your teeming shore,
Send these, the homeless, tempest-tossed, to me:
I lift my lamp beside the golden door."

That is what she says, Mr. Morley, this goddess of liberty!

MR. MORLEY

The good thing about liberty, my friends, is that it can be shared. I dare say that we could not have enjoyed our own freedom half so much had we not shared it with others. And now, John, suppose you read those words of Thomas Paine which I have marked in his book called *Rights of Man.*

JOHN

(*Reading slowly.*) "The world is my country,
All mankind are my brethren."

MR. MORLEY

The word I want you particularly to notice is the word "brethren." What do you suppose that means? Can our listeners tell us?

THE VOICE

Brothers are men of one father.

MR. MORLEY

That is but one meaning of the word, my friends. The time has passed when a man can say, "This is my brother because we were born of the same father," or "He is my brother because we were born in the same country." It has been many years since Thomas Paine said "*All* mankind are my brethren." It was a new idea then. Today it is an accepted fact. No race, no creed, no nation, can isolate itself. Tell us why this is, Pat.

PAT

Well, the world seems to have shrunk in size in the past fifty years. That's because of transportation being what it is. As a matter of fact, all the world seems just about as familiar as our own back yard since we've been reading about these six-hundred-mile-an-hour airplanes and jet planes and all. They make the world seem awfully small. And a smaller world makes the inhabitants depend on each other more. It makes us realize that we've just *got* to get along together, the same as any big family should! But with such a tremendously *big* family that takes some smart planning.

MAX

Planning like the United Nations! That's what Pat means. They have to adopt a plan to live by. That is how the Declaration of Human Rights came into being.

MR. MORLEY

You have learned about the United Nations in school, Max. It is too large a subject to explain now. We are concerned with the code that was drawn up by the United Nations. You mentioned it just now, the Declaration of Human Rights. Tell us about it.

MAX

It was rather like when our forefathers drew up the Declaration of Independence. They had to have something to live by and live up to. So a Commission on Human Rights was named by the U.N. This Commission worked hard for two years to get it all just right, because it was the most important document in years. Anyway, the Universal Declaration of Human Rights was adopted in 1948 by the United Nations General Assembly, representing 58 of the nations of the world.

MR. MORLEY

Max, we won't have time today to mention the thirty articles of that wonderful document. But I do want you to read Article One, if you please.

MAX

(*Reading.*) "All human beings are born free and equal in dignity and rights. They are endowed with reason and conscience and should act towards one another in a spirit of brotherhood."

MR. MORLEY

Please repeat those last dozen words.

MAX

". . . and should act towards one another in a spirit of brother-hood."

MR. MORLEY

Please note the word "brotherhood." Now I am going to ask Pat to tell us very briefly the story of the four chaplains.

PAT

It was during World War II. One of our troop ships was hit while crossing the Atlantic Ocean. Aboard her were four chaplains. They gave their life preservers to four enlisted men. When the boat went down, six hundred men were still on board. On the deck were the four chaplains, their arms around each other's shoulders. One was a Catholic priest, one a Jewish rabbi, and two were Protestant ministers.

MR. MORLEY

The boys of the club here, in talking over this program, decided they wanted to tell the story of the four chaplains. They feel this true story illustrates better than anything we could say the real meaning of brotherhood. Those four men of God acted in the truest sense of brotherhood. (*He turns to* BILL *at the controls.*) I think you had better check to see if our audience is still with us, Bill.

BILL

W3BXAU asking for station identification. Can you hear us? Over.

THE VOICE

(*Not very loud.*) We can hear you. We are interested in this universal brotherhood of which you speak. Are we to understand that this is your prescription for the ills of your world? And do you believe that brotherhood has helped mankind to progress toward good? Over.

MR. MORLEY

Oh yes, yes! The brotherhood of man is the answer! Every good and right-thinking person must realize that. As one of our poets has expressed it, "Life's final star is Brotherhood."* When that

*From "Brotherhood" by Edwin Markham.

day has come that the peoples of the world will say, "All men are my brothers because we are all sons of one Father"—then life's final star will shine down on mankind, and God will grant peace to his wayward world.

(MR. MORLEY *motions to the entire assembly to rise. Men, women, boys and girls join hands, all except* BILL, *who remains seated before the controls.*) Christina, will you please end this program with our final message to Mars?

CHRISTINA

We have all joined hands to signify our feeling of kinship. In this one room, in just one very small corner of the world, there are all kinds of people—white, black, yellow, red and brown; Jewish, Protestant and Catholic; descendants of many different nationalities; and yet here we are, united by that invisible chain called brotherhood. And so that is our message to you, our unseen friends of another planet—a message of brotherhood.

BILL

Is that all? Shall I switch over to them?

MR. MORLEY

Yes, Bill, that is all.

BILL

This is W3BXAU about to sign off. We have finished our broadcast for today. Is there any comment? Over. (*He switches the dials and waits. All eyes in the room are on the set, waiting.*) I can hear a voice, faintly, but I can't make it out. (*He works with the dials busily. Then switches to sending once more.*) Can you hear us, Mars? This is W3BXAU waiting at this end, over.

(*There is complete silence.*)

TOM

Well, you'd think they'd at least thank us for the program!

BILL

I can't get through. There is no one there.

BOB

They've gone! Like that!

MR. MORLEY

Perhaps never to return. Well, you gave them your message, boys and girls, on brotherhood. A program worthy of a Rotary Club performance.

(*All the boys look at* MR. MORLEY *with questioning glances.*)

TOM

Say! Isn't that a coincidence? Or is it? He wanted us to help him with a Brotherhood Week program. Well, by golly, we did!

curtain

E.H.S.

The Fire Demons

CHARACTERS

FOUNDATION STONE

STICK OF WOOD

AUTOMOBILE FENDER

BUNDLE OF HAY

FIRE DEMONS (*as many as desired*)

FIREMAN

FIRST GIRL

SECOND GIRL

THIRD GIRL

FIRST BOY

SECOND BOY

THIRD BOY

COSTUMES

No costumes are needed for STONE, WOOD, AUTOMOBILE FENDER *and* HAY, *but each child may carry something to portray his character. A fairly good-sized stone, a burnt stick, an old car part and a bundle of hay. The* FIREMAN *should wear a fireman's hat.*

ACT ONE

PLACE: *A roadside.* FOUNDATION STONE *is sitting on the stage, groaning, his head in his hands.*

STONE

Oh my, oh my! I certainly feel awful. That's the first time in all my life that I ever had a house burn right over me. And it was such a nice house too. Oh my, oh my!

(STICK OF WOOD *comes stumbling on.*)

STONE

Who are you and what do you want? Can't you see that I don't want to be disturbed?

WOOD

Well, you can't feel any worse than I do. Look at me. Once I was part of a noble pine tree. And this is all that is left of me now. Just a burned stick. No good at all.

(*He sits down and begins to cry. Just then there is a clatter and* AUTOMOBILE FENDER *comes in.*)

AUTOMOBILE

Do you mind if I sit down and rest? I've just had a terrible experience—a shock to my whole nervous system. Let me tell you about it. It happened like this—

STONE

(*Interrupting.*) Pardon me, but I think I see someone coming who needs help. (*He limps off stage and comes back helping* BUNDLE OF HAY. HAY *seems exhausted and* WOOD *and* AUTOMOBILE *help him lie down.*)

STONE

There! Are you comfortable? You'll be all right after a while. When you get your breath you can tell us what happened to you. Oh, what were you going to tell us, Mr. Automobile? You look as though you had been in a bad wreck.

AUTOMOBILE

Wreck indeed! There wouldn't have been a wreck if that man had only used his head.

WOOD

Did you go over a bank?

AUTOMOBILE

No, nothing like that. There was just a little trouble in my engine. My feed pipe got clogged and made me sputter and choke. You would have thought that man would have known what was wrong with me, but no—he had to light a match and go poking around. That was just too much for me. I blew up then and there!

STONE

Wasn't he hurt too?

AUTOMOBILE

Oh, he might have had his eyebrows singed a little, but look at me. My poor old fender is about all that's left. He'll have a hard time even selling me for junk. But say, you look a little scorched yourself. Were you in a fire too?

STONE

I should say I was. Why, my house burned right over my head!

WOOD

I suppose it was from an overheated chimney.

STONE

Of course not. Not in this kind of weather. Why, we didn't even have a fire in the furnace. It was worse than that.

AUTOMOBILE

Do you mean that yours was caused by carelessness too?

STONE

That's exactly what I *do* mean. Everybody in my house puts everything off until the last minute. So of course when they were getting ready to go away for the week end nothing had been done. Everyone was hurrying and the electric iron was never turned off. The first I knew about it was when it dropped through to the basement after burning through the floor. But it was too late for me to do anything then. No one even discovered it until the whole place was ablaze on the inside. That family is going to get an awful shock. None of the neighbors even knew where they had gone. There's not a thing left.

(HAY *begins to move about and look around dazedly.*)

WOOD

How do you feel now? Better?

HAY

Wh-wh-where am I? Wh-wh-what happened to me?

WOOD

I don't know what happened to you. All I know is that we saw you stumbling along the road and tried to help you.

HAY

Oh, I remember now. (*Shudders.*) It was terrific. I'll never forget that fire. You see, there I was. The farmer had just finished cutting his hay and he had put it all in the barn. Then someone came in with a lighted cigarette in his hand. Right after he went out I began to smell smoke and all of a sudden the whole thing burst into flames. Spontaneous combustion, the farmer thought, but I know better. It was that cigarette and of course they'll never blame the right person. It's a shame!

AUTOMOBILE

That's the way sometimes. The innocent suffer instead of the guilty.

WOOD

You're right. Look what happened to me. A lovely moonlight night, and one of the nicest picnics I ever saw. They had such a good time. They sat right beneath me. They made their fire, roasted steaks and marshmallows and had such fun. It smelled good too. Then they all sat around the fire and sang. It was late when they left and maybe they thought the fire was out. I don't know. But soon after they had gone a terrific wind came up and scattered those embers all around. And it wasn't long before that whole woodland became a fiery furnace.

HAY

How did they ever manage to get it out?

WOOD

Well, as soon as it was discovered a ranger called for volunteers. Lots of men and boys helped but not before it had destroyed two houses too.

AUTOMOBILE

That's worse than my fire. After all, mine did no damage except to the person who was careless.

WOOD

Yes, it seems to me there can be no greater waste than a forest fire.

STONE

(*Excitedly*.) Look who's coming!

(FIRE DEMONS *dance in, singing to the tune of "Solomon Levi."*)

FIRE DEMONS

We are the Fire Demons
And we love to see things burn
We make our visits to those folks
Who never seem to learn;
They throw their lighted matches
And their cigarettes about
And never stop to take the time
To see that they are out.
Oh Fire Demons,
Demons, tra la la la
Oh Fire Demons,
Demons, tra la la la la la la la la
We are the Fire Demons
And we love to see things burn
We make our visits to those folks
Who never seem to learn;
They throw their lighted matches
And their cigarettes about
And never stop to take the time
To see that they are out.

STONE

Come on. Let's drive them away. Don't let them mock us like this.

(STONE, AUTOMOBILE, WOOD and HAY *make futile efforts to drive the* DEMONS *away. After laughing at them and their attempts to move quickly the* DEMONS *scamper off.*)

WOOD

Is there no help for us? Is there nothing to be done?

(*They all seat themselves, looking very miserable.*)

curtain

ACT TWO

PLACE: *Same as Act One.* STONE, WOOD, AUTOMOBILE *and* HAY *are sitting in the same positions as before. They do not move while the other characters in Act Two are on the stage.* FIREMAN *and several boys and girls come in.*

FIRST BOY

I liked that talk, Mr. McCarthy. I learned a lot too. I've seen my dad sometimes flick his cigar ashes into the wastebasket. I'm going to see that he has an ash tray right beside him whenever he's smoking.

FIRST GIRL

Yes, and in the wintertime I used to hang my wet leggings near the stove. I never knew before that it was dangerous.

FIREMAN

You see, the danger comes, Lucy, in forgetting that they are there. First thing you know they are apt to scorch and then catch on fire if you are not around.

SECOND GIRL

Mr. McCarthy, my mother always has candles lighted on our din‑ ner table at night. Is that dangerous too?

FIREMAN

It doesn't have to be. If everyone would be careful with candles they could be used with safety. Just be sure that you use a candle‑ stick that is the proper size so that they won't tip over. And of course you should never use a cloth or paper shade on them. Candles give a lovely light but you must be careful never to go out of the room and leave them burning.

THIRD GIRL

My daddy has told me that when he was little they always had a Sunday school Christmas celebration. He lived in the country and in their church they had a big tree lighted with candles. Every year when the children were speaking their pieces it would catch on fire and they would have to stop everything and put all the candles out.

FIREMAN

They were lucky that the whole church didn't burn. Christmas trees should never have any fire near them. People should even be careful about smoking too near them.

SECOND BOY

We just moved into a new house and my mother was delighted because it has a nice open fireplace. I certainly am going to tell my father what you said about always having wire screens in front of them.

FIRST GIRL

Mr. McCarthy, what did you mean when you talked about spon— spon—something or other?

FIREMAN

Spontaneous combustion. That is when a fire starts itself. Sometimes oily rags, moist hay and certain other things left to themselves may grow hotter and hotter and burst into flames. That's why it is very bad to put a cloth that has been used for cleaning and is covered with oil into a warm, dark closet. It might start a fire and gain headway before anyone discovered it.

FIRST GIRL

I'm going home right away. I helped Mother dust yesterday and I know I did that very thing. (*Runs off stage.*)

THIRD BOY

I certainly was sorry to hear about those leaves being so dangerous. In the fall we fellows always have so much fun raking them all up and then burning them in a big bonfire.

FIREMAN

You wouldn't think it was so much fun if you could see some of the accidents that are caused by bonfires. They are apt to blow and catch clothing on fire if anyone is standing near. Terrible things have happened because of bonfires.

FIRST BOY

It seems as though *everything* we do is dangerous.

FIREMAN

(*Laughing.*) No, not that bad. It's just that we must all be careful. If everyone would just take care there would not be any danger from fire. It's the carelessness that does all the damage.

SECOND GIRL

This has been awfully interesting, Mr. McCarthy. I hope our school invites you to come and see us again.

(*The children and* FIREMAN *start to leave stage. Just before they leave he speaks.*)

FIREMAN

Thank you. I hope you'll all remember what I've told you too.

(*After they go the* STONE, WOOD, AUTOMOBILE *and* HAY *slowly come to life.*)

STONE

Did you all hear that?

WOOD

I certainly did. If those picnickers had heard that I'll bet I would still be a tree in a forest.

AUTOMOBILE

And not one of those children will ever be so silly as to light a match around gasoline, either.

HAY

Well, I feel better anyway. I know now that there are some people in the world who know how dangerous fire can be. Hey, hey, look who is coming back!

(FIRE DEMONS *dance on singing their song.*)

FIRE DEMONS

We are the Fire Demons
And we love to see things burn
We make our visits to those folks
Who never seem to learn—

STONE

Come on now, let's show them that we really mean it this time!

(STONE, WOOD, AUTOMOBILE *and* HAY *drive the* FIRE DEMONS *from the stage.*)

curtain

J.W.

First Aid in the First Troop

CHARACTERS

ANNOUNCER, *to read introduction to play*
MRS. CLARKE, *Girl Guide leader*

MARY	FLORA AND DORA, *twins*
HELEN	MRS. BROWNELL, *Mary's mother*
EUNICE	MRS. SMITH, *Flora's and Dora's mother*
LESLIE	MRS. CARTER, *Eunice's mother*
FRANCES	MRS. DAVIS, *Leslie's mother*
ISABELLE	SUSAN, *the maid*

COSTUMES

It is preferable that the girls wear Girl Scout uniforms. But if old-fashioned ones are not available they can wear ordinary dresses. They can be made to look like those of 1910 by having them longer than girls wear today and by adding huge sashes. They must wear long stockings and should have their hair tied with big ribbon bows. The mothers wear long skirts and high-

necked shirt waists. Their hair is worn high on their heads. SUSAN
*is dressed in a black dress with a little white apron and a maid's
cap.*

PROPERTIES

*Scene I: benches, straight chairs, table, cupboard, bookshelves,
books, bandages, splints, iodine and other first-aid materials. Scene
II: living room furniture, cookies, teapot, cups and saucers.*

*(Before the curtains open, a uniformed Girl Scout or Brownie
gives this introduction to the play.)*

ANNOUNCER

In our play today we go back to the time of the very first Girl
Scouts of America in the summer of 1912. The play is based on an
incident which actually took place in one of the first troops formed
in the United States. All names except that of Mrs. Low are fic-
titious.

The founder of the Girl Scout movement had started the first
troops in her home city of Savannah, Georgia, just a few months
before our play begins. As all Girl Scouts know, the mother of Girl
Scouting in America was Mrs. Juliette Low, known to her friends
as "Daisy." We will not take the time now to tell you how hard
Mrs. Low worked to get the movement started, for it is a long story.
Although Mrs. Low was a native Georgian, she had married an
Englishman and gone as a young woman to live in England. There,
after the death of her husband, she became interested in the Girl
Guides. She formed several new troops in Scotland and in London.
After seeing these troops successfully established, she determined
to take Girl Guiding to her own country. And that is what she did.
In a very short time, back in Savannah, she had started six troops
of Girl Guides.

You notice that we say Girl Guides, for it was not until later
that the name was changed to Girl Scouts.

The action in our play takes place while Mrs. Low is in England
to learn more about the Girl Guides and how she can further her

great ambition to spread the movement to every part of the United States.

We now present "First Aid in the First Troop."

SCENE I

TIME: *Summer of 1912, late afternoon following a Girl Guide meeting.*

PLACE: *Savannah, Georgia, Girl Guide Headquarters in the carriage house at the rear of Juliette Low's home. There are several benches and straight chairs, a long wooden work table, a cupboard, a bookcase containing books, curtains at the windows and several potted plants on the window sills.* MRS. CLARKE, *the leader, is putting away the bandages and splints which the girls have been using in their first-aid lesson. The girls are helping her.*

MRS. CLARKE

Now we must carefully put all these first aid things away in the cupboard so that the other troops can use them in their first-aid lesson.

MARY

I think first aid is the most fun of *all* the Girl Guide projects.

FLORA and DORA

So do I!

MRS. CLARKE

It may seem like lots of fun to you girls who are just learning, but you must never forget that it has its serious side too.

EUNICE

Oh yes! In case of accidents or emergencies, our first aid will come in handy.

FRANCES

I can hardly wait until our next meeting when we can bandage each other again.

MRS. CLARKE

You girls were very adept.

HELEN

Does that mean we were good at it?

MRS. CLARKE

Yes, you were very good. Of course you will all need practice.

EUNICE

I wish I had some brothers and sisters to practice on. Perhaps I can make the cat stay still long enough to bandage her!

MRS. CLARKE

Now, I'm all ready to leave. Everything is set to rights. Are you girls going home now?

GIRLS

Oh, no. Not yet!

LESLIE

We always go over to the drugstore for sodas first.

MRS. CLARKE

Well, I wish I could join you, but I have an appointment. Good-by, girls.

GIRLS

Good-by, Mrs. Clarke.
(MRS. CLARKE *goes out.*)

MARY

I'm not hungry today. I'm not going to get a soda.

GIRLS

(*In great surprise.*) *Not getting a soda?*

MARY

No. As a matter of fact, I have another plan for my spending money. A much more *exciting* plan than throwing it away on a soda. Just think, girls—*five* whole cents for a chocolate soda that is gone in two minutes!
(*The girls crowd around her.*)

FRANCES

What do you mean, you have a plan?

ISABELLE

Yes, what is so exciting? Tell us.

MARY

Well, you say you want to practice first aid. What are you going to use for bandages?

(*All the girls look at each other as though for an answer.*)

FLORA

We could make homemade bandages.

DORA

And some homemade splints.

MARY

Not me! I want to practice my first aid with the real thing. I'm going to buy some gauze bandage with my soda money!

ISABELLE

That's a wonderful idea! I'm going to do the same.

LESLIE

Not me! I love chocolate sodas more'n anything.

HELEN

So do I, but—

MARY

Well, don't let's stand here all day! I'm going to the drugstore. You can each get whatever you want. *I* am buying bandage.

(*Exit all the girls. As they go out the words "bandage," "adhesive," "liniment," etc. can be heard. Curtain closes for one minute to show passing of time.*

When the curtain opens, all the girls re-enter with packages. They proceed to open them while they are speaking, disclosing bandage, adhesive, iodine, liniment bottles, etc.)

EUNICE

Mary, this is the most wonderful idea you've ever had!

MARY

Thanks. But it was your idea to come back here to Girl Guide Headquarters to practice our first aid, Eunice.

FRANCES

I wish Mrs. Clarke were still here. She could show us what to do.

ISABELLE

Oh Frances, the best fun of all will be to see how well we can manage by ourselves!

LESLIE

(*Unrolling some bandage.*) Did you see that Johnson boy drinking chocolate sodas? He was having his third, and bragging about it. The little pig!

MARY

Leslie, do forget your stomach! And come here and help me make a splint, will you?

LESLIE

Well, all right. But I'm not very good at it.

MARY

You can do it. Pretend this is an emergency. Let's suppose I just broke my leg.

FRANCES

What shall we use for splints? I think I just broke my arm, and I'll have to put it in a sling too.

EUNICE

I don't think Mrs. Clarke would mind if we borrowed these splints we used in class. (*She takes several board splints from the cupboard and places them on the table.*)

FLORA and DORA

(*Together.*) What can *we* do?

MARY

We'll get to you later. Where is the cotton we bought? And the iodine? Come on, girls, we must get busy.

(*The girls start to bandage each other. Some bind up arms and legs while others make slings. Patches appear on faces and arms, iodine is painted on imaginary wounds. This part of the play gives an excellent opportunity to the troop which has studied first aid to give a first-aid demonstration. However, too much time spent on it might tend to bore the audience.*)

curtain

SCENE TWO

TIME: *A little later.*

PLACE: *Parlor of* MARY BROWNELL'S *home.* MRS. SMITH, MRS. CARTER, *and* MRS. DAVIS *are seated.* MRS. BROWNELL *is pouring tea and* SUSAN, *the maid, is passing cookies. The ladies are just putting their sewing and embroidery into their workbags.*

MRS. BROWNELL

(*As she pours tea.*) Ladies, I hear that Daisy Low will be coming home from England very soon now.

MRS. SMITH

Yes. She writes that she is bringing back lots of wonderful new ideas for the Girl Guides in Savannah.

MRS. CARTER

Not just for Savannah! My dears, they say that Mrs. Low is going to take the Girl Guide movement to cities and towns all over the United States!

MRS. BROWNELL

Yes, they say that Daisy will go to Washington first to get a national organization started. I do believe she can do it too! Will you take one lump of sugar or two, Mrs. Davis?

MRS. DAVIS

Two, please. Oh yes, Daisy Low can do anything! She has such a winning manner. She really makes you believe in the Girl Guides.

MRS. SMITH

Well, not all the people of Savannah liked the idea of the Girl Guides at first, you know. They thought it would make tomboys of their daughters.

MRS. CARTER

But just see how successful it is! There are six troops here now and others ready to be organized.

MRS. BROWNELL

Well, it certainly has done a great deal for our Mary! She used to be so timid and shy. And she never cared for outdoor life at all until she joined the Girl Guides.

MRS. DAVIS

Our Leslie has improved too. She always ate too much and too often. But she's actually lost ten pounds since she's gone on hikes with the Girl Guides.

MRS. SMITH

Flora and Dora have learned to play tennis and other games. Those twins of mine simply adore the Girl Guide activities!

MRS. CARTER

Today is their meeting, you know. Eunice said they are to take their first lesson in—dear me, I forget now *what* they were going to study today.

MRS. BROWNELL

Well, you may be sure it is something very useful. And we'll certainly hear *all* about it when our daughters come home!

(*A knock is heard on the front door.*)

MRS. BROWNELL

(*To maid.*) Susan, there is someone at the front door.

(SUSAN *leaves the room to answer the door. Suddenly a scream is heard.* SUSAN *continues to scream as she runs into the parlor.*)

SUSAN

(*Wringing her hands.*) Madam, come quick! It's Miss Mary and the other girls! Oh, oh my!

(MRS. BROWNELL *jumps up quickly. All the women rise to their feet.*)

MRS. BROWNELL

What is wrong?

OTHER LADIES

Oh, what is it?

SUSAN

They're hurt! There's been a terrible accident!

(*At that moment all eight girls file slowly into the room, some hopping on one foot, some limping. All are swathed in bandages, on heads, arms and legs. Iodine is painted in conspicuous spots on faces, hands and arms.*)

MRS. BROWNELL

(*Screaming.*) Mary—my child!

MRS. CARTER

Eunice! (*She falls to floor in a faint.* EUNICE *rushes to her and begins to fan her.*)

MRS. DAVIS

Leslie, is that you? Are you killed?

MRS. SMITH

Flora! Dora! (MRS. SMITH *drops her cup and saucer and falls down on the sofa in a faint.*)

(*The scene that follows is one of great confusion on the stage with eight girls limping and hopping about, two mothers unconscious, the other two mothers crying and wringing their hands, and* SUSAN *continuing to scream at the top of her lungs.* MARY *tries to make herself heard.*)

MARY

(*Loudly.*) Mother! Mother, do you hear me? I'm all right! Stop crying. I'm not hurt, I tell you!

MRS. BROWNELL

(*Shouting.*) Was there a runaway horse? Oh, your leg is broken. Oh—Oh!

MRS. DAVIS

Was there a fire? Are you badly burned, you poor children? I smell liniment! Oh, your poor arms and legs. They must be badly hurt!

EUNICE

Help, help! Mother's fainted. Help me, girls! We must administer first aid!

FLORA

Our mother has fainted too. Dora, do you have the smelling salts?

DORA

(*Pulling a bottle of smelling salts from her pocket.*) Poor Mother! Here, hold her head down between her knees, Flora. Smell this, Mother! (*Holds smelling salts under her mother's nose. Her mother chokes and comes to.*)

MRS. SMITH

Flora! Dora! Are you alive?

MRS. BROWNELL

Susan, do stop that awful screaming this minute! The girls are very much alive.

MARY

We aren't even hurt, Mother!

MRS. BROWNELL

I can't understand this! You *must* be hurt! Look at your bandages!

EUNICE

We were just practicing our first aid! (*She holds the smelling salts to her mother's nose and fans her at the same time.*) I think Mother is coming to. Poor Mother—are you all right?

MRS. CARTER

Oh. OH! What terrible thing has happened? Eunice, are you all right?

(*The girls look at each other and begin to laugh.*)

MARY

I guess we gave you an awful fright! But we didn't mean to. We were just trying out our first aid.

ALL THE GIRLS

We were just practicing!

(*The four mothers look solemnly at each other, shake their heads, then shake their fingers at the children.*)

ALL THE MOTHERS

(*Slowly and with great emphasis.*) Don't—ever—do—that— *again!*

curtain

E.H.S.

The Imps' Defeat

CHARACTERS

IMPS (*two boys and two girls*)   MR. LEWIS

HEALTH FAIRIES (*two boys and two girls*)   TEDDY LEWIS

MRS. LEWIS   RUTH LEWIS

COSTUMES

IMPS *may be dressed in ordinary clothing but it is dirty and they look very unkempt. Faces are dirty, hair is uncombed.* HEALTH FAIRIES *are neatly dressed. They all wear cardboard crowns and each one has his name printed on the front of it. In Act Two* RUTH *has on dirty jeans, her face is dirty and hair uncombed. In Act Four she has on a pretty cotton dress and wears a blue ribbon around her hair. In Act One* TEDDY *looks half put together. His shoes are untied, his shirt half buttoned. In Act Four he is very neat.*

PROPERTIES

Acts Two and Four, dining room furniture and dishes. Act Three, HEALTH FAIRIES *carry articles that have meaning for each one. For example* GOOD FOOD *may carry basket with carrots, milk bottle, bread and fruit.* GOOD GROOMING *may carry hair brush, comb and toothbrush.* EXERCISE *may carry a baseball bat.*

SETTING

No setting needed for Acts One and Three. Simple dining room furniture for Acts Two and Four.

ACT ONE

TIME: *The present.*

PLACE: *Meeting place of the* IMPS.

FIRST IMP

I tell you I don't feel right. We have been too good lately. I know that I don't feel well if I am not bad more often.

SECOND IMP

I agree with you, Brother Imp. I think we should be up to some mischief too. But what is it going to be?

THIRD IMP

I have an idea! I've been thinking about it for a long time, in fact ever since yesterday.

FOURTH IMP

Well for goodness' sake! What are you waiting for? Can't you see how anxious we are?

THIRD IMP

Yesterday I just happened to drop into a meeting that was being held at the hotel.

FIRST IMP

(*Interrupting.*) Do you think we should go down and try to steal food off people's plates before they get a chance to eat it?

THIRD IMP

No, that's not my idea.

SECOND IMP

(*To* FIRST IMP.) Oh, hush! Let our brother get on with his story.

THIRD IMP

A group of men were having lunch together and talking about having a "Baseball for Boys" club this summer.

SECOND IMP

What does that have to do with us? There are not enough of us to stop them from having it.

THIRD IMP

I know that. But if we could just keep one boy from belonging, that would be something, wouldn't it?

FIRST IMP

What do you propose we do?

THIRD IMP

Why don't we think real hard and choose one boy who might be a good player. And then we can decide how we can prevent him from joining.

SECOND IMP

Goody! Goody! (*He jumps around.*) Then not only will he be disappointed but the others will, too, because they'll be losing a good player!

(*He goes over to* THIRD IMP *and seizes his hand and they hop around together.*)

FIRST IMP

Stop! Stop! We have work to do. Now everyone think.

(*They all walk around in a circle with their heads bowed and their hands clasped behind their backs.*)

SECOND IMP

(*Looking up suddenly.*) How about Tommy Gray?

(*The* IMPS *all stop and look at one another.*)

FOURTH IMP

No. He broke his arm last week. He can't play anyway.

(*They all walk around again.*)

FIRST IMP

How about David Dawson?

THIRD IMP

His people are taking him on a trip to Canada this summer. He won't do either.

(*They all walk around again.*)

FOURTH IMP

How about Teddy Lewis?
(*They all stop and look at each other.*)

THIRD IMP

He's healthy.

FIRST IMP

He can run fast.

SECOND IMP

He can throw a ball, and bat one too. I've watched him.

FOURTH IMP

Well, how about him? What do you say?

OTHER THREE IMPS

(*Together.*) Just the one we're looking for!

SECOND IMP

Now, just what shall we do? Have him break a leg?

THIRD IMP

Oh no. Nothing like that. Then everyone would feel sorry for him. Let's just help him to be bad.

FOURTH IMP

You mean disobey his parents?

THIRD IMP

Yes, like not going to bed when he should. Let's have him stay up so late he'll be too tired to play.

FIRST IMP

We could urge him not to eat the right kind of food.

SECOND IMP

Maybe we can get him to refuse to drink milk.

FOURTH IMP

(*Jumping around.*) Isn't this fun?
(*All the* IMPS *join hands in a circle and jump around singing this song. The tune is "Yankee Doodle."*)
We'll take away his rest at night,
We'll make him tired and weary,
We'll make him slouch and walk all stooped,
And make his eyes look bleary!

We'll take away his milk at meals,
We'll give him good strong coffee,
We'll take away his veg'tables,
We'll make him just a softie!

FIRST IMP

Now I'm beginning to feel better. This is more like it. If we could only think of something else we could do too.

FOURTH IMP

How about doing something to a little girl? There ought to be plenty of nice little girls we could persuade to become naughty.

THIRD IMP

Let's think the way we did before.

(*They put their hands behind their backs, bow their heads and walk slowly around in a circle.*)

SECOND IMP

I have it!

OTHER IMPS

Tell us! Tell us!

SECOND IMP

Well, I heard they are going to have a pageant on the playground this summer and choose a little girl to be queen. Now who do you think it might be?

FIRST IMP

Linda Smith?

SECOND IMP

No, she's too old. It will have to be someone younger than that.

FOURTH IMP

Rita Harris?

SECOND IMP

Could be, but I don't think so. She never is very friendly and they're apt to choose someone who is pretty and cheerful.

THIRD IMP

How about Ruth Lewis, Teddy's sister?

OTHER IMPS

Just the one! Just the one!

FIRST IMP

She's pretty and she's always neat and clean in appearance. We ought to be able to take care of that!

SECOND IMP

Let's persuade her never to wash.

THIRD IMP

Combing her hair will be too much trouble.

FOURTH IMP

And she'll *never* want to wear anything but dirty jeans.

(*They all join hands and dance in a circle singing to the same tune as before.*)

And Ruthie too, we'll not forget,
The change we'll make complete,
We'll urge her to neglect her looks,
She never must be neat.

We'll hide her toothbrush and her comb,
For soap she'll see no need,
She'll look a mess and we'll be pleased,
On this we are agreed!

FIRST IMP

Stop! Stop! We must get busy. There's a lot to be done in a short time. We'll use our own short-wave radio station IMPS. We'll send over signal after signal. It may take a little time but we'll manage.

SECOND IMP

We can work in pairs. You and I (*he points to* FOURTH IMP) can take Ruthie. And you other two take Teddy. (*They pair off and go off stage in opposite directions. Two are singing* TEDDY'S *song and the other two* RUTHIE'S.)

curtain

ACT TWO

TIME: *A few days later.*

PLACE: *The Lewis family's dining room.* MR. *and* MRS. LEWIS *are seated at the breakfast table.* MR. LEWIS *is reading a newspaper.* MRS. LEWIS *gets up and goes over to the door.*

MRS. LEWIS

Ruth? Teddy?

RUTH

(*Off stage. Very bored.*) Yes, Mother.

MRS. LEWIS

Breakfast is ready, dear. Please come right away.

RUTH

(*Still off stage.*) Yes, Mother.

MRS. LEWIS

Teddy? (*Pauses, then, louder*) TEDDY?

TEDDY

(*Sleepily, off stage.*) Yes?

MRS. LEWIS

Teddy, you come down to breakfast right away. Do you hear me?

TEDDY

Yes, Mother.

MRS. LEWIS

(*Coming back to table.*) Honestly, I don't know what has happened to those children. Both of them seem to have changed over night.

MR. LEWIS

(*Lowering paper.*) I beg your pardon, dear. Did you say something?

MRS. LEWIS

Yes, I did. I said I can't understand Ruth and Ted. They seem to have changed completely. Ruth used to be so particular and neat in her appearance and now look at her. She looks positively awful all of the time. I'm so ashamed of her. I have to *force* her to wash behind her ears. And Teddy! He's grumpy, lazy and very disagreeable lately. What do you suppose has happened to them?

MR. LEWIS

Yes, I've noticed. It's worried me too. I wonder if we should take them to a doctor for a check-up.

(*At this moment* RUTH *comes in. Her hair is not combed, her face is streaked with dirt and her jeans are absolutely filthy.* MRS. LEWIS *takes one look at her.*)

MRS. LEWIS

Ruth Lewis! You go right back upstairs and get cleaned up. I told you to take a bath last night before you went to bed.

RUTH

Oh, what's the use of taking baths? You only get dirty again and have it all to do over.

MR. LEWIS

That will do, Ruth. Do as your mother says. And haven't you a dress to put on? It seems to me that I haven't seen you in anything but those dirty jeans for days.

(*At this moment* TEDDY *comes in. He is yawning widely and dragging his feet. He looks as though he might not make it across the room.*)

TEDDY

Hi, everyone.

MRS. LEWIS

Good morning, Teddy. You are late again. Now, come and eat your breakfast.

TEDDY

(*Looking at table.*) I don't want anything you have.

MR. LEWIS

Ted! Don't you dare speak to your mother like that. You have eaten cereal, milk, toast and orange juice for breakfast many times. What is wrong with them now?

TEDDY

All I want is some good old coffee.

MRS. LEWIS

Why, Ted Lewis! Of course you can't have any coffee. It isn't good for growing boys and girls, as you well know. What has come over you? You have eaten scarcely anything now for a week.

TEDDY

Oh, I'm sick and tired of old vegetables, that's all. Cakes and pies are all I want.

(RUTH *in the meantime has quietly sat down and is fairly shoveling food into her mouth.* MRS. LEWIS *suddenly becomes conscious of her.*)

MRS. LEWIS

Ruth! I thought I told you to go upstairs and get cleaned up. I absolutely will not have anyone with uncombed hair and a dirty face at my breakfast table.

(RUTH *gets up and flounces over to the door.*)

RUTH

Oh, all right if you have to be so mean!

MR. LEWIS

Ted, are you going out for baseball practice today? I hear they are going to have the team tryouts soon.

TEDDY

Oh, I don't know. It's so much effort to bother.

(*He gets up and drags himself across the floor and out of the door.* MR. *and* MRS. LEWIS *look at each other.*)

MR. LEWIS

I had so hoped that Teddy would be interested in the Baseball for Boys. Especially since I have been asked to be one of the sponsors.

MRS. LEWIS

And they're planning that nice playground festival this summer. But I know Ruthie won't even be asked to take part. Who would want her around, the way she looks and acts lately. Whatever shall we do with them?

curtain

ACT THREE

TIME: *A few days later.*

PLACE: *Meeting place of the* HEALTH FAIRIES, SLEEP, GOOD FOOD, GOOD GROOMING *and* EXERCISE *are on the stage.*

SLEEP

I have called you together, Health Fairies, to present to you a little problem. You know we have always been proud of our friends Ruth and Ted Lewis. But something terrible has happened to them. Good Food, have you anything to say?

GOOD FOOD

Yes, indeed. Ted has always been my pride and joy. He has always eaten everything his mother put before him at the table. He loved his fruits and vegetables and he drank lots of milk. But no more.

SLEEP

He keeps his light on until all hours. He can hardly get out of bed in the morning. Have you seen him lately, Exercise?

EXERCISE

Yes, Sleep, just yesterday. He was having trouble running to first base. He was all out of breath and panting terribly. I know he'll never make the baseball team.

GOOD FOOD

What has happened to him? Have you noticed anything, Good Grooming?

GOOD GROOMING

I guess I have been more concerned with his sister Ruth. She used to be so attractive and sweet that people liked having her around. But now—you should see her. She is certainly a mess!

SLEEP

Well, I think it's high time we did something about it. Personally, I have an idea that our old enemies the Imps have had something to do with it.

GOOD FOOD

(*Excitedly.*) Of course! That's just who it is. Last night I was trying to get our signals through from our radio station HEALTH. It sounded as though the air was full of words like "no sleep," "no vegetables," "no washing." All sorts of bad advice was being sent out over the air waves.

EXERCISE

We must do something about it right away. We can't let those Imps win out over us like this.

GOOD GROOMING

Our signals are stronger than theirs. Let's really jam the airways with *our* slogans. Then they will finally be forced to stop and we'll get ours across.

(*They all join hands and dance around singing to the tune of* "*Comin' Through the Rye.*")

We'll jam the airways, make them hum.
With slogans strong and true.
We'll force the Imps right off the air
They won't know what to do.

Good Food and Grooming, Exercise
And Sleep are hard to beat,
We know that we are in the right
And never will meet defeat!

curtain

ACT FOUR

TIME: *Morning a few days later.*

PLACE: *Same as Act Two.* MR. *and* MRS. LEWIS *are seated as before.* MR. LEWIS *is reading his paper.* MRS. LEWIS *gets up and goes over to the door.*

MRS. LEWIS

Ruthie?

RUTH

(*Off stage.*) Yes, Mother. I'll be there in a minute.

MRS. LEWIS

Teddy?

TEDDY

Yes, Mother. I'm coming.
   (MRS. LEWIS *goes back to table and sits down.*)

MRS. LEWIS

Honestly, I don't know what has happened to those children. Both of them have changed overnight.

MR. LEWIS

{*Lowering paper.*} I beg your pardon dear. Did you say something to me?

MRS. LEWIS

Yes, I did. I said I can't seem to understand Ruth and Ted. First I was worried because they suddenly were so careless and lazy. Now this morning I heard them arguing over who was to have a shower first.

MR. LEWIS

(*Laughing.*) Well I wouldn't worry over that. (*Then he grows serious.*) Or *do* you think it's something to worry over?

(*Voices are heard outside.*)

RUTH

Don't you dare mess my hair, Ted Lewis. I just got it combed.

(TED *and* RUTH *enter. They are both neatly dressed.* RUTH *has on a pretty cotton dress and has a blue ribbon around her hair.* TED *slides halfway across the floor and crash lands in his chair.*)

TEDDY

Hi, Mom. What's cookin'? Fill up the cereal bowl to the top please. I'm starved. (*Picks up his glass of orange juice.*) Oh, boy, does this look good! (*Drinks it down in a hurry.*)

RUTH

Mother, do you like this blue ribbon around my hair or do you think I should wear a yellow one with this dress?

MRS. LEWIS

(*Faintly.*) There's plenty more cereal in the kitchen, Ted. Ruthie, that blue ribbon looks very nice.

TEDDY

Dad, are you coming to the baseball tryouts this morning?

MR. LEWIS

I thought I would try to get over for a while. How are you doing, Ted?

TEDDY

Better than a couple of days ago. Today I feel as though I can knock one over the fence.

RUTH

Mother, do you mind if I go to town with Mrs. Stone today? I help her with the baby while she does her marketing.

MRS. LEWIS

Of course, dear. Go right ahead. Just make your bed before you go.

RUTH

Of course, Mother. Don't I always do that?

(MR. *and* MRS. LEWIS *look at each other as though not quite believing their ears. Just then the* HEALTH FAIRIES *tiptoe in and begin dancing softly around.*)

MRS. LEWIS

What is that I hear? It sounds like someone singing.

(*Everyone listens but they don't look at* HEALTH FAIRIES.)

HEALTH FAIRIES

(*Singing softly.*)
We'll jam the airways, make them hum
With slogans strong and true.
We'll force those Imps right off the air
They won't know what to do.

Good Food and Grooming, Exercise
And Sleep are hard to beat,
We know that we are in the right
And never will meet defeat.

TEDDY

Oh, that must be some children playing in the street.

(HEALTH FAIRIES *tiptoe out.*)

RUTH

I don't know why it is, but I feel so good this morning. Just as though something nice were about to happen.

MRS. LEWIS

Somehow I think it *has* happened.

MR. LEWIS

Come on, Son. We'd better be going.

(MR. LEWIS *and* TED *leave.*)

RUTH

Good-by, Mother. I'll see you later.

(RUTHIE *skips out of room too.*)

MRS. LEWIS

Good-by dear.

(*Starts to clear table and finds herself humming song of* HEALTH FAIRIES.)

curtain

J.W.

Suggestions for Production and Selection

Boys and girls like to have a part in the selection of the play they are to produce. They should also be given a voice in helping to assign the characters. It has been shown that very successful casting can be accomplished if the director starts by having the play read with the cast chosen at random. After reading a few pages those who are not suitable for the roles are succeeded by others. It may require several readings, but in this way the children themselves will be in complete agreement with the final selection of the cast.

The children will realize that some of their group will do their best work as production managers, property men, or prompters. The artistic ones will quite naturally be suggested to do the scenery. This co-operation among the young people will be a tremendous help in building up enthusiasm for the amount of work entailed in putting on a play.

The adult director of the play will find the children's hearty co-operation invaluable. But there are, as every director realizes, certain responsibilities which only he or she can assume in making the play a success. The plays under consideration must fit the age group, for there is nothing more disastrous than to assign work that is too difficult or is beyond the talents and capabilities of the group. Although most of the play-production projects will be undertaken by the children themselves, it will be up to the director to block out the action of the cast for every single minute on stage so that the play will present a well-balanced picture to the audience. Above all, the director should see that the actors face their audience and speak clearly.

In those plays where scenery and costuming are necessary, simplicity should be the keynote. Even when no special costuming or scenery is used, if the suggestions above are followed the children will play their parts so effectively that the audience need not feel their omission. In other words, the actors will have learned that "the play's the thing," and that dialogue is the messenger of the play.

Although the plays included in this book were written for specific holidays, many of them may be adapted for use on other occasions. As in most collections of plays, some of these require only a small cast, while others call for many characters. Several of the plays can be adapted to more or fewer characters than we have specified in the presentation offered here.

Considering these variabilities, we decided that some suggestive lists for selection might be helpful to producers who are looking for a play for some specific group. We offer the following:

PLAYS WHICH CAN BE GIVEN ON MORE THAN ONE OCCASION

DAYS AND DAYS (see *New Year's Day*), for special anniversaries

THE GREAT TREE COUNCIL (see *Arbor Day*), for Founder's Day, Fourth of July, May Day, Boy Scout or Girl Scout Week, or almost any school, club or playground project

CHARLIE'S MAY BASKET (see *May Day*), for any occasion during the season when flowers are in bloom

EACH STAR A STATE (see *Flag Day*), any patriotic occasion such as the Fourth of July, Inauguration Day, Election Day, or Admission Day

THANKSGIVING PROCLAMATION—1863 (see *Thanksgiving*), for Lincoln's Birthday

THE GOOD OLD DAYS (see *American Education Week*), for grade commencement or any school production

MARS CALLING! (see *Brotherhood Week*), could be produced by Boy Scouts, Boys' Clubs, or Recreation Centers

THE FIRE DEMONS (see *Fire Prevention Week*), excellent for Safety Week

THE IMPS' DEFEAT (see *National Health Week*), equally appropriate for Child Health Day or any occasion when health is stressed

PLAYS WHICH CAN BE PRODUCED WITHOUT SPECIAL COSTUMING

THE DONKEY'S MISSION (see *Easter*)

CHARLIE'S MAY BASKET (see *May Day*)

MOTHER OF THE TOWN (see *Mother's Day*)

EACH STAR A STATE (see *Flag Day*), with the exception of Columbia

A PICNIC FOR FATHER (see *Father's Day*)

MOTHER GOOSE GIVES ADVICE (see *Be Kind to Animals Week*), with the exception of Mother Goose

RADIOS VERSUS DOUGHNUTS (see *Boy Scout Week*)

MARS CALLING! (see *Brotherhood Week*)

GEORGE WASHINGTON SERVES HIS COUNTRY (see *George Washington's Birthday*)

PLAYS ESPECIALLY SUITED TO OUTDOOR PRODUCTION
GREAT TREE COUNCIL (see *Arbor Day*)
EACH STAR A STATE (see *Flag Day*)
A PICNIC FOR FATHER (see *Father's Day*)
THE UNITED NATIONS, THE HOPE OF THE WORLD (see *United Nations Day*)
THE FIRE DEMONS (see *Fire Prevention Week*)

PLAYS ADAPTABLE TO MARIONETTES OR PUPPETS
DAYS AND DAYS (see *New Year's Day*)
THE QUEEN OF HEARTS' PARTY (see *St. Valentine's Day*)
THE WITCHES' COMPLAINT (see *Halloween*)
THE SANTA CLAUS COURT (see *Christmas*)
MOTHER GOOSE GIVES ADVICE (see *Be Kind to Animals Week*)
THE FIRE DEMONS (see *Fire Prevention Week*)
THE IMPS' DEFEAT (see *National Health Week*)

PLAYS FOR LESS THAN TEN CHARACTERS
LINCOLN'S SECRET JOURNEY (see *Lincoln's Birthday*)
MY HONEST FRIEND (see *George Washington's Birthday*)
THE DONKEY'S MISSION (see *Easter*)
CHARLIE'S MAY BASKET (see *May Day*)
MOTHER OF THE TOWN (see *Mother's Day*)
A PICNIC FOR FATHER (see *Father's Day*)

PLAYS FOR TEN TO TWENTY CHARACTERS
DAYS AND DAYS (see *New Year's Day*)
GEORGE WASHINGTON SERVES HIS COUNTRY (see *George Washington's Birthday*)
THE WITCHES' COMPLAINT (see *Halloween*)
A HALLOWEEN SURPRISE PACKAGE (see *Halloween*)
THANKSGIVING PROCLAMATION—1863 (see *Thanksgiving*)
THE SANTA CLAUS COURT (see *Christmas*)
THE GOOD OLD DAYS (see *American Education Week*)
MOTHER GOOSE GIVES ADVICE (see *Be Kind to Animals Week*)
RADIOS VERSUS DOUGHNUTS (see *Boy Scout Week*)
MARS CALLING! (see *Brotherhood Week*)
THE FIRE DEMONS (see *Fire Prevention Week*)

FIRST AID IN THE FIRST TROOP (see *Girl Scout Week*)

THE IMPS' DEFEAT (see *National Health Week*)

PLAYS FOR LARGE GROUPS

THE QUEEN OF HEARTS' PARTY (see *St. Valentine's Day*)

GEORGE WASHINGTON SERVES HIS COUNTRY (see *George Washington's Birthday*)

THE GREAT TREE COUNCIL (see *Arbor Day*)

EACH STAR A STATE (see *Flag Day*)

THIS DREAM CAME TRUE (see *Columbus Day*)

THE UNITED NATIONS, THE HOPE OF THE WORLD (see *United Nations Day*)

THE GOOD OLD DAYS (see *American Education Week*)

THE WONDER WORLD OF BOOKS (see *Book Week*)